The Christos Connection

The Christos Connection

KRISHNA....CHRIST....BUDDHA

**Three Divine Messengers of Three Different Eras
All With One Common Message**

The Divine Essence

**That Energetic Fragment of Kingdom Consciousness
Where Truth Abides in Fullness is Within You.**

Michael R Mundy

Taran Nam Singh

First edition published 2023 by Michael R Mundy

NATIONAL LIBRARY OF AUSTRALIA

A catalogue record for this book is available from the National Library of Australia

ISBN 13: 978-0-9876228-4-6(paperback)

Dedicated to my mother, Doris Jewell Mundy...1906-2002.

❧

Doris Jewell Mitchell was born in a small gold mining and dairy farming community in a town named Gympie in Australia in 1906. She grew up, married, and had nine children, one of whom, a daughter, passed away at a very young age.

At the age of forty two years, Jewell as she was known, fell pregnant with her ninth child, at which time she was advised by her physician that because of her age it would be dangerous to both herself and her unborn child to continue with the pregnancy, and that it would be wise to consider having the pregnancy terminated. This was the common belief of most doctors in that day. She shared this story with me when I was around eight years of age.

Jewell went home from her appointment and considered the implications of continuing with the pregnancy. Being a woman of faith she decided to consult with her good friend the Reverend Gray A. Parker from her local Gordon Park Baptist Church. The Reverend Parker visited her, prayed with her, wisely counselled her as best he could, and then advised her that regardless of what he thought, the final decision must be jointly decided between Jewell and her God.

On Sunday morning June 6th. 1948, Jewell went into labour, with her baby signalling its intention to come forth into the world of form, and on Monday 7th. June, 1948, her ninth child, a son, was born. In gratitude for the safe birthing she named him Michael Robert. Why did she choose the names Michael and Robert?

The name Michael is of Hebrew origin. It is found in the Old Testament, notably in the Book of Daniel. She had named him Michael after the Archangel Michael, one of the seven archangels mentioned in the Book of Enoch. These seven are said to be Holy Angels here to watch over humanity, each archangel corresponding to a day of the week; the Archangel Michael's day being Sunday; the same day Michael as a child in the womb signalled his intention to come forth.

Michael is recognized in ancient scriptures as the conqueror of Satan and one who would lead those willing to their spiritual destiny. The popular meaning of the name Michael is "a gift from God", the popular meaning of the name Robert is "light."

As a loving mother Jewell always went about her time confidently and diligently, patiently dealing with the traumas and tantrums that continually arose, as five boys and three girls under the same roof interacted and argued their way through their teenage years and into adulthood.

Being a woman of faith with Christian beliefs, regardless of the busy life she led as a wife and mother, Jewell visited her local Baptist Church regularly every Sunday, whilst at the same time always encouraging Michael to attend the church classes for young people known as Sunday School, but never demanding that he do so.

For the sacrifice of her own safety in giving birth to me, for the fragment of faith I was exposed to through attending those weekly Sunday School classes that revealed the concept of the existence of a Supreme Being called God, which was the beginning of a long spiritual, psychological, and physical pilgrimage that would eventually lead to the writing of this book, for all these things, I am extremely grateful.

From outward things, whatever you may believe,
There is an inmost centre in us all,
Where truth abides in fullness;
And around, wall upon the wall, the gross flesh hems it in,
Hems in this perfect, clear perception, which is Truth,
A baffling and perverting carnal mesh blinds it and makes all error;
And to know,
Rather consists in opening out a way,
Whence the imprisoned splendour may escape,
Than in effecting entry for a Light supposed to be without.

An excerpt from the English Playwright and Poet Robert Browning's poem Paracelsus, speaking of the Kingdom of God our True Self, The Divine Essence, which lies in stillness within our being, waiting to be recognized, harmonised, and thus released into our lives. Freeing it to function fully in our outer experience as our True Self, our true "I Am".

Table of Contents

"In the physical world illumination occurs as incandescent light displaces the material darkness. In the spiritual world illumination or enlightenment occurs as the one transcendent light of the Krishna, Christ, or Buddha Mind, transports us thru the psycho-spiritual darkness by displacing the veil of ignorance that blinds us from a true knowledge of the Mind of Infinite Intelligence as the Eternal Light. Jesus expressed it this way saying: "I am the Light of the world who takes away all darkness."

Preface

"To everything there is a season, and a time for every purpose,
under heaven: a time to be born, and a time to die, a time to
plant, and a time to uproot, a time to kill, and a time to heal,
a time to break down and a time to build, a time to weep, and
a time to laugh, a time to mourn, and a time to dance, a time
to cast away stones, and a time to gather stones together."

— ECCLESIASTES 3...BEREAN STANDARD BIBLE.

Many years ago, whilst wandering around some book displays in a
Barnes and Noble bookstore in New York, I picked up a newly
released hardcover book by a mostly unknown author at the time named
Eckhart Tolle, and quickly browsed the Preface and Introduction.

The book was titled The Power of Now, and Eckhart Tolle by choice
had used both the Preface and the Introduction to share some details of
his own personal journey, his own personal psychological and spiritual
pilgrimage leading up to the writing of that book.

It was detail that I felt was compelling enough in the moment to
prompt me to purchase his book so as to find out more. I came to see
later in life that it was no coincidence that I was in New York, and in that
bookstore at that particular time of the book's release.

That seeming coincidence, birthed out of "curiosity," and aligned with that deep seated longing for spiritual truth that is part of the psychological DNA of all human beings, was not in fact a coincidence, but a perfect example of the "compelling nature of the Spirit of Infinite Intelligence" directing my thoughts and subsequent behaviours intuitively towards a specific objective it had, in terms of my own personal spiritual development, and my specific pilgrimage of consciousness.

The renowned scientist Albert Einstein once said: "coincidence is God's way of remaining anonymous". The renowned psychologist Carl Jung once said: "there are no coincidences only synchronicities."

Synchronicity is a causal connecting principle. Synchronicities in the scientific, psychological, and spiritual world, are what I would describe as "metaphysical meaning filled moments". They are things that happen for a specific reason. Synchronicities are links, and whilst many interpret them as mere coincidences, they can be a form of Divine guidance and a powerful "wink from the Universe" telling us that "we are on the right track in our pilgrimage of discovery."

This curiosity aspect of human nature that all human beings possess, is almost always purely a yearning for truth. And this applies not only to truth pertaining to the visible material aspects of our world, but also to truth pertaining to the unseen spiritual aspects of our universe; which includes a deeper understanding of the concept of the existence of an eternal God watching over us. This noble desire to find truth, for the scientist, is not dissimilar in intent from that of the psychologist, nor from the intent of the spiritual seeker.

The scientist looks for truths pertaining to the physical aspects of the world, the psychologist looks deeply for truths pertaining to the invisible workings of the mind, and the spiritual pilgrim looks to find the truths of the metaphysical nature of the universe, things that cannot be reached through objective study; more particularly truths pertaining to the workings of the inner being, the spirit soul partnership.

And that is the key difference between the scientist on the one hand and the spiritual seeker and the psychologist on the other. The scientist is seeking to find or understand truths pertaining to the outer world, that which is visible, but the psychologist and the spiritual seeker are both trying to find the truths of the inner world of the human being birthed in the invisible realms of the universe. Truth which cannot be witnessed to visibly, but nevertheless truth that does functionally exist.

It is truth with an ongoing eternality attached to it, and truth that every human being needs to have at least a basic understanding of in order to successfully navigate their physical and psychological present existence in this ever changing and sometimes chaotic world, and in doing so transmigrate successfully in a joyous and peace filled state to their next life whatever that might look like.

For the scientists of all fields, in their search for absolute truth, the end goal is humanity's outer progress and with that the glorification of the art of science and the human nature of humanity, but for the spiritual seeker the end goal should always be solely about one's own personal inner progress, about "being and becoming", and with that the glorification of the eternal in man, the True Self, not the glorification of the outer egoic false self.

In the spiritual pilgrim's search for truth, in their own personal process of becoming, the true seeker's desire centres on one primary thing. To come forth from that quiet deeply personal pilgrimage into the unknown invisible world, with their mind and heart firmly grasping precious slivers of truth, spiritual truths, Pearls of Divine Wisdom that they can apply to their everyday experience to enhance and accelerate their journey of consciousness. Truths which so far in life they may have been blindly ignorant of.

My personal spiritual pilgrimage for Ultimate Truth was played out through my love of literature. From a very early age I have had in terms of the creative arts two primary interests, literature and music.

Concerning literature and music, for most of my life particularly from my pre-teen years onwards, I have been possessed with what might be described as a fascination for the written word, all manner of books and nowadays blogs too, regardless of what genre they belong to, and a deep admiration for those creative people in the world of literature and in the music industry, who dare to explore their hidden gift and then create something in order to bring some sort of psychological or even just emotional blessing to their audience.

The decades following my teenage obsession with comics would see me read works of fiction, biographies of influential leaders, books about world history, about health and wellness, about science, about philosophical thought, about spirituality and religion, and books about the evolution of society over the last two thousand years traditionally, culturally, socially and religiously.

Some of these I read in full, and with others, finding no Pearls of Wisdom in them that quelled my curiosity on the subject matter at hand, I respectfully set them aside and moved on to another.

During my exploration into religious groups, I commenced reading and contemplating the sacred writings of the largest religions in the world; the Bible of the Christian faith, the Quran or Koran of the Muslim faith, various teachings of the Hindu faith including the Bhagavad Gita and the Upanishads, the Tao Te Ching of Confucianism, and with Buddhism as much as I could find on the teachings of Gautama Buddha including the Dhammapada. I also explored experientially different types of Eastern yoga practice, meditation, and for a while Ayurvedic medicine.

With regards to the Bible the Holy Book of Christian tradition, after reading the Old Testament with a particular focus on the Book of Psalms and the Book of Proverbs, I then read and studied the New Testament four times, paying particular emphasis to the life empowering teachings of Jesus in passages of work such as the Sermon on the Mount, which includes the Beatitudes and the Lord's Prayer, and gave much attention to the metaphysical mystery hidden in much of the Apostle Paul's writings.

Later in my adult life this fascination for religious and spiritual literature drifted into exploring the achievements of creative scholarly people, those unselfish students of spiritual history who possessed an inner drive to translate the writings of ancient sages, mystics and prophets, into a language that the modern reader would be familiar with. Their aim being to share the spiritual wisdom and truth from the world of yesterday, with the world of today and with those who would come searching tomorrow.

I was drawn to those tireless translators responsible amongst other things for the most popular English translations of the Sanskrit text of the Hindu Bhagavad Gita, and the Upanishads. I had read that one Spanish translator took twenty years to complete his task of translating some of the ancient Indian Sanskrit scriptures into English.

I discovered that for some of these scholarly translators, it was not just a process of taking one ancient language and translating it into English, more importantly the "spirit of the Divine Principle (Divine Law)" embedded in the writing had to be taken into account.

For with regards to rules or laws, there are two possible ways to approach them. There is "the letter of the law" and there is "the spirit of the law." To obey the letter of the law is to follow the literal reading of the words of the law as did religious leaders in the Old Testament days and in the early days of Islam, and unfortunately as some religious extremists still do to this day.

For even after the coming of Christ and Muhammad, some religious extremists, particularly of the early Catholic and Muslim faiths, refused to allow the spirit of those laws, life principles that Jesus or Muhammad taught such as love, compassion, and forgiveness to be the final guiding principle in all situations.

They refused to allow the spirit of the law to have preference over the letter of the law. They continued to strictly advocate for the punishment principle to remain in force making no allowance for the forgiveness principle, which saw many early Christians crucified or burned at the stake and many Muslims beheaded, for what in this modern day would appear to be minor offences.

For the translators of these ancient scriptures, the self-sacrificing goal of every true translator was to produce a translated document that was "true to the Spirit" in which it was originally written. A clear, concise, accurate, natural, and acceptable translation, able to be read and understood unambiguously by the people for whom it was translated, those not familiar with the original language in which the scripture was written; whilst in the same process still revealing to the reader the original intent of the ancient Divine Truth, God's intent.

Over time I started to realize that scriptural translators are in fact participating in the process of "progressive revelation". The process of revealing in a new way and in a different language to a different culture, timeless spiritual truths that were originally revealed to humanity, but truths that were lost to many over time due to the emerging isolated nature of growing cultures around the world, and the evolving language differences.

You see progressive revelation is:

"A movement from truth to more truth, and so eventually to full truth."

The ethos of a culture or society is its collective spirit or character, the fundamental or underlying beliefs and attitudes that have always influenced its customs and practices. So those Divine Revelations given to Krishna, Christ, the Buddha, and Muhammad, are still as relevant in this modern day as they were when they were first given. Specific Divine Wisdom and Truth through revelation, no matter which society or culture it is originally birthed in, is given for all time to all of humanity, not just a few.

It is given as a pathway to guide and instruct for the entirety of humankind's benefit, and will, if applied in daily life, metaphysically influence the outworking of an individual's or a society's attitudinal and behavioural life; no matter who it was birthed through culture wise, and no matter what era it was birthed in, and no matter what religious umbrella it was birthed under.

The first few years of my progressive writing journey occurred as I travelled and lived full time in a mobile home so as to experience the multi-dimensional side of societal existence, and in some way explore the inner hippie mystic in me that I felt had been suppressed by a life of attachment to things of form; particularly to work success, to the possessions that success enabled me to buy, and to specific personal relationships.

For me it was a time of non-attachment to the primary egoic influences of life. A non-attachment to anything that gave my ego boasting rights. And to me this meant non-attachment to the comforts of a home, non-attachment to the desire for personal possessions that enabled me to keep up with the Jones's so to speak, and non-attachment to the confines of a personal long term relationship.

At different times in different places I interacted personally and sometimes simply observed from a distance the different societal mix, from the seemingly affluent people all wearing fine designer clothes, and outwardly appearing to be enjoying life, to the seemingly materially destitute poverty stricken members of society, who in their time worn apparel, bare feet and apparent homeless state, likewise seemed content and unfazed by what appeared to others to be their physical lack and their psychological isolation in life.

Most seemed to have both psychologically and physically adapted to what others might see as their apparent lack of material possessions and relationships. It appeared to me that many had surrendered to their current state of existence, their non-attachment to things of form including people, merely accepting it as "their life", and wanting for nothing more than food for sustenance and shelter from the storms.

I regularly strolled the different local weekend market places in various beachside and bushland settings, and casually watched the early morning arts and crafts stalls being set up by a group of focused and purpose filled vendors. A diverse group of people from farmers to fashionistas, from budding musicians and folk singers to those with an obvious creative desire, all seeking some sort of personal acknowledgement or even just some modest financial reward for the effort they had extended in their chosen creative pursuit.

And I marvelled at the variety of creative forms that had been so cleverly constructed so as to bring the seed of an idea having germinated in the mind of one person for a measure of time, into some sort of useful goods of form that could be shared unselfishly with others for a reasonable price. Whilst I occasionally saw what appeared to me to be the odd profit monger disguised as a humble vendor, on most market days it was a rare thing to be seen. Such was the beauty of the local marketplace.

On many occasions I sat on a sandy beach watching the local surfboard riders embracing their chosen wave whilst marvelling at some of the skills they displayed, achieved no doubt through hours and hours of disciplined practice, and at other times I simply sat on a park bench and quietly observed the close knit group of Hare Krishna devotees gathered in the local park chanting their mantra of hope, as they bore witness to their faith in that which is above all.

It was at one of those particular times I recognized such was the irony of the moment, that in the same visual picture, not far from where those devotees in their orange garbs were gathered, in their apparent state of collective inclusivity, lay a homeless man, alone, asleep in the early morning shade of a big oak tree, resting in his own chosen state of singular exclusivity.

And I reflected on possible events that may have occurred in the lives of both the Hare Krishna devotees and that homeless man that had led each individual to make the personal decision to embrace or surrender to their current lifestyle. Had it been a conscious decision or was it something that was unavoidably forced upon them through unforeseen circumstances, and thus as a means of escaping those forces.

Was it wisdom through some sort of Divine providence that dictated their choice? Or was it a decision made at some stage as a way of escaping the forces underpinning what is referred to as a supposed "normal life." Forces which they felt had so relentlessly rallied against them that the supposed normal life became to them quite an abnormal life.

My time on the road became a time of outer peace-filled freedom for me. Freedom from the regimented routine of deadlines and demands that life had thrust upon me in my driving desire to achieve success in the ego dominated business world and in relationships, both things supposedly containing the financial and emotional security that I had come to believe was the sole purpose of one's existence, and the only thing that measured up to societal expectations.

But more importantly than a time of outer freedom, it became a time of inner contemplation and reflection for me, which cautiously and quietly ushered in a measure of inner freedom, freedom from the relentless machinations of a restless roving mind. Freedom from the insidious energetically draining demands of desire and attachment.

In moments of reflective silence watching the early morning sunrise or the late afternoon early evening sunset, I came to see more clearly that in order for a life to leave a realistic legacy, it does not necessarily have to be locked into societal expectations.

I came to see that in order for a human being to leave a realistic legacy, the life lived must first of all have the right measure of "wisdom, integrity, and selflessness" attached to it, that changes some aspect of current or future life around them for the better. In other words what measure of eternality exists in all we achieve in this earthly life, and thus what seed of eternity is left behind to continue to influence after our Spirit/Soul transmigrates.

Is the only thing we leave behind temporal things, specific evidence of material success, including a successful career and a capacity to successfully procreate many times, all these things having a temporality attached to them. Yet these are usually the things which many people get accolades from others for at their funeral service. But even those accolades are temporal, for after the curtain falls on all stage plays the initial rapturous applause of the audience eventually fades into silence as the audience heads back out into their own self-absorbed journey.

For very soon after our funeral service, where we see friends and family gather to give we the deceased one last egoic accolade, much of what we gained, achieved, or conquered, just morphs into the dust and decay of thousands of forgotten yesterdays; the only evidence of their existence being time worn photo images in a dust covered photo album, sitting on the top shelf of the bedroom closet.

A career may go forward and backward, finances fluctuate up and down depending on circumstances, and unfortunately family dynamics fracture at times because the whole principle of family dynamics is centred on relying on each other for emotional, physical, and economic support, which opens the family dynamic up to relationship insecurity or stress if personal needs are not being met.

The most important thing that all of humanity must come to understand is that whilst the temporality of life has its place, it is the eternality of life that should be our first priority.

During my mobile physical and spiritual pilgrimage, I came to realise that Godly Wisdom is the only thing that endures eternally. Everything else rusts and decays. Success dissipates, looks fade and wither, the early joy of material possessions gets lost midst the gathering of more, and the early passion of an intimate relationship tempers over time.

The getting of Wisdom, and with that the subsequent application of Wisdom gained, for the physical, psychological, or spiritual benefit of others, is the only thing that truly matters; it is the only thing that truly impacts in the present moment, and the only thing that has unlimited potential to leave a lasting legacy for the future.

The Book of Proverbs in the Old Testament tells us that the getting of skilful and Godly Wisdom should be our primary task in life before anything else, describing Wisdom as "the summit of life". We should not settle for the base camp of the mountain of life, but rather strive to reach the summit of Wisdom. This should be our first and foremost priority above everything.

Reaching the Summit of Wisdom, this is the great adventure of life, this is the great journey we alone must undertake, no one can do it for us. Yes others who have walked that path can give us directions and thus can point out a particular way, but it is we who must find the Path of

Wisdom and travel the Path of Wisdom, one step and one day at a time to its peak.

For it is not until we have reached the top of that mountain of wisdom that we are able to see in full glory the view that lives on in spite of the dangerous boulders and slippery slopes that blocked that view on the way; and a view that lives on in spite of the concerning creatures of darkness sometimes disguised in human form that hid in the rock crevices along the way appearing purely to tempt us in another direction, an unwise direction, purely to disrupt and suspend the progress of our consciousness climb.

And during that climb, if we are willing with courage to withstand these hindrances and strive in a patient and faith filled way to complete our pilgrimage, we are not left alone to walk the Path, for glimpses of the Light of Wisdom emanating from the summit like a lighthouse will progressively illuminate our path and guide us through those physical and mind centric obstacles to that glorious summit, to itself.

Alternately, if with haughtiness of heart we continue to deny the presence of that Light of True Wisdom sent to guide us, if we with a subtle arrogance birthed as we steadfastly hold on to our ego driven achievements of the material, intellectual, and emotional kind; or if we hold fast to uncompromising belief systems born out of the theologised or ideologized deceptions still witnessed in the beliefs of many institutionalised religions and political establishments in this modern day, how can we ever hope to place our flag firmly at the peak.

Or even if just purely through laziness or dullness of spirit, we continually set aside the inner promptings for Truth, how can we hope to find True Wisdom, for our hearts will become progressively hardened, firmly closed to the truth that God earnestly desires to reveal to all of us. It is we and it is we alone who can open the door of our hearts and let the Light of Wisdom in.

We need to with a discernment that separates the wheat from the chaff, grasp hold of every spiritual sliver of Truth knocking on our door, the slightest sliver that may in whatever circumstance or through whatever channel be lovingly bestowed upon us by Infinite Intelligence the God of the Universe. Whether it comes forth from a sincere friend, from a book, through a spiritual guide of some kind, or perhaps through what we have labelled all our lives as "merely a coincidence."

For myself after searching for spiritual Truth and Wisdom for many years through books, through seminars, through institutionalised religion, through gurus, and through a variety of spiritual practices, trying to find the guide to take me to the summit of Wisdom, in the quiet and peacefulness of the early morning, as I sat on a beach silently watching the glorious colours of the early morning sunrise, I had an epiphany of sorts.

I came to realize the true reason I had spent my whole life searching for spiritual truth was simply because I believed that if I discovered spiritual truth I would find ultimate happiness and peace.

And whilst much of the information I had gathered over many years had been beneficial in separating the wheat from the chaff of all the knowledge I had been harvesting, beneficial in separating the True Wisdom from that which was mere foolishness, I also discovered that not all the time and energy and financial cost spent in doing this was absolutely necessary to my inner goal of finding True Wisdom and with that ultimate happiness and peace.

After many years of wandering aimlessly around the base camp of an authentic spiritual life whilst in a semi-illusionary way believing that the climb was rigorously progressing, I discovered that these precious slivers of spiritual truth, these fragments of a faith forgotten, these glory filled glimpses of Light and Truth that we need to appropriate to light our path through the potential minefield or what you could call "mind-field of life", were in fact all that time lying in stillness in the Kingdom of God, the Divine Essence within me, silently and patiently waiting to be birthed into my conscious existence and thus my personal outer experience.

You see an ongoing search for happiness, or a measure of pleasure, is the underlying reason behind everything we do in life, even if we won't admit it to ourselves. And it is a goal that continually separates or distances us from an experience with the container of True Wisdom, the Christ or Atman within, the Kingdom of God within, whose essence already possesses amongst other things the qualities of pure wisdom, pure joy, pure happiness, and pure peace. All being character qualities desiring earnestly to come forth into the sphere of our outer experience according to their Divine designated role..

I came to see that:

"True authentic spirituality is not about letting the Light in, it is about letting the Light within us out".

As a child in the Christian Church I can clearly remember the children in the class singing with gusto every Sunday morning, "into my heart, into my heart, come into my heart Lord Jesus, come in I pray, come in to stay, come into my heart, Lord Jesus." We should have been singing, "out of my heart, out of my heart, come out of my heart Lord Jesus, come out to play and there to stay, come out of my heart, Lord Jesus."; because the Kingdom of God in all its fullness was already in there wanting to express itself in every child's outer experience.

And that has been one of the great deceptions of much of institutionalised religious teaching and in this modern day some secular teachings. True abiding outward joy is not something that can be gained through an objective experience, something that can be brought in from the outside. True joy is purely an outer expression of that joy already residing within, a particular characteristic of the nature of the Kingdom of God or the Divine Essence within us, rising to the surface of our outer experience.

Our outer happiness and peace is purely an outward expression of that pure happiness and peace that has already been imprinted within us. It was imprinted in us when the fragment of God Consciousness was imbedded into our being to give us animated life, a life created in the image of the Infinite Intelligence we commonly refer to as God.

"We do not become whole in body and soul by trying to be whole, rather by recognising the wholeness that is already in us, and then detaching ourselves from anything that would stop that wholeness from emerging".

But through a lack of wisdom we don't realise this and think that in order to be happy I must do or acquire something that will make me happy. Something to add to my current experience of life. So we continually look for the next experience or activity that will make us feel happy. The underlying intent attached to every new endeavour or activity we undertake is to give us a measure of pleasure or happiness that wasn't there before.

This may take the form of starting a new relationship, getting a degree, getting a job, making money, buying a new car or house, going on a holiday, having sex, eating our favourite ice-cream, buying a dog, getting married, having children. All of our desires originate because of this subconscious desire all human beings have for an encounter with true happiness, which in its shortened state, when it comes in short bursts, is described as a pleasurable experience.

But if happiness is caused directly by some kind of objective experience then that same experience would make everybody happy. For instance if wealth was a true source of happiness, why are many rich people unable to cope with life and others of less means for example a Mother Teresa so fully embracing of life. If the objective experience of being rich causes one to be happy why are so many rich people unhappy and so many poor people extremely happy.

Torrential rain may bring joy to the heart of a drought stricken farmer, but untold misery to a community trapped in rising flood waters. But self-induced happy periods subside over time as do flood waters. They are temporal and short lived. They do not create or empower us with the enduring happiness, joy, and peace that Jesus spoke of. And subconsciously we know this which is why we attempt so often to preserve these happy times in photo or video format.

The happiness we found as a child eating an ice-cream no longer brings us the same intense joy as an adult. The happiness we found in a scholastic achievement can quickly turn to disillusionment when we find ourselves unable to secure employment. The temporary happiness we found as a teenager in partying with our friends on Saturday night, can turn into the longer and more miserable experience of a splitting headache on Sunday morning, or an alcohol problem later in life.

The happiness we find in the experience of "falling in love" one day, can over time soon dissipate into an objective experience of miserableness when breaking up. The sweet happiness we found in getting married can easily turn into the bitter reality of an acrimonious divorce. The new car happiness as an adult is not as intense as the first car happiness as a teenager. The joy we found on waking up Christmas morning becomes less extreme as we age.

So whether it be an ice-cream as a child, a first love as a teenager, a new car as a teenager or the joy of the birth of our first child, regardless of whatever is the catalyst that brings about a happiness hit, that happiness hit is not eternal but temporal, and lasting happiness and peace cannot be achieved through an objective experience. But we keep seeking this elusive butterfly of happiness through objective experiences.

We are addicted to seeking out happy experiences or rather experiences we feel will bring happiness or a measure of pleasure with it. Drug addicts will seek out more powerful drugs to give themselves the same intense happiness hit that they experienced in their first venture into drug taking. Thrill seekers will seek greater thrills. The athlete will hunger after the gold medal after initially finding happiness in the bronze. The scholar will seek out another more prestigious degree.

So throughout our life, having established in our mind as a child and then reinforced as an adult, that happiness is connected to the acquisition of something or the experience of something, or an experience with someone, we continue to embark on an endless and subsequent fruitless search for a happiness that stays put.

Believing that this can only be accomplished by attaching ourselves to something we like or through the attainment of something we desire, something that appeals to us; attaching ourselves to an objective experience that brings forth a pleasurable emotional experience, even if it is something as simple as a pleasurable bodily sensation.

And what does that have the potential to do? It opens the door to unwise decisions. It did that for me as I am sure it did at some time for most people. It causes us to, so many times, make some of the most ignorantly conceived and most unwise life decisions we could possibly make, seeing us go on to justify those dumb decisions as being right and appropriate for us.

But in the end they can, if not conceived through a measure of Wisdom, be decisions that become not only hurtful and damaging to others but, due to the eternal law of reciprocity, more broadly damaging to ourselves and subsequently our own personal spiritual evolution. If there was one thing I had to name that was of the most benefit to me during my physical and spiritual observational pilgrimage in my mobile home during those years, I would most assuredly say it was that "wisdom is what truly matters," and in particular Divine Wisdom.

That's a portion of the external story of who I am, and how I got to this stage of my life, the credentials and background that I bring to this particular undertaking, the writing of this book. But more important than the happenings that occurred during my external pilgrimage into the world of non-attachment, were the internal learnings of both the psychological and spiritual kind that were gained during that journey when the highway met the heavens. I share these insights, these Pearls of Wisdom gained along the way, in the following pages.

"I have gone round in vain the cycles of many lives ever striving to find the builder of the house of life and death. How great is the sorrow of life that must die.

But now I have seen the housebuilder: never more shalt thou build this house. The rafters of sins are broken, the ridgepole of ignorance is destroyed, the fever of craving is past: for my mortal mind is gone to the joy of the immortal Nirvana."

— THE BUDDHA...THE DHAMMAPADA 153, 154.

Introduction

❦

"He who in early days was unwise but later found
Wisdom, he sheds a light over the world "like
that of the moon when free from clouds."

— THE BUDDHA...THE DHAMMAPADA 13:172.

There is a phrase we see written in the New Testament that Jesus uses repeatably, "the Kingdom of Heaven," or "the Kingdom of God" is within you, and Jesus also speaks of that Kingdom being "at hand," meaning present in the here and now.

Jesus was continually alerting his followers to the truth that the Kingdom of Heaven is not a pipe dream of the future, or merely a future Kingdom to be established in a physical sense on earth. Jesus taught that it exists as a life force in the present moment in all individual life forms, and that it is an energetic force which not only created those life forms, but sustains, supports, and preserves all those existing life forms enabling them to stay alive and animated.

In saying "the Kingdom of God is within you," Jesus is referencing a dimension of spiritual presence, a Divine Essence or Divine Consciousness that is within us, you, me, right now in the present moment. When he said that "the Kingdom of Heaven is at hand," he was telling us that we don't have to die in the hope of finding it in some magical afterlife experience, for it is here now. He was telling us that we simply have to "acknowledge its existence" and "awaken to its influence", in this present life experience.

When Jesus, similarly as did other ancient Hindu, Muslim, Buddhist, and Christian Mystics, spoke about this essence, this "oneness that pervades all", the Kingdom of God that is within us, and around us, he was talking about a complete mutual indwelling and an all-encompassing outer dwelling.

Jesus was saying I am in God, God is in me, you are in God and God is in you; we are all a part of one Universal Consciousness, one all-pervading essence of life energy, which he referenced in the New Testament's Book of John as:

"The Spirit of Truth who dwells with you and will be in you."

That Divine Essence or Breath of Life in our neighbour, is the same Breath of Life that is in us. Our Consciousness is a fragment of the Divine, the Pure, or Kingdom Consciousness, similarly as is our neighbour's Consciousness. We are not two individual life forms; we are all a part of one Universal life form together immersed in the one and the same Essence, breathing the primary Breath of Life, God, Pure Consciousness, the Supreme Para Brahman.

However Christianity is not the only religion that espouses this truth. This is one of the central teachings of the Hindu Upanishads, in that there is a True Self within us that is eternal and unchanging, which is our True Nature, our Divine Nature; and it is in coming to an awareness of that True Self and acknowledging its presence that we enter a state of peace and happiness or bliss as it is described, in the present moment.

The Upanishads also teach that it is the Divine Force or Supreme Intelligence supporting, sustaining, and transforming all things, and that we can interact with this Divine Force if we so choose.

And as such as the nature of that Divine Essence or Kingdom Consciousness is within us, so the Mind of that Kingdom Consciousness is within us. In Christianity it is described as the Christ Mind, in Hinduism the Krishna Mind, and in Buddhism the Buddha Mind. It is within us, waiting to release its stored up Wisdom into the circumstantial experiences of our conscious awareness.

And we are in control of that. Only we can decide as to whether we keep the Divine Essence, the True Light of Wisdom within us imprisoned, or do we open up the gates and allow that imprisoned splendour to escape into the external circumstances of our life. It is we, not God, who are the arbiters, the primary influencers of our own evolutionary pilgrimage of Personal Consciousness, and as such our own personal journey of life.

And how do we primarily influence our personal level of Conscious Awareness? We do it by as the Apostle Paul said to the people of Philippi, "by allowing the same mind that was in Christ Jesus" to express itself in our own intentions, attitudes, and behaviours. By giving the Consciousness of Christ permission to go about its work freely and unhindered in us.

The Apostle Paul, in writing to the people of Philippi said, "let the same mind be in you that was in Christ Jesus." A Hindu disciple might say, "let the same mind be in you that was in Krishna." A Buddhist disciple might say, "let the same mind be in you that was in the Buddha."

Paul was speaking of us seeing the world through the eyes of Christ, feeling the world through the emotions of Christ, and responding to the world, with the compassion and kindness of Christ, the key components of living an authentic ethically based spiritual and practical life. The ultimate aim being that we become psychologically whole, and spiritually holy, continually manifesting the Nature of God, or the character qualities of God in all our interactions with each other and with all other life form.

That is our primary purpose as a human being. Having been given, according to the ancient scriptures, dominion over all things, there is an expectation that we, having been given that sovereign rulership, will conduct ourselves in accord with the principles that underpin the nature of our sovereign God, principles of love, compassion, kindness, and forgiveness.

And what does that bring to ourselves and the earth? It brings "peace on earth, and goodwill to all men." That is why we see Jesus being described in the New Testament as "the Prince of Peace", and that is why we see Jesus in the New Testament preaching, "blessed are the peacemakers." Peace on earth and goodwill to all men is not just an angelic slogan we roll out at Christmastime. It is God's eternal purpose for humanity.

Now whilst a lot is being written and taught in this modern day about the practice of Self-Enquiry as a means of realising or recognizing the Kingdom of God within, as a means of knowing our "True Self," and thus understanding the consciousness of our being versus the unconscious false self, all of which is helpful, that alone does not make us a whole and thus holy individual before God; that alone will not change us into the holy image of Christ, Krishna, or the Buddha.

For even when we come to acknowledge the existence of our True Self, to accept the presence of that Divinity within, we must also understand that it is only the human being, the mental, moral, volitional human being who can fully declare the nature of that Divine Essence within that it has come to realise it is in precious possession of. And it is only the human being that can manifest the character qualities of that Divine Consciousness or Essence that we have come to understand we truly are. It is firstly about recognizing our True Self, and secondly and even more importantly, about living that True Self.

It is we who must set about determinedly developing a Kingdom Consciousness, a Christ Consciousness; what the Hindu might term as a Krishna Consciousness; what the Buddhist might term as a state of Buddha Mindedness.

Yes, as Jesus said, the Kingdom of God is within us, but it sits in silence "waiting for us to imprint on its characteristics", its nature, and it is we who do the imprinting. God does not take over and miraculously change us to be more like him. We imprint God's character qualities on ourselves, which automatically then sees us begin manifesting Christ-like, or Krishna-like, or Buddha-like attitudes and behaviours in all our interactions with all other life form.

We take over, and, as an act of our own will, set about changing ourselves into God's image, and the Divine Essence within our being and outside our being will spring into action and support and sustain us in our undertaking. Authentic spirituality, no matter what institutional branding it has, is not lazy spirituality. It is not just a matter of popping down to the church or mosque once a week and tossing some pennies in a plate. It is purposeful, and purpose filled.

We deliberately imprint the personality characteristics of Christ, Krishna, or the Buddha, over our own self-developed characteristics, that false sense of self we have identified with all our life thus far. And with that imprinting the old self, the "old me" is veiled from sight, not permanently in the first instance, but progressively it will be if our resolve, our willingness to change is resilient.

To imprint something on ourselves is to stamp ourselves in the same image. Imprinting is important for raising the young, as it encourages them to follow their parents. This is referred to as "filial imprinting". For example, in the wild, animals learn to hunt, while watching their parents hunt. And with humans, babies learn to speak, by mimicking their parents speech, by their own choice of imprinting their parents characteristics on their own personality.

Similarly as Krishna, Christ, and the Buddha in their awakened states all chose to harmonise their attitudes and behaviours with those of the Father of Consciousness, chose to manifest the characteristics of Light, Life, and Love, in their dealings with the rest of humanity, so we too, once "the imprinting" has occurred, begin working "in harmony with the God Mind," and manifesting those qualities in our daily lives.

As such we begin acting virtuously and ethically with all human beings and all other life form that contain a measure of conscious life, a fragment of the Divine Essence in them. And at times we may need to remind ourselves of that fact. All life forms do have a fragment of the Divine Essence in them, regardless of whether it's characteristics manifest in their individual outward attitudes and behaviours.

The Kingdom of Heaven at hand is consciousness at hand, Divine Consciousness, the eternal source of every life form, the root and source of all beings. It is the Holy Breath of Life, that preserves us, and keeps up alive and animated.

And when in the final stages of our life that Breath of Life leaves us, and returns to the source from whence it came, all that is left is a bag of bones and flesh, that we have spent a lifetime fussing over, which having lost the eternal seed of its existence, that gave it its animation and aliveness, eventually decays to dust.

The Islamic Mystic and Poet Rumi once said: *"Paradise is not a place; it is a state of Consciousness"*. And this is something that we may need to remind ourselves of occasionally until we have removed any theologised programming from our awareness.

Heaven is not a Kingdom in the sky that we go to when we die, sometime in the future; rather heaven is an **"evolved state of consciousness"** in our present circumstantial existence; and hell is not a place of fire and brimstone in the bowels of the earth, that some go to when they die; rather hell is a **"devolved state of consciousness"** in our present circumstantial existence.

So the essential way to successfully navigate this earthly kingdom we have been born into, to evolve our state of conscious awareness, is through the harmonisation of the essential expressive elements of our Personal Consciousness, being our Soul attributes of our Human Mind, Emotions, and Will, with the essential expressive elements of Pure Consciousness, being the Soul attributes of God's Mind, Emotions, and Will.

But to successfully "harmonise", we must in the first instance "familiarise". That is what in the first instance this process of imprinting is all about. That is what the process of attaining a state of Krishna

Consciousness, or Christ Consciousness, or Buddha Mindedness is all about. It is about in the first instance getting to know and understand the Divine Nature, the Kingdom of God within us, and then we deliberately choose to begin starting to express that nature in all our personal thoughts, attitudes, intentions, and behaviours towards all other life forms.

To imprint is to choose in the first instant to familiarise. We must get to know the character qualities of the Divine Nature within. Prior to our coming to an understanding of our True Self within it really didn't matter. Now it does, because self-realisation alone, an understanding of who our True Self is, is not enough. It gives us a false sense of reassurance of our eternal wellbeing, and certainly does not create a whole and holy person capable of responsible dominion or rulership over this earth.

We need to consciously integrate the God Personality or God Identity within, into our Personal Personality or Identity that is visible to the world. Jesus described this as being "a witness to the world."

We must first come to fully understand mentally the things that impact on harmonisation, both the good, to preserve and strengthen that harmonisation and also come to understand and be aware of those bad things we have "attached ourselves to", perhaps unwittingly, whose singular intent is to block that harmonisation from occurring by whatever means in you it finds to exploit. And then when found we through the Spirit co-operate to suppress or veil them or alternately destroy and eliminate them. It really is as simple as that.

Our True Self, the Kingdom of God within waits patiently to be recognized as the only realm of true lasting happiness. Waiting, watching, and ever desiring to come to the conscious surface of our external experience and express the qualities of its inherent eternal nature, ethical qualities which carry with them the blessings of true joy, true happiness, and true peace.

This is the true battle for the Soul of humanity that is continually in progress. This is the message the Buddha was continuously trying to covey to society when he spoke of the "principle of non-attachment to things." And this is the subtle message that Jesus was trying to convey to the people when he said, "sell all you have and follow me", or "let the dead bury the dead".

Both the Buddha and Jesus were trying to direct our thoughts and subsequent behaviours away from attachment to earthly things and redirect our primary attachment to heavenly things, attitudes and behaviours aligned with the principles of the Kingdom of God. Because both Jesus and the Buddha understood that when our primary attachment is to things of form or things of the flesh, a psychological veil positions itself to further separate us from our knowledge of God or desire for the things of God. And consequently we continue to prioritise pleasure over peace, and wallow in the waters of uncertainty.

One of the most important things we must understand as we navigate our earthly life looking for peace and happiness is this:

> *"The acquisition or achievement of some objective thing is not what specifically brings about the happiness hit that we are experiencing at the time.*
>
> *Rather it is the fact that this acquisition or experience in the moment simultaneously brings to an end for a length of time, the activities of seeking or desiring, or resisting, all being the primary tools of the egoic self to distract us from our relationship with our true self, the Divine Essence within."*

All our life we have referred to ourselves continually as "I." We say I like this, or I hate that, or I want this, or I need this. Or in describing ourselves we say, "I am tall" or "I am strong," or "I am smart" or "I am in love" or "I am an adult." It's always been I, Me, or Mine in referencing ourselves in our everyday life. And that referencing has always been tied to some objective experience or concept.

But our True Self, the root and ground of our very existence or life, is not this image of itself we have that is tied to innumerable concepts and experiences. Our True Self is that which underpins our very existence, that fragment of God's Consciousness that is at the centre of our existence and without which we don't exist, we do not have conscious life, and as such do not have the ability to even have an aware objective experience.

Similarly as the waves of the ocean whilst coming forth from the ocean are just manifestations of that ocean, and very soon are displaced by another emerging wave, so are concepts and experiences, there is a temporality attached to them.

But when we as an act of our will disassociate or cease from actively desiring or striving for some sort of objective experience, it brings to an end those active components of the ego or false self that are continually manifesting trying to veil our understanding of our true inner self, our true nature, as the wave manifests to take us away from an awareness of the ocean, particularly if storms are in play. I mean in cyclonic weather who stands on the beach, gazes out past the huge waves and says, "wow look at that ocean." No, our attention is firmly fixated on the huge waves.

Our true nature does not have to be strived for, it just needs to be set free from the prison of flesh, bones, concepts and experiences that we have encased it in. That is the part we have to play in all this. and we do have a part to play. There are some things we may need to detach ourselves from in the first instance. But when we with our egocentric tendencies back off, when we get out of the way, it opens a pathway for Divine Wisdom to manifest through us and participate in our life.

First comes the recognition and then the acceptance that this person who we thought we were, the "I" or "Me" that needs an outer objective experience to enjoy life is not our True Self in our innermost being, not who we really are, simply an illusionary self. This is the first conscious decision we must make. A simple recognition of the fact that this, perhaps slightly mixed up person that I have always thought I was, in truth is not who "I am" in the depths of my being.

That this slightly and for some fully mixed up person who we may have spent our whole life being disappointed in, and thus continually pre-disposed to trying to enhance or change it in some way, physically or psychologically, thus usurping that responsibility from the Holy Spirit of Christianity or Shiva of Hinduism, is in reality just a big bag of bones and flesh and intellect continually chasing an objective experience to try and find some, even if small, measure of pleasure, happiness, or financial, social, and emotional security.

Once we just carry out that simple act, the act of recognizing that our True Self is contained in that Fragment of God Consciousness within, the Kingdom of God in our innermost being, not in the outer shell, that act in a sense turns back the hands of time to our own personal beginning. We are starting all over again as if we have been born again. Thus comes an initial state of peace. It is as if a great weight has been lifted off our shoulders.

But subsequently if we want to continue in that initial state of joy and peace and to grow that state, so that the ever present threat of the false egoic self has no opportunity to re-emerge and cause confusion in our life, when we inadvertently let our psychological guard down, we must grow in Grace and our knowledge of Him as the Bible expresses it, through feeding that existing realisation of our True Self with an ongoing measure or pathway of nurturing wisdom.

The Soul is no different from the body in the sense that as the body needs ongoing nutrient rich food to sustain it and to keep it strong, so the Soul needs ongoing nutrient rich spiritual food to sustain its resolve and evolve or strengthen its level of consciousness or awareness. And that nutrient rich food to sustain it and cause it to grow in Grace and Wisdom can be simply found in the Divine Pathways outlined in the timeless teachings of three timeless masters, Krishna, Christ, and the Buddha.

Krishna in the Bhagavad Gita speaks of the Path of Love, the Upanishads of Hinduism speak of the Path of Light, and the Buddha in the Dhammapada encourages us to embrace the true Path of Life. And the historical records of the Christ in the New Testament and the

Gospel of Thomas, reveal to us concrete accounts of his every word and deed showing that Christ followed all three paths, the Path of Love, the Path of Light, and the Path of Life.

Christ followed the Path of Love as seen in the Bhagavad Gita,, Christ followed the Path of Light, as seen in the Upanishads, and Christ also followed the Path or Way of Life, as seen in the Dhammapada. The Christ of the Christian religion lived the paths that the religion of Hinduism teaches and the paths that the religion of Buddhism teaches. All three masters sharing with us in their teachings their own specific Divine Blueprint that illuminates the heart and mind of the hearer with the Ultimate Truth.

It being that the Kingdom of God, the Divine Essence with all its characteristics of wisdom, joy, peace and happiness is within us all waiting to be released and thus consciously expressed in our earthly life. Our inner being call it our heart if you like, then becomes the river of life from which the tributaries or arteries of love, kindness, compassion, and integrity find their freedom to flow effortlessly.

But in order to understand the practicality of that Divine Blueprint for the virtuous and ethics based functioning of this earthly kingdom we live and move in, and before we develop enough intuitively to automatically tap into that blueprint, we must in the first instance simply spend time familiarising ourselves with the will and ways of God as revealed in the teachings of the masters.

We must spend time re-educating the thoughts of our mind so that the rational mind instinctively accepts the emergence of Divine Thought. We need to get to know the will and way of Divine Thought sincerely. We encourage that thinking Mind that was in Christ, or Krishna, or the Buddha, to be in us also. It is what I describe in this book as the harmonisation of our Soul, our Mind, Emotions, and Will, with the Soul of God, the Divine Mind, Emotions, and Will.

We re-educate, realign, and thus transform the thoughts of our unregenerated rational mind with the thoughts of those chosen messengers of Divine Thought, who have in their respective lives most influenced the spiritual existence of the world since recorded time. And the more we psychologically ingest their teachings, and imprint them on ourselves attitudinally and behaviourally, the more they become the automatic response, the go to position in our time of need.

However it is important to understand this. Whilst mental understanding is in the first instance necessary, long-term it can become useless, unless it is linked to a direct experience of that which is understood mentally. It just becomes part of the religious clutter, albeit good clutter, that we have absorbed throughout our life.

The most important thing in the whole transformational process is **"to move from a mental understanding to a continuous realisation, and as such an ongoing manifestation in every aspect of our lives and relationships".** We become doers and not just hearers of Divine Wisdom.

"We go from familiarisation to mental understanding, to practical experiencing or manifesting."

Faith or belief lodged in our mental understanding without a corresponding level of application, is dead faith. For some religious people whether Christian, Hindu, Muslim, or Buddhist, this means "having a form of religion, but inwardly denying the power of it." Mental understanding, the renewing or transformation of the mind, is the very beginning of the process of Soul harmonisation, but actualisation through application of Divine Principle, the Law of The Kingdom, is the gateway to the joy that Christ spoke of.

One then has to stay the course, to stick with that understanding and turn to it through all circumstantial experiences, until the mind, emotions, and will have been replaced by a complete fixated realisation that, as Jesus put it, "I am " or as he expressed on the cross, "not my will. but thy will be done."

Very soon you will find that you respond in a Christos Way in all situations automatically. You have psychologically been changed into the image of Christ, or Krishna, or the Buddha. The Apostle Paul described this as being "changed into the stature and the fullness of Christ."

And this is not a difficult or time consuming task. It can be simply achieved through mediation and then contemplative reflection on the Divine Truths, revealed through those Divine Messengers of the Mind of All Minds, those representatives of Pure Consciousness, Krishna, Christ, and the Buddha in their respective scriptural writings. Which then sees those Divine Truths, the Will and Way of the Christos, begin to permeate every nook and cranny of our physical and psychological life.

The Divine Truths of Krishna can be found in the messages of the Upanishads and the Bhagavad Gita, the Divine Truths of Jesus can be found in certain passages in the New Testament, such as in the one described as the Sermon on the Mount, and in his many parables, and also in his teachings in the Gospel of Thomas, and the Divine Truths of the Buddha can be found in the Tripitaka and the Dhammapada.

Whether from Krishna, Christ, or the Buddha, all are Divine Truths that not only correspond and reaffirm each other, but perfectly align with the eternal purpose of Soul Harmonisation. What is Soul Harmonisation? It is a realignment of our personality with the Personality of the Divine to progressively bring about a complete harmonisation of the Soul of each individual human being with the Soul of God, which when realised is known in Eastern spiritual teachings as a state of Enlightenment, and in Western spiritual teachings as "a life lived in the Spirit."

Divine Wisdom sheltering our existential existence is the most essential ingredient needed to navigate life's sometimes chaotic and confusing physical, psychological and spiritual evolution. And it is only when true Wisdom, that Godly Wisdom which comes from the storehouse of the Kingdom of God within, a different energetic frequency than that of the rational mind, shelters all the decisions that we make in all areas of life, it is only then that a truly successful legacy is assuredly left for others to aspire to, lay hold of, and voluntarily emulate.

Throughout this book, I will make references to the concept of the existence of a Being or Presence or Essence that pervades the universe. A Divine Essence that I will sometimes refer to as Kingdom Consciousness, sometimes Universal Consciousness, sometimes Pure Consciousness, sometimes as the Holy Breath, sometimes as the Universal Mind, and sometimes as Infinite Intelligence.

Over the centuries, this Essence has been referenced by a variety of different names, according to the cultural, religious, or philosophical tradition of a society, but more commonly referred to by people of all faith, and also by people of no faith throughout the ongoing evolution of societal existence, simply as God. It matters not what name you use to refer to its existence, what matters most is your acceptance that is does exist. That is the starting point.

As you progress further through the pages of this book, you may find yourself reading certain truths or understandings that you have already read in a previous chapter, perhaps with the phraseology or understandings expressed in a slightly different context. You are not imagining it. In certain chapters I have deliberately returned to a specific truth or learning because I have felt it is vitally important that you get a firm grasp on it.

Our mind very easily takes some teaching of a spiritual nature in, and too quickly tosses it out and forgets it before it is enabled to impact on our conscious understanding. How many readers who attend some sort of institutional place of worship can remember the message that the religious leader of that place delivered a month ago, far less how many put it into practice.

Repetition reinforces it on our conscious awareness. The mind is a psychological sponge, continuously taking in things that are presented to one or more of our sense realms in the present moment. So one thought comes and is quickly displaced by the next thought. Repetition reinforces retention. The more we see, hear, taste, touch, or smell something, the more likely we are of retaining that in our conscious and subconscious awareness.

Throughout this book, mostly in italic font, you will see scriptural examples of teachings that it is important we come to comprehend more deeply. They are scriptural truths from Hinduism, Christianity, and Buddhism that align with each other and confirm each other. Try to pause on them for a reflective moment to mentally absorb them.

They will be either the Wisdom Truths contained in the teachings of Christ in the New Testament and the Gospel of Thomas, the Wisdom Truths of Krishna as taken from the Bhagavad Gita and the Upanishads of Hinduism, part of a collection of the sacred books of Hinduism known as the Vedas that deal primarily with Knowledge and Wisdom, or Wisdom Truths of the Buddha taken from the Dhammapada, a collection of teachings of the Buddha in verse form.

These timeless teachings of the Masters of The Ages do not conflict with each other, rather they confirm each other; and their correlation with each other, is a witness to the timeless existence of the field of Infinite Intelligence and Ultimate Truth, the indisputable Oneness, that Divine Essence from which they were originally birthed in the beginning, in all their uncontaminated and non-theologised purity.

If you have trouble taking that first step of exposing yourself to teachings that are of a supposed contrary religious belief system to the one you have been familiar with all your life thus far, let this not concern you. I am assured that the eyes of your understanding will be opened to see clearly that the teachings of Hinduism and Buddhism and Christianity do not conflict with each other even though certain elements of religious society have long since stressed this to protect their own brand.

Rather the teachings of all merely confirm the teachings that have gone before. The Wisdom of Buddha confirms the Wisdom of the ancient sages and mystics of Hinduism, and the Wisdom of Christ merely confirms and adds to the Wisdom teachings of both Hinduism and Buddhism. That mental resolution should bring peace to your undertaking.

For myself, through times of meditative reading and contemplation, as I have immersed my mind in the timeless teachings of Krishna, Christ, and the Buddha, I have come to see more clearly that these three spiritual masters of different eras and supposed different religious beliefs and brands do not compete with each other, rather they complement each other, as their respective teachings go about their task of continually "restoring, realigning, supporting and harmonizing our Soul with the Soul of God."

How did the Buddha describe the outcome of this harmonisation principle at work, the end result of the ongoing harmonisation of his Mind with the Mind of God? Whilst quietly resting under a Bodhi Tree, the Ficus religiosa, the large sacred fig tree he said:

> *"The rafters of sins are broken, the ridgepole of ignorance is destroyed, the fever of craving is past: for my "mortal mind is gone" to the joy of the immortal Nirvana." (The Buddha...The Dhammapada 154.*

Whilst this book focuses primarily on the eternal nature of our Being, as witnessed and agreed on by the great spiritual masters, Krishna, Christ, and the Buddha, it also explains how our state of eternality impacts on our current state of temporality, our practical experience as a human being navigating this temporary and sometimes chaotic existence we call life.

The contents of this book will reveal the intended relationship between **our Spirit,** the key component of our eternality, and our **Soul and Body,** the key components of our temporality. They will give clarity as to **why** our thoughts affect us, from a spiritual perspective, and **how** the energetic power of those thoughts influence us from a psychological and thus behavioural perspective.

And since the energetic influence of thought cannot be removed only transformed, this book will also reveal how to harmonise the spiritual aspects of our nature with the psychological aspects of our nature, enabling the practical side of our existence to be energetically transformed, and as such to step off the "wheel of becoming" and "rest harmoniously in peace in the centre of Being."

"That spark of consciousness we are born with, that fragment of Kingdom Consciousness, that portion of the Divine Essence that is the Christ within, can be likened to one singular star witnessed at night on a dark cloud filled sky, waiting patiently to expand.

Comes the removal of that veil of cloud revealing in all its splendour a singular unlimited expanse of sparkling shining light, a star studded sky, a demonstration of the fullness and splendour of our Universal God.

This is enlightenment defined, a revelation of the hidden Christ or Atman within, and with that an understanding of the unlimited potential of our Soul."

CHAPTER 1

The Concept of the Divine Essence and its Relationship with Consciousness

❦

"I have felt a presence that disturbs me, with the joy of elevated thought; a sense sublime, of something far more deeply inter-fused, whose dwelling is the light of setting suns, and the round ocean, and the living air, and the blue sky, and "in the mind of man". A motion, and a spirit, that impels all thinking things, all objects of all thought, and rolls through all things."

— WILLIAM WORDSWORTH, ENGLISH POET.

The religion of Hinduism teaches that all human beings have the Spirit of God within them, a Divine Essence of an impersonal nature, which they refer to as the Atman, our True Self or True Nature as against our False Self, the ego I. Atman is a Hindu word that means, Spirit Soul.

Essentially it refers to the real person inside an individual, their "true being." It is made in part of the Spirit of Brahman the Absolute. Brahman in Hinduism being the name given to the one true ultimate God Hindus follow. Therefore the Atman it is not something that can be seen or touched, for it is invisible and eternal.

The Swiss psychiatrist and psychoanalyst Carl Gustav Jung acknowledged his indebtedness in his work to this Hindu concept which he referred to as "the Atmic or Undiscovered Self." Historically, according to Jung, the Self signifies the unification of consciousness and unconsciousness in a person, representing the psyche as a whole. It is realized as the product of individuation, which in his view is the process of integrating various aspects of one's personality or nature with the personality or nature of the Divine.

The end goal of Jung's treatment process, collectively called Jungian Therapy, was this individuation, an ongoing process in which different aspects of the individual personality are cultivated to function harmoniously and authentically with each other. and at the same time even though perhaps differentiating, still co-operating.

It is the re-uniting of two aspects of the psychological world of the individual. What you could describe as Soul Unification or Harmonisation, the harmonisation of differing aspects of the Soul, being the Mind, the Emotions, and the Will, but only of the individual, human Soul, not the harmonisation of humanity's collective Soul, humanity's collective Mind, Emotions, and Will to create universal harmony.

His theory being that in order for there to be societal harmony, we must first attain individual harmony. We cannot extend the hand of peace if we are not at peace within ourselves. It merely becomes the hand of compromise perhaps birthed in fear. First comes inner peace, and then outer peace.

In the early centuries of humanity's known existence, this concept of there being a Kingdom or Universal Consciousness, a Divine Essence or Infinite Intelligence, was not only central to most religious thought, it was central to some non-religious thought such as scientific thought, and also in certain philosophical thought. In fact in many cultures it was essential to their lifestyle or at least parts of it.

That concept of the existence of a Divine Essence or Pure Consciousness is becoming more and more in this modern day a focus of many spiritual teachers. Many referring to it as "a presence" or "a oneness that is all and in all."

In simple terms the Divine Essence is the Nature of God, as mentally distinguished from the persons and attributes of God. Consciousness, our personal consciousness, our capacity to breath and thus stay alive and animated, is an intrinsic part, a fragmented portion of the totality of the Divine Essence.

Probably the biggest disservice institutionalised religion did to itself was when in its attempt to make spirituality more palatable to the people, it began humanising God through the introduction of names, symbols and certain rituals, that in some religions took people away from the meta-physicality of God.

Thus the whole concept of God being a Divine Essence or Pure Consciousness pervading and permeating the entire universe and all it contains was set aside, in favour of teachings and practices that the human mind found easier to navigate and digest.

The term the Divine Essence attempts to explain the relationship between an eternal, and infinite creator, and the mortal finite universe. The Oxford dictionary defines essence as "the intrinsic nature, or indispensable quality of something, especially something abstract, which determines its character". It is speaking of the basic nature of a thing: the quality or qualities that make something what it is, and thus determine what it does.

In Philosophy the concept of the Divine Essence is represented in two arenas, being Philosophical Theism and Philosophical Pantheism. In Philosophical Theism it is believed that this Supreme Being or Divine Essence exists or must exist independent of the teaching of any particular religion. It represents a belief in God entirely without doctrine, except for that which can be discerned by reason, and by the contemplation of natural laws.

In Philosophical Pantheism it is believed that reality, the Universe and the Cosmos are identical to Divinity and a Supreme Being or entity. The physical universe is thus understood as an "immanent deity", still expanding and creating, a deity which has existed since the beginning of time.

The term pantheist designates one who holds that everything constitutes a unity, and that this unity is Divine, consisting of an all-encompassing, manifested God. And as such the many astronomical objects, the natural bodies that float in space, such as stars, planets, meteoroids, moons, and other space objects, are all viewed as parts of a sole deity.

The theory of there being an "immanent deity" in Pantheism holds that the Divine encompasses or is manifested in the material world, and that the spiritual world permeates the mundane. This theory gives credence you could say to the words of Jesus as we see in Gospel of Thomas where he says:

> *"I am the light that is over all things. I am all: from me all came forth, and to me all attained. Split a piece of wood; I am there. Life up a stone and you will find me there."*

Amongst some of the people known to have embraced Pantheism, we find Adi Shankara, the 8th century Indian Vedic scholar and teacher of Advaita Vedanta, Laozi who wrote the Tao Te Ching, Baruch Spinoza the Jewish-Dutch philosopher, Friedrich Nietzsche the German philosopher and cultural critic, and Carl Gustav Jung, the Swiss psychiatrist and psychoanalyst.

In terms of Science we have Albert Einstein, the German-born theoretical physicist, Nikola Tesla, a Serbian American inventor, and in terms of the arts we have Ludwig van Beethoven the German composer and pianist, the poets Ralph Waldo Emerson, Alfred Lord Tennyson, Walt Whitman, and English writer and novelist D.H. Lawrence,

Major religions who embrace pantheistic concepts include Taoism, and some schools of Hinduism. An important example of a pantheistic concept is Tao, which is the foundation of Taoism. Tao is a unifying principle that provides the substance and activity of the universe. Pantheistic ideas appear in many schools of Buddhism also.

But the God of the universe does not refer to itself as a Pantheist or God, or Yahweh, or Allah, or Brahman, or any other institutionalised names, when describing its Divine Essence or Immanence, its Universally Conscious Being. In spiritual writings the Divine Essence describes itself purely as "I Am". In the New Testament Book of John we read that when Jesus was attempting to describe to the hostile crowds who in essence he was as "a fragment of God's Consciousness" he simply said, "before Abraham was "I am."

The term Divine Essence then, is an analogy for the true being, the true I am, describing the metaphysical Essence of the God being in all life form, that is meant to determine what we are and what we do. It is the essential nature or substance of God, as contrasted with the essential energies of God. The essential energies of God are those external actions and influences through which the Divine Essence is made manifest. I speak of these vibrational energies in Chapter 8.

The word Ousia is a philosophical and theological term, originally used in ancient Greek philosophy, then later in Christian theology. It was used by various ancient Greek philosophers, such as Plato and Aristotle, as a primary designation for philosophical concepts of "essence or substance."

The word itself is an ancient Greek noun meaning "to be, I am." It is similar in a grammatical sense to the English term "true being." However since there was no equivalent grammatical formation in Latin, it was translated as "Essentia or Substantia," as Essence or Substance.

In this chapter I will try to simplify the concept of the Divine Essence and the subject of Consciousness as much as possible, whilst at the same time drawing attention to the extreme importance of us having even just a basic understanding of it, and its relationship and involvement in the spiritual and functional life of humanity.

Ramakrishna, the Indian Hindu Mystic and Spiritual Leader once said:

"Many are the names of God and Infinite the forms through which He may be approached.

Similarly the ancient Greek Philosopher and Polymath Aristotle said:

"God has many names, though He is only one Being."

Consciousness, or more specifically our personal state of consciousness, that brings with it a capacity to be aware, is simply "a fragment of God's Consciousness", the Divine Essence, or what you could call God's Holy Breath or God's Energetic Influence, that has been impregnated into our being to give us animated life. Without this Holy Breath we have no physical breath, and without that physical breath we have no capacity to be aware, and as such no ability to be animated.

"The Divine Essence or Holy Breath is the breath of life within our breath."

The word breath in ancient scriptures means far more than the physical exchange of air in and out of the lungs. It is one of the most profound symbols in scripture. Breath is equated with God's Spirit, the Spirit that gives life and animation. Ancient scriptures tell us:

"God breathed into Adam's nostrils the breath of life, and man became a living being."

The Apostle Paul in the New Testament's Book of Acts described our connection with the Holy Breath in the following way:

"For in Him we live and move and exist, that is in Him we actually have our being."

The Kaushitaki Upanishad of Hinduism speaks of the God Consciousness or God Breath in this way:

"I am the breath of life, and I am the consciousness of life, adore me and think of me as life and immortality."

It then goes on to say:

> *"The breath of life is one; when we speak, life speaks. When we see, life sees. When we hear, life hears. When we think, life thinks. When we breathe, life breathes. It is the consciousness of life which becomes the breath of life and gives life to a body. The breath of life is the consciousness of life, and the consciousness of life is the breath of life."*

Our personal consciousness is a fragment of Divine Consciousness or God's Breath, a fragment that Infinite Intelligence has purposefully sacrificed to become localised in our body to give life to this magnificent creation, our individualised unique combination of mind and body; to animate this individual grouping of flesh and bones and organs, that we all refer to as our body and our mind. Without that "Holy Breath within our conscious breath" that sustains and supports all our physical and mental faculties, there is no life.

Without consciousness there is no life, there is no animation, and as such there is no functioning perception or awareness through the senses. Without consciousness we are not aware of what is going on around us or inside of us. So a non-conscious person, say a person asleep or in a coma, has no movement, no animation, and certainly in most cases appears to have no demonstrable awareness of what is going on around them or inside of them.

They are still physically alive only not in an animated way, because animation needs a measure of awareness to activate it. We react in some sort of physical or emotional animated way to that which we are made aware of through one or more of our five senses, taste, touch, sight, smell, or hearing, and in doing so demonstrate the existence of a measure of conscious energy within our being.

However it is important that we understand this. Even though the physical body in a coma is "unconscious", not responsive in an animated way, and consequently not visibly impacted on by outside stimulus, the internal genomic structure of the unconscious human being is still alive and relevant.

What do I mean by that?

The Biblical Old Testament Book of Genesis says: "so God created man (human) in his own image, in the image and likeness of God he created him: male and female he created them." This scripture is not saying that the human being has been created in the same physical image as God. It is referring to the human being as being created in the same "genomic image" of God. And there is an eternality of existence attached to that genomic image, rather than the temporality of existence most believe they have.

What is a genomic image?

We have all heard I am sure reference being made to a person's genes, particularly in relation to generational "disease of the body transference". A gene is a specific segment of DNA that tells the cells of our body how to function. A genome is the "entirety of the genetic material" inside an organism.

It is believed that the human genome consists of between 20,000 and 25,000 genes. "Genetics" refers to the study of genes and the way that certain traits or conditions are passed down from one generation to another, however "Genomics" describes the study of the totality of a person's genes together, the genome of the individual.

By linking genomic analysis to behavior, psychologists can now explain, predict, and possibly, so some believe, even alter human behavior. Indeed, it is believed by some in the scientific world, that in the future, psychologists will no longer be able to model behavior without reference to genomic data; the field of psychology will therefore be transformed into genomic psychology.

Where does genomic DNA come from?

Your genome is inherited from your parents, whose combined genomic seed from a physical perspective created you; created you, the physical and psychological form. That creation process was initiated through the unification of two gametes, one being a reproduction cell of a male known as sperm, and the other being the reproduction cell of a female known as the ova. Each gamete is unique which explains why siblings from the same parents do not look the same.

However, whilst DNA is a unique chemical code that guides our physical growth, development, and health, and as such plays a critical role in these processes of determining your outward appearance and inner organ functioning, it does not by itself create the personality traits of the individual; and as such the instincts or behavioral patterns of the child are not preprogrammed or hardwired into the child at birth. They are developed and influenced over time in what has been termed the formation of an individual's identity.

All things with a measure of conscious existence, regardless of whether those created things are deemed good, or bad, or ugly by human rationale, have in their original creation still been given, through breath transfer, (remember God breathed into Adam), the genomic signature of God, signifying that this Universal Mind, the Divine Essence, is real-izing itself in this visible functioning universe in some sort of concrete phenomena; some measure of form and structure with some level of conscious awareness, varying from specie to specie.

That genomic image of God and genomic likeness to God was gen-erously and sacrificially given to us or impregnated in us when we were gifted at birth "the fragment of God's Consciousness" or God's Holy Breath that gave us animated life and continues to sustain and support our animated life.

Now I said that our personal consciousness is a fragment of Divine Consciousness purposefully sacrificed to create us as an individual liv-ing breathing soul. What happens when one sacrifices something? In simple terms they just give it up as an offering or set it aside in favour of something else or someone else, some greater and more noble cause or being than their own.

This principle of self-sacrifice was at the core of the teachings and self-example of Jesus the Christ, whether it was in the early stages of his earthly mission when he was instructing his disciples, metaphorically some would say, to sell (sacrifice) all they had and follow him.

Or in the middle stage in incidents like the story of the loaves and fishes, or in the parable of the prodigal son who having crossed over into the world of carnal pleasure chose of his own volition to give up that self-determining, happiness seeking, and pleasure directed lifestyle of the flesh, and to return to his father the seed of his existence.

And of course we see this principle of self-sacrifice at play at the end stage of Christ's earthly visitation in the profound sacrifice Christ, a fragment of God Consciousness in flesh, made of himself on the cross to become what the Christian religion teaches as a redemptive ransom for all of humanity.

This same principle, the principle of self-sacrifice, is not only seen in Christ's teachings, it is also a foundational principle built into the teachings of the Buddha and seen in the teachings and counsel of Krishna.

We see in the Hindu scriptures in talking about the characteristics of a Yogi, one who has sacrificed the pleasures of life in favour of a more austere life whilst simultaneously focused on establishing and maintaining a consciousness that is in harmony with God Consciousness, Krishna in the Bhagavad Gita Chapter 4 speaks of the many "sacrificial ways" in which one can progress that harmonisation.

It speaks of the sacrifice of wasted time in favour of the path of work. It speaks of the sacrifice of our own mindlessness in favour of mindfulness, and of the sacrifice of our own rationalistic wisdom and knowledge in favour of Godly Wisdom and Truth. It speaks of the sacrifice of material possessions such as the sacrifice of personal wealth, and it also speaks of the sacrifice of breath as in the practice of meditation.

The sacrifice of breath in Hinduism is called Pranayama, which refers to a meditative breathing exercise that clears out energy blockages that we have attached ourselves to, attachments that create physical and emotional roadblocks in our life, thus freeing the human breath to release the flow of prana, the life energy of the creator, the flow of the Spirit through our person.

And Krishna reiterates that every sacrifice done as an act of love for God, is in its own right, a pathway to a psychological harmonisation of our mind with the Mind of God.

The Bhagavad Gita Chapter 4 Verse 31 tells us that:

"Neither this world nor the world to come is for him who does not sacri-fice; and those who enjoy what remains of the sacrifice go into Brahman."

So when did this happen, when did that "fragment of God's Consciousness" become localised or impregnated into our body? It happened in an instant at our birth as an individual fragment of God's Breath or God's Conscious Energy selflessly and voluntarily came into our bodies giving our body its own individual animated life, and with that its capacity for awareness and perception through the realm of the senses.

You see developing babies need oxygen in the early stages of a woman's pregnancy. But the baby won't take their first breath by themselves until birth. This means that babies don't truly breathe in the womb. Instead, the umbilical cord provides the baby with oxygen until their first breath is taken. Immediately a baby is born they are checked at one minute and five minute intervals for heart and respiratory rates. No breath, no perception, no animated life. A baby's first cry is the initial sign of animated life, which means the baby is alive and breathing.

The umbilical cord is the vital connection between the foetus and the placenta. Umbilical cord development begins in the embryologic period, around week three of the pregnancy, with the formation of the connecting stalk. The baby is connected to the placenta by the umbilical cord. Together the placenta and the umbilical cord act as your baby's lifeline while it is in the womb. The mother in a sacrificial way "shares her breath of consciousness" with her baby.

Prior to our birth as we lay in safety, silence, and seclusion in our mother's womb, we had no need for our own breath of consciousness. For secure in the womb we shared the consciousness of our mother, with the mother's placenta assisting us to breathe while we were growing in the womb. Which gave us a measure of animation as evidenced in a baby's pre-birth kicking, but not full animation. There was no obvious activity of any of our senses, they too were in the developmental stage.

And then we were born. And in that instant, when that fragment of God's Consciousness, a fragment of Divine Conscious Energy, became embedded in us, it took over as it were from the umbilical cord the responsibility for our aliveness, and we rose up and came alive. We came forth with Divine approval, stamped with the King of Consciousness's image as a coin would be stamped after its minting with the image of the king of the day.

And as such in that moment of our birth in accordance with our Divine Birthright as heirs of Pure Consciousness, we became partakers of the genomic nature of God and all the Divine Qualities relative to it, including the resurrection principle.

The resurrection principle is the Divine promise that, as Buddhism teaches, life and death are a continuum. Meaning our individual fragment of consciousness will continue its journey after our physical death and may be reborn again into another physical form or alternately may return to the source from whence it came, Pure Consciousness, if it has attained liberation from the cycle of life, death, and rebirth.

That genomic signature of Pure Consciousness, the Divine Essence, call it God if you like, has not only been stamped on all human beings, but has been stamped on all created life forms that contain a measure of conscious awareness.

Jesus as seen in the Book of Luke in describing this essence said: "the Kingdom of God is not something people will be able to see and point to. For the Kingdom of God is within you." Jesus was referring to the fact that the genomic imprint of the Divine Nature with all the Divine character qualities has been imprinted on every human being and on all form with a measure of conscious life.

All created forms with a measure of conscious life, able to create after their own kind according to their own level of individual consciousness, have been imprinted with the genomic signature of Infinite Intelligence. All life forms with a measure of awareness are unique individual fragments of Divine Consciousness, heirs of our Divine Father, and as such are all partakers of the character qualities or nature of that Pure Consciousness.

That same genomic imprint has been stamped on the life and beauty of the animal world, whether it be upon the fowl of the air that soar to great heights, or on the multitudes of fish that swim in the depths of the sea. It has been stamped upon the beautiful butterfly, the menacing wasp. and the fragrant and beautiful flowers that ignite and excite our senses.

Whether upon the sun, the moon, or upon the starry skies, whether upon the seasons or upon the rich soil of the earth that brings forth specific food in each season, Infinite Intelligence, the Divine Essence has impressed its genomic image upon all life form, all form with a measure of conscious energy.

But perhaps most importantly, that same genomic image has been stamped on every human being that inhabits this earth. Thus all human beings, the good, the bad, and the ugly of all society, having been given the genetic signature of God. And no matter how buried and stifled for educative or ego driven purposes in a corruptible body some appear to have become, all human beings are still inseparable from God, eternally linked to the Mind of their Infinite Originator, their Creative Father, Pure Consciousness, the Holy Breath.

And as the human being needs God in its journey towards complete self-realisation, its Divine end goal, the harmonisation of its Soul (mind, emotions, and will) with God's Soul, so God needs the human being as a vehicle for its own happiness seeking self-manifestation. Ancient scriptures tell us that not only has Infinite Intelligence created all things, all things were created for God's pleasure.

Even the genomic sacrifice Infinite Intelligence made in empowering Jesus with the Holy Breath and all the qualities of that Breath, was done to bring happiness or pleasure to God. The Book of Colossians in the New Testament tells us that "it was for the Father's good pleasure for the fullness of God to dwell in Jesus".

What is the fullness of God in man. It is the fullness of the Divine Nature, embedded in that fragment of God's Consciousness full of God's Character Genes, that gives conscious life and animation, and what you could describe as Godlike character qualities; the capacity to love, forgive, show compassion, emanate peace, express benevolence, etc, etc.

From which we can logically deduce then that as it was for the Father's good pleasure that the fullness of God dwelt in Jesus, so too it is for the Father's good pleasure that the fullness of God dwells in each and every one of us also. Because that same Breath of Life that dwelt in Jesus dwells in us also, as the scripture puts it:

"The same Spirit that resurrected (brought to life) Jesus, dwells in us."

We are all fragments of the one Universal Divine Essence. And out of all the life forms with a measure of conscious life, the human being is the crowning glory of the Creative Originator and as such has been given a special role in the ongoing evolutionary journey of this universe.

It has been given a delegated dominion over all life forms by God to manifest towards all life form that same measure of love and care and sacrifice given by the Creator when it initially breathed the breath of conscious life into all things. The human being is the Divine Caretaker of the universe.

Thus as all life forms proceed on their personal evolutionary journey of consciousness, the human being must maintain its God given responsibility to be the watchman for the continual wellbeing of all that life form. The watchman not only over themselves, but over all other human beings and all animal and vegetable forms with a measure of conscious life. How do we know that a form has a measure of conscious life? It is evidenced in its capacity to create or procreate after its own kind.

And whilst the ancient scriptures tell us that "the heavens declare the glory of God and the earth shows his handiwork", it is only the human being, the mental, moral, volitional human being who can fully declare the nature of God and manifest the character qualities of God.

Which is why the human being has been given dominion over all things. For as God's power is revealed throughout the universe, so God's

Full Nature is revealed in the thinking, functional, animated, human being. The human being is therefore of special interest to the Divine in its ongoing creative self-manifestation.

We are all individual fragments of the God Consciousness, having been impregnated with that fragment of God Consciousness purely to give us life, to animate us, and as such to enable us to fulfil our Divine responsibilities to be vehicles for the creative manifestation of God's desires.

But in addition to this we have a God given responsibility to maintain correct dominion over all the earth and all it contains, over all of God's creative desires that have already been manifested into some sort of conscious life form, and all of God's future creative endeavours. And if we fail in that responsibility we fail God, and consequently fail ourselves and the rest of humanity.

And in so much as the human being, impregnated with the genomic signature of God, has been delegated responsibility as a vehicle for the ongoing wellbeing of the outer earth and all it contains, so also the human being is responsible for the ongoing wellness of its own inner being, that place of inner stillness within where that fragment of God Consciousness that we have been given dwells, the Kingdom of God within us as it is described by Jesus. We have a responsibility to keep the "house of God within" clean and tidy and in virtuous order.

Once again this is the true meaning of the words of the Apostle Paul in the Book of Acts in the Christian New Testament where Paul said: "In him we live and move and have our being." In other words, we exist, and we are all animated, thinking, aware pieces of human form or flesh and bones simply and only because that fragment of God's Consciousness is in us.

And when our personal fragment leaves our body, when we breathe out our final breath as can be witnessed as one watches someone passing, our flesh and bones, our visible form or structure, having lost its breath and thus its animation, has no alternative but to return to the dust of the earth, to rot and decay. Cryogenics won't help. No human being has been cryogenically frozen and revived back to life. That fragment of the Holy Breath that was localized in that cryogenically frozen body, has long since moved on to continue its life journey or returned to its Source.

Everything in the physical world with a measure of consciousness and as such a measure of animated life, regardless of how it looks and behaves, is what it is by reason of a common spirit-organism or mind-form which relates it to the Universal Mind. And the Universal Mind is that Divine activity which the Book of John in the New Testament calls the Word, the Logos, the Originator in creative activity. John 1-3 says: In the beginning was the one who is called the Word, and the Word was with God, and the Word was God. Through him all things were made; without him nothing was made."

That Logos, that Originator, that Infinite Intelligence is Pure Consciousness, the Divine Essence, the birthplace and seed father of all ongoing awareness and alertness in all life forms. And when we grasp this, we come to an understanding of who our True Self, who this person we refer to as me, or I, or I am, really is.

We come to understand that "I am" not just a bag of flesh and bones with a sometimes out of control thinking mind, but rather an immortal, eternal being with a Divine responsibility. And when this happens, we lose all preoccupation with fear that is the underlying emotion behind all strife in our individual and collective life. Fear of loss, fear of failure, fear of pain, fear of suffering, fear of the future, fear of other people, fear of death. all fear goes. The Hindu scripture known as the Isa Upanishad puts it this way:

> *"Who sees all beings in his own Self, and his own Self in all beings, (who sees both as common connected fragments of the one God Consciousness) loses all fear. When a person sees this great Unity or Oneness, what delusion or what sorrow can ever be near him."*

But unfortunately, many human beings don't understand this, thinking in a contaminated and thus semi-delusional state of mind that they are a totally separate being from all other beings, the sole master helmsman steering the way on their individual ship of life, and that the truth of what is going on around them lies solely in their individual awareness and subsequent personal interpretation. This is not so.

This world is ruled and controlled by the Infinite Mind and not by finite matter, by things of visible form, which probably gave rise to that saying, "things are not as they appear". But we in a semi-delusionary state of mind think the world is ruled by matter, and that this is all that matters.

And in that semi-delusionary state of mind, thinking that we are the victim of our circumstances, we attempt to manipulate or change in some way the appearance of matter whether form or circumstance to a new state that aligns with our opinion on how it should appear or behave. We focus on the form of all things rather than the underlying formator of all things, forgetting that there is a mother father Soul in all things and that Primary Soul is Pure Consciousness, the Divine Essence.

That is the true philosophy regarding all of creation, from the minutest atom to the magnificent prehistoric animal of times past. Everything with some measure and quantity of animated form has been embedded with a principal, a genomic signature, a life, a purpose, and a degree of consciousness or awareness which is appropriate to its position in the scheme of all things.

The humanity of the human, and the beauty and majesty of the world around us is stamped with God's imprint, whether that be the mountains, the forests, the oceans, or the heavens. And whilst everyone's level of consciousness differs in magnitude and intensity in its capacity to manifest, that which it manifests is always in accord with the initial level of consciousness it has been sacrificially gifted with, appropriate to its position in the Divine scheme of all things.

It is higher in an insect than in a flower, but higher still in an animal, and even higher in a human being. The human being has been gifted with a higher level of consciousness and thus awareness than that of the animal, vegetable, or mineral, which is why the scriptures tell us that the human being has been given dominion over all things. The greater the level of consciousness the greater the level of human responsibility. The word dominion comes from the Latin dominus meaning lord or master. The human being has been given sovereign responsibility under God for all conscious existence.

Infinite Intelligence has delegated the responsibility for the ongoing conscious existence, welfare, and ongoing multiplication and replication of all life form on earth to all human beings. We human beings are responsible for the ongoing preservation of all life forms. However, when the human being with the higher level of consciousness fails to fulfil its obligation to Infinite Intelligence, fails to fulfill its moral responsibility to sustain and protect all life form, then God in that moment takes back that responsibility, handing it back to Nature.

And Nature, the natural process of things set up in the beginning takes over that responsibility originally given to the human and sets about bringing things back into balance and thus Divine order. A process many human beings unknowingly refer to simply as being "nature at work," or "nature taking its course."

When the writer of that passage of scripture in Genesis, traditionally thought to be the Prophet Moses, wrote of the human being as a life form "stamped with the image of God," he was stimulating thinkers of future ages to consider a human being's unique place in the cosmic order, and a human being's true relationship to that Universal Originating Spirit, the Divine Essence.

When the human being understands this, understands that they have been stamped with the genetic imprint of Infinite Intelligence, they are well on their way to what is known in ancient teaching as **"an enlightened state of being,"** and in more modern spiritual teaching as **"a realization of one's True Self."**

For once the human being knows this and accepts this, once a human being knows and accepts that their True Self is that Divine Nature within, the Divine Essence of Kingdom Consciousness within, no matter at what age they are in their physical journey or what stage they are at in their psychological journey, they open the way for that Divine Nature to become a reality in every aspect of their waking existence.

Once this Divine Truth is both known and accepted, one becomes fully aware of their capacity to volitionally set free so to speak that Divine Nature within from the confinement of flesh, bones, concepts, and experiences it has been continuously immersed in; giving it its freedom to actively participate in both the inner (psychological) and outer (physical and social) sanctums of every aspect and experience in everyday life. They have as the poet Robert Browning put it, "opened out a way whence the imprisoned splendour may escape."

"The Kingdom of God is within you". With these words, Jesus gave voice to a teaching that is Universal and Timeless. They were a reaffirmation of the truth that nothing can ever really change the central current of humanity's purpose, and regenerate the nature of each individual, but the clear recognition of one's dignity, one's responsibility, and one's potentiality, as a vehicle for the manifestation of the Nature of God."

CHAPTER 2

The Human Being Created in The Divine Image. A Vehicle for The Manifestation of Kingdom Consciousness

❧

"The Book of Psalms in the Old Testament tell us that the heavens declare the glory of God, and the earth is an example of His handiwork. But what we must truly understand is this. It is only the human being, the mental, moral, volitional human being who can declare the True Nature of God and manifest the life-enhancing primary qualities of God's essential character, the qualities of love, compassion, and forgiveness."

"Render to Caesar what is Caesar's" is a well-known quote that appears in the New Testament's Book of Matthew and is part of Jesus' response to a joint attempt by the Herodians and Pharisees, the Jewish political and religious leaders of the day, to make Jesus stumble in front of his followers and thus impact his credibility.

The Herodians were a non-religious Jewish party who supported the dynasty of Herod and the general policy of the Roman government. They believed that the pure spiritual teaching of the Christ, combined with his emerging social influence, were together antagonistic to their interests.

The Pharisees on the other hand, were members of an ancient Jewish sect who believed in the strict observance of oral traditions and the written Law of Moses. They didn't believe that Christ was the Messiah, despite the many miracles he performed during his earthly ministry. But although Herodians and Pharisees were at opposite ends of the political spectrum, their common hatred of Christ was enough for them to join forces to try to destroy him.

The New Testament story tells us that Jesus had just returned to Jerusalem for the final time and was addressing the crowds. When he had finished sharing several parables with the people, a parable being a relatable story with some sort of moral significance, the Herodians and Pharisees saw an opportunity to put Jesus on the spot in front of his followers, to embarrass him and hopefully discredit him.

So they said to Jesus, "Tell us, then, what you think. Is it lawful to pay taxes to Caesar, or not?"

It was of course a trick question, and it was deliberate. For they knew that if Jesus answered, "No," the Herodians, the keepers of the purse could charge him with treason against the laws of the Roman government. If He said, "Yes", the religious leaders, the Pharisees, would accuse Him of disloyalty to the Jewish nation, and He would lose the support of the crowds. That was the reasoning behind the question put to Jesus, and his response was immediate and powerful.

For being aware of their ego driven malice towards him, Jesus said, "Why put me to the test, you hypocrites? Show me the coin used for the tax." And they brought him a denarius. The denarius was a coin used as the tax money at the time. It was made of silver and featured an image of the emperor with an inscription describing him as "divine."

The Jews considered such images idolatry, forbidden by the second commandment. This was another reason why, if Jesus answered, "Yes, "he would be in trouble. His acceptance of the tax as "lawful" could have been seen as a rejection of the second commandment, thus casting doubt on his claim to be the Son of God. For the second commandment forbids the honouring or worshipping as Divine any man-made image.

With the crowds and officials watching on and the coin displayed in front of them, Jesus, pointing to the coin said, "Whose likeness and inscription is this?" The Herodians and Pharisees, stating the obvious, said, "Caesar's of course." "Then," said Jesus, "render (give) to Caesar the things that are Caesar's, and to God the things that are God's." The Scripture tells us that upon hearing this, the enemies of Jesus just shook their heads and went away.

You see these Pharisees were no obscurantists, they were religious thinkers of a curious exploratory mindset. Some of them were Essenes, a Jewish sect or School of Philosophy, some were Therapeutic, of the branch of medicine concerned with the treatment of disease, and some were Mystics, spiritual pilgrims involved in exploring religious experiences that embody the act of revelation itself, an intuitive mystical encounter with God.

So when Jesus asked, "whose is this image," their minds would automatically have reverted to the profound declaration of human origins in the Book of Genesis which says, "so God created man in his own image, in the image of God created he him." They would have realised that the question was a suggestion for a thought excursion. They would have realised that the question of Jesus, "whose is this image," was a hint at the transcendent truth of the elemental non-severability of God's Nature and the nature of a human being.

It was an appeal to a Divinity Principle within the human being. It was a reiteration of Christ's statement, the Kingdom of God or the Kingdom of Heaven is within you. It was a reaffirmation of the truth, that nothing can ever really change the central current of a human being's purpose, and regenerate a human being's nature, but the clear recognition of one's dignity, one's responsibility, and one's potentiality, as a vehicle for the manifestation of God.

Thus when Jesus said, "Render to Caesar the things that are Caesar's, and to God the things that are God's," He was drawing a sharp distinction between Two Kingdoms. There was an earthly kingdom, a kingdom of the world, and Caesar held power over it, but there was another kingdom, not of this world, and Christ was and is still its King. We see Jesus speak of this in the Book of John, where he says, "my Kingdom is not of this world."

All human beings are existing in both Kingdoms, regardless of what religion we may have aligned ourselves with. When we are born we are birthed into Two Kingdoms, an earthly kingdom, and a Heavenly Kingdom. And as such we are told to "be in the world, the earthly kingdom, but not of the world."

We are spiritual beings, physically and psychologically sojourning in a foreign land so to speak. The Gospel of John in the New Testament of the Christian Bible, portrays a prayer of Jesus Christ, addressed to his Father, placed in context, immediately before his betrayal and crucifixion. In the Book of John we see the words, "be in the world, but not of the world,." and one of the most difficult challenges for humanity is to be in the world, but not of the world.

This doctrine makes it clear that we must live in this world to achieve our eternal destiny, complete union or harmonization with Supreme Consciousness. And as such under the laws of this earthly kingdom, we have certain obligations that involve material and thus temporal things. But under the laws of the Kingdom of God, we have other obligations mostly attitudinal and behavioural, virtuous things, the things that bring about peace filled relationships with all created life form and evolve and strengthen our level of personal consciousness.

Now the message hidden in a mystery that Jesus was trying to get across here in this discussion with the Pharisees and the Herodians is this. Caesar demanded money of his subjects, and as king of his earthly kingdom this was Caesars's right, and the citizens of the day were legally obliged to give him what was due.

This is why his image was imprinted on all their coinage, a declaration of his ownership of certain aspects of the material earthly realm. And Jesus was saying, "so if Caesar's image denotes ownership" pay your dues aa loyal servants of Caesar to enable this earthly kingdom to function in an orderly way, to keep the House of Caesar functioning harmoniously..

However Jesus was also saying, that even as Caesar has minted the currency of the earth, evidenced by the imprinting of his image on all coinage, and as such has ultimate ownership, so similarly God has "minted the Human Soul". And as such the human being has a Divine Responsibility to ensure the attributes of its Soul, its Mind, Emotions, and Will are in complete harmony with the Divine Soul, the Mind, the Emotions, and Will of God that are contained within that genomic image that has been stamped on it.

The human being has a responsibility to keep its personal state of divinity in Divine balanced order to ensure its own inner household is orderly, swept clean of all untoward influences, and thus functioning virtuously and harmoniously with all other life form. So, render to God what is God's due to enable this to occur.

God has stamped His image on everyone and everything that has consciousness, everyone and everything that has the Divine Breath in them. The Divine Breath is God's signature of ownership, and as such God is the primary owner or master of our being. For without the Divine Breath giving life we cease to exist, and if we cease to exist we can't pay taxes or do anything else in relation to this earthly kingdom.

So yes, give Caesar his due, this is our earthly Kingdom responsibility, but at the same time make sure to give to God His due, which is our responsibility as citizens of the Kingdom of God. And the primary responsibility we have as a citizen of the Kingdom of God in terms of paying our dues for God's sacrificial gift of the Holy Breath, is to offer ourselves without question as "instruments of righteousness" and thus earthly vehicles for the manifestation of God's Nature on earth.

In the New Testament's Book of Romans 6:13, Paul gives the people a command to not offer any parts of their bodies to sin, as instruments of wickedness, but rather offer themselves both psychologically and physically to God, as instruments of righteousness. Righteousness is one of the chief attributes of God as portrayed in the Bible, it's chief meaning being "ethical conduct". You cannot be an instrument of righteousness whilst still attached to non-virtuous or unethical conduct in thought, word, or deed.

Jesus, in what are known as the Beatitudes said, "Blessed, joyful, nourished by God's goodness, are those who hunger and thirst for righteousness, those who actively seek right standing with God, for they will be completely satisfied."

What does it mean to be an instrument of righteousness in practical terms?

To be an instrument of righteousness on earth is to be an instrument of peace and harmony with all life form, human, animal, vegetable and mineral. It is to be at peace and in harmony with this earthly kingdom and all it contains.

In practical terms it means that where is hatred we sow love, where there is injury we pardon, where there is doubt we sow faith, where there is despair we sow hope, where there is darkness we sow light, where there is unforgiveness we sow forgiveness, where there is sorrow we sow joy, where there is heartlessness we show compassion, and where there is indifference we sow understanding.

We do not seek to be consoled rather to console others, we do not seek to be loved but rather to love others, we seek not to be understood, but rather to understand others. This is what it means to be an instrument of harmony and peace. Which means that we sacrifice our ego driven needs, and deliberately offer ourselves up, attitudinally and behaviourally, as vehicles for the manifestation of God's Nature on earth.

And in the first instance it means getting our psychological and spiritual house in order. You cannot be a true instrument of peace if you are not at peace withing yourself. And the getting of internal peace will involve the setting aside or sacrificing of old manner of thought and embracing new manner of thought. For how we can ever hope to be instruments of righteousness on earth that we are called to be if we continue to embrace unrighteous thoughts, wrong intentions, and subsequent unrighteous behaviours in our everyday lives.

In the first instance it all centres on getting the faculties of our Soul, our Soul centres, being our Mind, Emotions, and Will, in right relationship or harmonisation with the faculties of the Soul of God, being God's Mind, Emotions, and Will.

You see first comes the thought, and then comes the attitude or intent setting, bringing about the behaviour applicable to that thought. So change the thought and you change the intent which then sacrifices the behaviour that that particular type of thinking had the potential to create. What are we doing? We are changing the energy dynamic associated with that type of thought or thinking.

For our own continual progress in our spiritual evolution of consciousness, attachment to the supposed rational thought process must be our primary target of sacrifice. The rational thought process must become the servant of the intuitive thought process, the Christ or Krishna, or Buddha Mind within, rather than the master we have enabled it to become for the purpose of self-interest.

"Fix the thought and you fix the intent; fix your intention and you fix your behaviour; fix your behaviours and you alter the physical or psychological effect, the specific energetic influence that that original thought has on the wellbeing of yourself or others."

However the only way you can maximise the neutralisation of a habitual harmful thought is through the continuous process of displacement; which involves not only the sacrifice or setting aside of a specific thought or pattern of thinking, but in addition the filling of the void created with a faith filled thought, its specific opposite.

Willpower is not enough. For there is a creative energy dynamic cemented in place through habit that needs to be addressed. And energy cannot be destroyed, but it can be transformed. And that is where the Divine Essence enters the picture.

Quantum Physics has now reduced all material things to a primary ether or essence, universally distributed, whose numerous particles are in absolute equilibrium, moving and revolving, and regenerating, and restoring, and dancing together creating all things beautiful in perfect order as per their original Divine design. So all these particles are joint participators, and all are equal and necessary contributors to the ongoing functioning of the universe.

Science has also revealed to us that the initial movement, that which started this Divine Dance, that which began to concentrate certain material substances out of the ether and create some sort of form, could not have originated with the particles themselves, and as such we are logically compelled to acknowledge the presence of an invisible Creative Intelligence, a Divine Essence exercising volition, exercising its own free will as it chooses.

That Creative Intelligence, exercising volition, that Mind above All Minds, has impressed its image and subscription, declared its Kingdom ownership, upon all created things with a measure of life or consciousness. I say with a measure of conscious life to distinguish it from anything of form that man has created. Remember Jesus did not say, "look at a rock or in a rock and you will find me, he said, "look under a rock and you will find me."

The Mind of All Minds has imprinted its image upon not only all human life, but on the life and beauty of the animal world, upon the marvels of the vegetable world, and upon the abundance of fruits, and upon all flowers of the earth. Upon all that is beautiful.

So in order to come to a greater understanding of how this earthly kingdom works, both the seeming good and the seemingly bad, we must rise to some conception of that Invisible Intelligence, that Mind above all Minds methodically working and thus realising itself or manifesting its existence in earthly animated forms.

If in the first instance we can grasp this principle, that the Universe, having been created by the God Mind, and ongoingly supported and sustained by the God Mind, has a Primary Soul, it being the Soul of God, then as such we are able to accept that the true philosophy of creation is that within every molecule and every atom, there exists a degree of Supreme Consciousness, a Fragment of God's Consciousness or the Divine Breath appropriate to its position in the universe.

At the same time we must remain acutely aware that all fragments do have the capacity to manifest something, to create something beautiful after their own kind. We all have a calling to participate in the virtuous functioning of this universe, with the words, "be fruitful and multiply" as seen in the Book of Genesis, but how that calling manifests and how much manifesting occurs is all related to the level of Divine Consciousness we have progressed to.

And as such we must then logically conclude, that in the great scheme of things, each Fragment of God's Consciousness, alive and functioning in some individual life form, will differ in magnitude and differ in its capacity to manifest. But whilst the operation of that God Mind differs in the density and quality of its manifestation through each individual vehicle, there is one thing that we can be assured of. It is that the quality and frequency of that manifestation will always be in proportion to the receptive capacity of the matter, in which it is impregnated.

It will be higher in the insect than in the fruit or vegetable, higher in the animal than in the insect, and occasionally be higher in specific animals, where evidence has shown the existence in the animal of shrewdness, which implies observation, and close reasoning; and of course the quality and frequency of that manifestation is at its highest point in the human being, which is why the human being has been given under God, dominion over all other life form.

As human beings we are told in ancient scriptures that we have been delegated the highest capacity to manifest and as such have been given dominion over all things on the earth. But most people have no realisation of this in their lives, and rather allow the things of the earth, including psychological things, the thoughts of the human rational mind, to have complete dominion over them.

You see to grow in consciousness it is not sufficient for us to intellectually affirm the Presence of God manifesting itself in a blade of grass, or in a flower, or in a beautiful butterfly, for having been given dominion over all things we have a responsibility to carry the thoughts higher, and to not rest, until we have realised that Divine Presence manifesting itself in a far more intense degree in ourselves.

The deeper our level of consciousness, the greater our capacity is to influence metaphysically the things within that cause us to manifest non-virtuous behaviour rather than virtuous or Kingdom Consciousness behaviour.

If you wanted to relate what I have just said back to institutionalised religion. In Christianity it is not enough to merely recognize and accept the sacrifice of Christ and the subsequent indwelling of Christ, and in Hinduism it is not enough to merely recognize and accept and implement the process of self-enquiry leading to what is termed self-realisation, and then in both cases say, "Well, I'm done, all good, my eternal insurance policy is in place, now all I have to do is mark time until I end up in heaven."

For whilst both these things, the salvation experience and the self-realisation experience, are helpful in the first instance in our evolution of consciousness, neither of these things are our primary purpose.

Our egoic false self however will tell us that salvation or self-realization is sufficient. Our egoic false self will say okay, you're all good, you are now saved, so go and open a mega-church, or alternately okay, you're all good you are now enlightened, go sit in a cave and mediate on the sound of OM.

Our primary purpose in this earthly Kingdom Life, after going through the recognition or acceptance process, the Self-Realisation or Salvation process, is to be a vehicle for the manifestation of the Nature of God, in thought, word, and deed, and thus an active instrument of righteousness.

And if we don't know how God's Nature expresses itself we need to find out, and then implement those Divine Principle into our earthly activity, in both thought, intent and in subsequent behaviour. The Bible refers to this as "working out your salvation." We must work out our salvation, if we are of the Christian faith, or we must work out our self-realisation, if we are of the Hindu or Buddhist faith.

We are fashioned in the Divine Image upon receiving the Divine Breath at our birth, and with that we have been given dominion over all things, and as such our Soul, being our Mind, Emotions, and Will, is readily receptive to Divine Thought. But being fed with a small measure of Divine Thought, perhaps through public attendance at a church, mosque, or holy place, will not eliminate entirely the onslaught of lower thought, the many machinations of a decades long mis-programming of our mind.

Present moment mind strongholds, vain imaginings, in most cases are not new, they are usually strongholds that we have indelibly imprinted into our personal consciousness over many years of cultivating our own personal identity, thus veiling from sight our realization of the Presence, or conscious understanding of the reality of the Kingdom of God within us.

Albert Einstein put it succinctly when he said:

"You can't solve a problem with the same level of consciousness that created it".

You can't remove a lifetime of accumulated vain imaginings with the same level of consciousness that created it. They can only be transcended with the aid of a higher level of consciousness, Kingdom Consciousness. The Essence of Supreme Consciousness, the Kingdom of God our Divine Nature within, waits patiently for permission to bring the characteristics of its higher nature to the outer circumstances of our lives.

Both the influencing aspects of our lower nature and the influencing aspects of our higher nature lie dormant, waiting and watching for an opportunity to come out to play in our own personal pilgrimage of consciousness. In terms of our higher nature in a good way like a sunken ship wanting to float to the surface of our life to reveal its treasures, but in terms of our lower nature in a detrimental way, like a shark prowling around the ocean of our consciousness, like a sea stalker, waiting for the right moment to attack.

In our ingrained self-survivalist way of life, we personally are occupied with one little corner of consciousness, the lower corner and that has to change. We have to stop being in the earthly Kingdom and of the earthly Kingdom, one foot in each camp, and rather become one who whilst being in the earthly Kingdom, is primarily a loyal subject of the heavenly Kingdom.

Our shared but mostly unconscious and unnoticed personality profile containing specific self-developed attitudes and patterns of behaviour, knows how to express itself through us, in other words how to come to the surface of our ephemeral existence.

It knows how to embed a particular aspect of itself into our life circumstances. It knows our weaknesses and our points of vulnerability. How does it know? Because it is the psychological storehouse, call it memory bank if you like, of all our thoughts and behaviours and potential vulnerabilities collected up until this stage of our life.

There is a war raging in the heavenlies. A war between the energetic forces of Light and the energetic forces of Darkness which flows down to this visible existence we commonly refer to as life, the life of humanity. In other words life as we know it, everyday life is continually being impacted on by these opposing forces of Light and Darkness both striving to achieve pre-eminence in the lives of all human beings. There is the visible side to our existence and there is a non-visible side to our existence.

We live in an ephemeral world, and a spiritual world, a physical world, and a meta-physical world, an earthly Kingdom and a Heavenly Kingdom, both meant to be harmoniously co-existing with each other, but which in many cases are not; they are in a state of ongoing mutual opposition or conflict, and thus disharmony.

Our old habitual way of thinking that has been imprinted on our consciousness will lie in stillness waiting to come to the surface of our lives at the first opportunity, unless, and herein lies the secret:

"Unless our thoughts have imprinted on them something more energetically powerful than the energetic or vibrational power of a self-interested thought."

And the only thought that is more energetically powerful than a thought emanating from our lower nature, is the thought that emanates from our higher nature, our True Self, the Kingdom of God within us, the thought of Infinite Intelligence.

The human being is the jewel on the crown of creation, and when Jesus took that coin in his hand, and asked the question "whose is this image," he was stimulating the thought process of those present to consider the human being's unique place in the cosmic order, and its true relation to the universal originating spirit, the Divine Essence.

The eternal purpose is everywhere. When the heart grows faint and the hands weary, how sustaining and encouraging it is to know that life is not just simply a game of chance. Everywhere around us and within us there is purpose, intelligence, evolution, and love. and man's true relation to the originating, universal spirit; and when an individual has really found that, they are well on their way to the region of understanding and True Self-realisation.

Pure Consciousness or Infinite Intelligence has expressed itself by materializing its thoughts in the phenomena of the universe, but the human being is the highest expression of that Creative Intelligence, of that Originating Mind. The embodiment of Pure Consciousness was in a man called Jesus in a particular era, and whilst that man did not stay long in the limitations of the flesh, we saw him stay long enough to manifest the splendid Divine potentiality of a person in whom an understanding of the Kingdom Principles of Life dwell.

Similarly, the emergence of the human forms of Krishna and the Buddha in their respective eras of earthly existence were given to humanity to help humanity brush off the centuries long dust of accumulated dogmatic limitations, and theological schemes of salvation, and all the rest, that in many cases had brought misery and suffering to those caught in the middle, rather than the joy and peace that is humanity's Divine birthright being fragments of God's Consciousness.

All Hindus, Christians, and Buddhists are products of Pure Consciousness expressing itself sacrificially in an individual life form. The word Christ comes from the Greek word Christos, which means "the anointed one". The word Krishna in Greek is the same as Christos. A colloquial Bengali rendering of Krishna is Christo which is the same as the Spanish for Christ".

We are all a part of the Christos Connection, all imprinted with the Divine Nature of Infinite Intelligence. All the characteristics of the Christos, the personal attributes of Christ and Krishna and the Buddha, and as such of Divine Consciousness itself are within us, lying in stillness in what Jesus described as "the Kingdom of God Within You," waiting for us to imprint the fullness of truth it contains into our outer practical experience. But it is we who must do the imprinting.

To imprint as a human being is to attach ourselves in a strong and permanent way to some specific influence of someone or something. Imprinting is a form of learning in which a particular life form gains its sense of species identification. A bird does not automatically know it is a bird when it hatches. The bird visually imprints on its parents during its critical period of development.

A baby bird does not fully understand it is a bird until it has imprinted the truth that "I am a bird and birds can fly," truth that its mother bird has made available to it. After imprinting it will identify with the behavioral characteristics of that species of life form for life.

But until the baby bird in a practical sense acts out that which it has imprinted on its consciousness taken from its mother regarding its ability to fly, or if through indifference or self-will the baby bird rejects this learning, it will never fly no matter how hard it tries. Imprinting behaviour in dogs is essentially how they bond with their pet parents. Dogs typically pick one human being to imprint on, although they can still warm to other members of the family.

Similarly a human baby when it is born is not aware it is a human being, nor a Divine Being capable of expressing God-like qualities. It is a learned process during childhood and into early adulthood. And the type of human being it thinks it is as an adult all depends on what particular imprinting it has absorbed during its early years of physical and psychological growth.

This is the hidden message in the teaching of Jesus as seen in the Book of Matthew where he says: "I tell you the truth, unless you change and become like little children, you will never enter the Kingdom of Heaven."

He was saying go back to being a sponge for learning, go back to being a sponge for learning as an innocent uncontaminated child is when first it discovers its powers of perception. He was talking about humbleness and willingness. Being humble enough to realise that what you have absorbed so far into your thinking faculties hasn't worked too well, so sacrifice that, and in its place embrace a willingness to try a new way, as if you had been born again, by imprinting God's Nature into your own personal conscious awareness.

When the Apostle Paul as we read in the New Testament said to those around him, "be imitators of me, as I am of Christ," he was not just saying, "copy me," he was saying indelibly imprint my attitudes and behaviours on your conscious awareness as I have with the attitudes and behaviours of Christ. It's the "fake it until you make it" principle. Yes in the first instance we copy them, but if we continue to copy them before long they become a conscious response or a response of our consciousness at all times in all situations; they become habitual.

All human beings upon taking their first breath of life at birth, automatically become containers of the Divine Creative Breath and as such psychologically ingest the Divine Nature into their being. And in that process all the qualities and powers of the Kingdom of God to successfully navigate human life on earth are made available to us.

They lie dormant within our soul desiring earnestly to manifest, and they will manifest through us **"once we imprint them on our conscious awareness."** But therein lies the key.

All those character qualities of the Godhead, having been impregnated into our Soul, the Kingdom of God within, can only guide us, and support us, when we, as an act of our own volition, imprint those characteristics into our conscious personality or identity, thus giving permission for the Divine Nature to manifest them through us. We are harmonising our personality with the God Personality, our underlying selfless intent to be an instrument of righteousness on earth.

"We don't have to continually petition God to give us something, we simply have to give God permission to be everything in us and through us, and that happens as we imprint the character qualities of Divine Intelligence into our state of awareness."

The measure of imprinting that has occurred, determines the measure of permission we give Divine Intelligence to act energetically on our behalf, and the measure of permission we give Divine Intelligence determines the measure of Gods' Grace that is manifested into our lives in return, for it is in giving that we receive.

All human beings are anointed creations of God, Divine caretakers of God's Universe, products of the Originating Mind, and as such have a responsibility to in a righteous, virtuous, moral, useful, and good way caretake the rest of God's creation whether things of form or things of flesh.

And as we recognize this Originating Mind as our true self, as we recognize that we are a localized fragment of God Consciousness having an earthly experience, and seek to strengthen and "manifest" the character qualities or Nature of that Originating Mind, through ongoing absorption of the life changing principles embedded in the teachings of Krishna, Christ, and the Buddha, we will all be able to eventually confidently say as did Jesus, "I and the Father (Universal Mind) are one; he that hath seen Me hath seen the Father."

The essential way to successfully navigate both this earthly kingdom and the Heavenly Kingdom is through the harmonisation of our Soul, being our Mind, Emotions, and Will, with the Soul of God, being God's Mind, Emotions, and Will.

To understand the practicality of that blueprint of the Divine Mind, before we develop enough intuitively or simply habitually to automatically tap into it, we in the first instance simply have to spend time imprinting, re-educating the thoughts of our mind bringing them into harmony with the thought processes of God.

We re-educate, realign, and thus transform the thoughts of our rational mind with the thoughts of those chosen messengers of Divine Thought, who have in their respective lives most influenced the spiritual existence of the world since recorded time.

And the more we psychologically ingest their teachings, the more we imprint them on our awareness, then the more we manifest them. And the more we manifest them the more often they will become the automatic response of our will in our time of need. Life then becomes Divinely habitual.

And this does not require any complicated schedule or overly disciplined ritual. It can quietly and progressively be achieved through contemplative reflection in those Divine Messages revealed through those Divine Messengers of the Divine Mind, Krishna, Christ, and the Buddha.

Divine Messages, that not only correspond and reaffirm each other but messages that are all embedded with one primary eternal seed purpose. To realign the Mind of Humanity with the Divine Mind of Infinite Intelligence, the Divine Essence, equipping the human being to become an effective vehicle for the manifestation of the character qualities of Pure Consciousness, and thus a purpose filled and active instrument of righteousness on earth.

"Although you appear in earthly form, your essence is Pure Consciousness. You are the fearless guardian of Divine Light, so come, return to the root, the root of your own Soul".

— JALAL AL-DIN MUHAMMAD RUMI....
13TH CENTURY POET AND SUFI MYSTIC.

CHAPTER 3

Our Pilgrimage of Personal Consciousness

❧

"Paradise is not a place; it is a state of Consciousness"

— RUMI.

A pilgrimage is the term often used to describe an individual's journey through life, sometimes as a general description of personal growth and exploration, outlining a particular spiritual focus or pathway which it is believed will lead to an encounter with God. Another term for pilgrimage is a holy expedition.

The Pilgrims Progress, is a Christian allegory, written by John Bunyan in 1678. It is regarded as one of the most significant works of theological fiction in English literature, and it is a book which has had a strong influence on gifted writers as diverse as C.S. Lewis, Charles Dickens, George Bernard Shaw, Charlotte Bronte, Mark Twain, John Steinberg, and Enid Blyton. The entire book The Pilgrims Progress is presented as a dream sequence narrated by an omniscient narrator.

The chief protagonist, a man called Christian, is an everyman character and the plot centres on his journey from his hometown, the City of Destruction (this physical world), to the Celestial City, (the Divine world, commonly called heaven). It's author John Bunyan, was working hard to finish another book when he conceived the idea of writing a story about the adventures that a devout Christian might have in trying to save their soul as they set out on a personal pilgrimage to heaven.

The above quote by Rumi, simply expressed, is of significant importance to all spiritual pilgrims, not just those with a leaning towards the Christian religion, but to those of all faiths who find themselves on a journey to find ultimate Truth; because it exposes a common deception that has been used over the centuries as a type of fear driven narrative to corral many spiritual pilgrims (seekers), into some particular institutionalist religious organization.

That deception being the "Heaven or Hell" screenplay of Christianity, or the "Paradise or Jahannam" screenplay of Islam; taught as a type of "faith or fear" it's your choice scenario. It is a deception that all spiritual pilgrims who truly want to succeed in their quest must avoid.

But even worse still it is singularly the most influential deceptive concept that has prevented humanity in general from not only pursuing a greater understanding of consciousness and thus the cosmic connectedness of all life form, but also in stalling the pilgrimage of personal consciousness evolution of many spiritual pilgrims who grow weary in their search for truth.

Seeing spiritual pilgrims who having searched the spiritual landscape for true spiritual water to refresh themselves, resigning themselves to the belief that in terms of authentic spirituality perhaps near enough is good enough. The thought comes, "I know I am going to heaven, and that's all that matters."

That religious ideological deception, the heaven hell scenario, regardless of whatever institutionalised brand it is attached to, or regardless of whatever teaching it is insinuated into, has been alongside the "whose God is the true God" argument, the key component underpinning the religiously motivated wars and genocides that witnessed the brutalisation and subsequent deaths of millions of innocents from the beginning of recorded time, not only in the Christian and Muslim religions, but in Hinduism and Buddhism as well.

Christianity, Hinduism, Buddhism, and Islam have all experienced both historical and ongoing religious persecution, many times from each other, and systematic violence, in the form of forced conversions, documented massacres, genocides, demolition and desecration of temples and places of worship, as well as the destruction of educational centres. This includes state supported acts, such as destroying or defacing religious icons and buildings, and targeting properties shared by religious communities during peace and war.

And even in this current day the Paradise or Jahannam deception is still the key component underpinning the insanity that drives an Islamic terrorist to in a selfish and premeditated way, sacrifice their own life and even the lives of their loved ones in favour of a successful mission of death and destruction against those of dissimilar beliefs.

A recruited Islamic suicide bomber is motivated by the obscene promise that after he or she carries out their mission of death and destruction, they will immediately transmigrate to heaven (paradise), and the Karmic life of birth, death, and soul rebirth (reincarnation) will be over for all time. They are promised that in this paradise (heaven) they shall recline on jewelled couches, be waited on with cups of the purest wine, given the fruits of their own choice and the flesh of fowls that they relish, and receive a gift of seventy virgins.

And whilst the average Christian's beliefs about heaven are not as sensual and pleasure driven as are those of the Islamist terrorist, there is still a degree of psychological and material comfort and reward attached to the average Christian's belief about what awaits them in heaven.

Many Christians believing that heaven is a place of peace and happiness, where streets are paved with gold, where the gates are made of pearl and the walls of the city of heaven are made of precious jewels. A physical place where there will be no sickness or sorrow and all of their needs will be met. A visible place, a paradise, somewhere up there in the clouds, where all our loved ones will be waiting to greet us and live with us happily ever after in physical form.

But what did the Islamic Poet and Sufi Mystic Rumi say in reference to these beliefs? He said:

"Paradise is not a place; it is a state of Consciousness".

In my previous book The Divine Dance of The Universe, Cosmic Consciousness Freedom from Body and Mind, I spoke on the subject of Consciousness looking at it from a spiritual, a psychological, and a physical perspective.

In simple language I spoke extensively on the relationship of this thing we call consciousness with our everyday thoughts and behaviours, and its influence on the truthfulness of our awareness and perception in everyday life, those key components of the mind and senses we use to understand and interpret life events, and then act accordingly.

In this present economic and social climate, now, perhaps more than ever before, consciousness is a subject that all human beings must have at least a basic understanding of in order to successfully navigate the current and future headwinds that life is going to impose as the storms of life circle and the winds of change blow through each individual life and society.

Our institutionalised religious beliefs, and our institutionalised doctrinal alignments alone will simply no longer cut it, for they do not contain the spiritual energy that is necessary to support us psychologically in this modern day of extremes, evidenced in the skyrocketing surge in mental illness around the world in recent years.

Rumi in his earthly life was a 13th century Persian poet, Islamic scholar, and Sufi Mystic, who lived that earthly life with a deep understanding that to seek after heaven as a physical place to retire to in the afterlife was not fact, but pure religious fiction. He fully comprehended that the purpose of life is not all about "a pilgrimage to a place in the afterlife", but rather a pilgrimage to a particular "state of being in the present life".

He understood that there was a spiritual journey to complete, yes, but that it was not just a physical journey to another place after death, rather it was:

"An expansion of our consciousness and thus awareness to a higher state of being, during our earthly life."

Rumi understood that our foremost priority in life is "the journey" not the destination. The "journey or pilgrimage of the Soul" through the three levels of conscious existence, starting at the lowest level called the Collective Unconscious which we are born into, continuing in its progressive pilgrimage to the level of Collective Consciousness, which gives us a greater understanding of the interconnectedness of all life and our shared humanity; and then in the third and final stage returning to our Source, Pure Consciousness, the Creative Originating Spirit from which our individual seed of consciousness first came forth.

Be comforted that there is an end goal but focus on the intermediatory journey of our Pilgrimage of Consciousness, our pilgrimage from the Collective Unconscious level to the Collective Conscious level, which centres on the harmonisation of our Soul with the Soul of God.

The Apostle Paul in the New Testament described it as "the attainment of unity of belief", and "a greater understanding and knowledge about Christ the Son of God, thus attaining the same stature (status) and fullness (power) of Christ."

Rumi understood that our consciousness is simply a fragment of God's Consciousness, or what you could call God's Holy Breath or God's Energetic Influence; a fragment that Infinite Intelligence has sacrificed to become localised in a physical body, and a fragment that is destined at the end of a particular earthly pilgrimage of supporting and sustaining an individual human soul, to return to its Source, Pure Consciousness from which it was originally sacrificed.

So why did God through the sacrifice of a fragment of his own Pure Consciousness make alive and animated an individual human being, and then dispatch that human being on its own personal pilgrimage of consciousness? The answer is not profound.

The human being was created, equipped, and dispatched on its earthly pilgrimage simply for God's own happiness and pleasure. The intention being that the human being in its role of lordship or dominion over all other life form, would in its role manifest the necessary aspects of God's Nature needed for the task, and thus give pleasure to the Father of Creation; similarly as a human father gets pleasure in watching their own child manifest the parents nature.

We have all heard the saying I am sure, perhaps laced with a hint of pride, in speaking of a child, "he gets that from his father", or "she gets that from her mother." The scripture tells us that "God created all things for his own pleasure."

What kind of pleasure? The pleasure that would be realised when God as a proud Father-Creator watched the human being, his creation, successfully navigate its earthly existence, eventually returning home to its source. I mean who doesn't like watching a diverse and intense true life stage play, full of twists and turns. The evolution of individual consciousness is the psycho-spiritual Prodigal Son/Daughter story, written, produced, and directed by Infinite Intelligence.

We are all prodigal sons and daughters of the Father of Consciousness, sojourning in a foreign land, and in that sojourning, since we human beings have the genomic imprint of God in our being we also have that happiness or pleasure seeking gene burned into us, into our own personal pilgrimage. And at times we will experience it manifesting in some specific way, sometimes in a good way but also sometimes in a bad way if that manifestation is purely motivated by self-interest.

This is perfectly exemplified in that parabolic story, told by Jesus, the Parable of the Prodigal Son written in the New Testament's Book of Luke; it is the story of a young man who left his birth family, went on a pilgrimage of pleasure to another place, and eventually returned to his seed father in his originating home after much disillusionment.

Every human being is an inherently pleasure or happiness seeking individual, mainly because to the human mind it appears to be the best option. No one deliberately seeks unhappiness, in fact most people resist it at all costs. So why do all human beings have this drive to find pleasure or happiness? Where did this drive come from? It was given us when the genomic imprint of God's Image including God's desires, likes and dislikes, was planted in us at our first breath.

It happened when that fragment of God Consciousness became localised in our body. It happened in an instant at our birth as the Breath of God came into our bodies and our body came alive, came into conscious existence, and with that we received the genetic imprint of God which amongst other things included the "happiness or pleasure drive or gene."

You see as mentioned prior to birth we were happily sleeping in the womb of our mother being nurtured or kept alive through the breath or consciousness of our mother, which also was a fragment of God Consciousness. So as a foetus, if our mother was happy we were happy, if our mother was unhappy we were unhappy. If our mother whilst consuming alcohol during her pregnancy damaged a few of her brain cells, we the foetus according to science had a few brain cells damaged also.

Then at our physical birth that responsibility for sustaining and influencing our existence was transferred to and taken over by the Breath of God. You could say we received our own personal fragment of God Consciousness as we ceased reliance on our mothers' breath and ceased primarily depending on our mother for our ongoing psychological and physical expansion and growth, which included our own personal happiness.

In the Old Testament's Book of Genesis in speaking of original creation it says, "God breathed into his Adam's nostrils the Breath of Life and man became a living creature." Or what is described in modern language as a conscious being.

The words "conscience" and "conscious" come from the Latin root relating to "two states of awareness". The first word **conscience relates to a moral awareness,** and the second word **conscious, relates to a physical and mental state of wakefulness or awareness of our surroundings.**

So you could say that when the Breath of God came into us at birth we not only received animation, a physical and mental wakefulness, but we also received an abiding moral awareness, a knowledge of right and wrong which would then manifest throughout our life as what is commonly described as our "voice of conscience".

And of course we received various other genomic influences including the happiness or pleasure seeking gene, that I just mentioned, which many times in life since it has it own separate set of needs will begin working against our state of moral awareness there to give us guidance,

So it becomes in the moment a war of two genetic guidance systems, and if our moral awareness gene capitulates to a pleasure seeking gene the end result is the committing of what is termed as some sort of sin against ourself or others. And it all depends on our existing state of personal consciousness or awareness. The greater or deeper our level of Personal Consciousness that contains our moral awareness, the more likely are we going to see our being choosing moral awareness over pleasure seeking awareness, and thus ethical conduct over unethical conduct.

Some of the earliest and most delightful, animated movements and sounds a baby makes is when the happiness gene kicks in and they begin smiling and giggling, which usually commences around three to four months of age, as they embrace some type of pleasurable awareness experience, brought to one or more of their five sense realms by something or someone.

That Breath of God our source of conscious existence or animation, that gives us awareness or perception, and thus the ability for the baby to observe something and think "yes, that makes me happy," which results in an emotional display called a giggle, is described in different ways in different religions, but all referring to the same thing, Consciousness.

But some babies in the same situation won't giggle but rather cry, for example say the case of a baby lying in a cot watching a bright colourful mobile go round and round. That colourful mobile that spins endlessly above a child's cot may for one baby, be a source of pleasure because of how it perceives it, and thus kick in the happiness gene creating an emotional response of a giggle, but to another baby whose perceptive abilities are different it may kick in the fear gene, creating an emotional response of a cry. And it all comes back to the baby's current level of awareness or perception.

Everything that happens in life is determined by our current level of conscious awareness, which contains the component of moral awareness, which is why something like a harmful impulsive act that affects someone else might be regarded by one person as right and appropriate in the circumstances, but the same act to another person of a deeper level of consciousness might be later seen as an endless source of guilt and regret. It all comes back to our current state in this instance of moral awareness, a component of consciousness.

As our pilgrimage of consciousness through the Collective Unconscious state, then into the Collective Conscious state, and finally into a complete unification with Pure Consciousness continues, many noticeable elements in our psychological and behavioural functioning will appear.

One will notice a higher level of perceptual awareness, of how we interpret life events, a higher level of moral awareness, how we judge situations and events, and also a new capacity for intellectual enlightenment or illumination will appear, what you could call the getting of True Wisdom.

Which places the unified individual on a higher plane of functioning existence than those still at the Collective Unconscious or Collective Consciousness stage. One has a deeper investment in the cosmic guidance system referred to in Christianity as being "led by the Spirit," or in everyday language "a state of knowing intuitively."

In a higher state of consciousness one begins knowing more deeply and being guided more continuously by the supposed unknowable, that which "exists in another dimension", in a different time and space. It is a level of knowing which cannot be realised through simple awareness which manifests in this existing time and space, using as its guide for understanding, the rational and many times irrational thought process.

In this higher state of consciousness, a person also comes to a greater awareness or sense of their own physical mortality and their Atman immortality, a conscious awareness of the eternal life that is already theirs, where prior to this the tendency for a human being is to see themselves purely as a mortal human being who eventually will die and then that is the end of life.

Which is why so many attach themselves to the heaven or paradise scenario. It makes the thought of death less scary. They have a known safe place to transition to, so the thought of death becomes slightly less intimidating. But when one through an increased level of Personal Consciousness comes to a true realisation of their own true immortality, rather than the mortal nature of human life, then the death principle becomes a thing not to be feared, but rather something to be embraced as another ongoing cosmic adventure.

The Apostle Paul of the New Testament, when he came to this realisation cried out, "death, where now is thy sting". In speaking of Jesus the Book of Timothy in the New Testament says, "who abolished death and brought life and immortality to light." The ancient Prophet Isaiah in speaking of the coming of Jesus said, "he will swallow up death for all time."

We alone decide through our own volition, through our personal Soul behaviours, Soul behaviours being the chosen attitudes and behaviours of our Mind, Emotions, and Will, which state of consciousness we want to exist in in this present moment. The Old Testament describes these choices very bluntly with the words, "choose life, or choose death." Meaning choose eternality or temporality.

Do we want to in this present moment progressively evolve in conscious awareness and as such create a heavenly life right now on earth, or are we content to progressively devolve our state of consciousness and thus languish in a continuous hellish circumstantial existence? Are we choosing through our attitudes and subsequent wise decisions and thus wise behaviours to live a heavenly life in this present moment, or are we content to wallow in restless uncertainty about our ongoing life?

We have been taught a deceptive concept, that here we are, in this physical world, psychically and physically separated from God, and that the only way to know and experience God will be when we eventually go to heaven to meet God after we die. When in reality there is no separation between humans and God, because of our mutual source, which expresses itself in the indivisible reality of Divine Consciousness or the Divine Essence within.

The Isa Upanishad of Hinduism in speaking of "this Divine Essence that pervades all and unifies all," this Pure Consciousness, puts it this way:

> *"He moves, and he moves not. He is far, he is near. He is within all, and he is outside of all. Who sees all beings in his own Self, and his own Self in all beings, loses all fear. When a sage (a spiritual seeker) sees this great Unity and his Self has become all beings, he loses all fear."*

Recently we have seen the terms "a Christ Conscious Person, or a Buddhi Conscious person, or a Krishna Conscious person" coming to the fore in the teachings of certain spiritual influencers.. They are all referring to the same thing, the Human Soul at oneness with the Soul of God, working as one in complete harmonisation with each other.

To be Krishna Conscious means to work and fully exist in complete knowledge and awareness that the Consciousness of God, the Divine Essence, the Vibratory Energy of God is indwelling in you. To be Christ

Conscious is to work and exist in complete knowledge and awareness that the Consciousness of God, the Divine Essence, the Vibratory Energy of God is indwelling in you. To be Buddhi Conscious is to work and fully exist in complete knowledge and awareness that the Consciousness of God, the Vibratory Energy of God is indwelling in you.

But along with this knowing and most importantly it is the alignment of the human will with that Vibratory Energetic Influence, God's Will, that gives it influence in our daily attitudes and behaviours, to enable it to function freely. Without the harmonisation or unifying of our will with God's will there will be no manifestation of the energetic influence of the Divine. The two wills must co-operate and align.

> *"To be in any of these three states of being or existing, to be consistently Krishna Conscious, Christ Conscious, or Buddhi Conscious, one is able to witness the physical phenomena going on around them, things occurring outside the body, and also witness the various psychological phenomena going on within them, meaning in their thoughts and feelings,* **without becoming consciously identified with them."**

You are expressing that you know without a doubt that you are physically and psychologically separate from them, and as such they have "no power to influence or affect you and your current attitude of willingness; unless you open the door of doubt or attachment" through some sort of conscious identification. To consciously identify with them means that you have opened the door of doubt in some way. You are in fact misusing your personal consciousness.

It means you have moved away from your state of Krishna, Christ, or Buddha Consciousness, and attached yourself to a particular physical or psychological phenomena in some way, perhaps in thought or perhaps through some habitual behaviour. And as long as we are encased in a physical body this can potentially happen at any stage of our life, no matter how "very spiritual" we may think we are.

You see the inherent nature of mind is to process thought. To merely attempt the cessation of a particular thought or a particular way of thinking goes against what is natural.

"The goal therefore is not the cessation of thought. The goal is cessation of identification with specific thoughts, and that can only come about through the displacement of that specific thought with one that is of a more powerful energetic vibratory influence."

Hence the ongoing influence and growth of our Krishna, Christ, or Buddhi Consciousness is dependent on how much attention we have given to the realm of our Soul, being our Mind, our Emotions, and our Will, during our life. How much attention we have given to keeping our Soul, the throne of the Christ or Krishna or Buddhi Consciousness within detached from concepts and experiences that are of no spiritual benefit.

Everything we do, experience, and learn through our awareness moves us along the inevitable path of consciousness evolution, the goal being the attainment of a fully conscious state of being. The Apostle Paul described this as "attaining the stature and the fullness of Christ."

When your mind is continually aligned with the Mind of God, and in everyday life you "cast down every vain imagination or thought that would oppose your inner understanding of God," then you can be said to be a Universally Conscious being, vibrationally aligned with God. You have become what the New Testament describes, "an imitator of Christ."

That is the universality of the faith that the Apostle Paul spoke of. He was not speaking of a universality of religious doctrine; he was speaking of "a universality of minds." When the Apostle Paul said, "let this mind be in you that was in Christ Jesus," he was saying harmonise your thoughts with the thoughts of Christ.

To harmonise one's mind with the Mind of God in the ancient days of the Hindu mystics and sages the "Krishna Conscious Way" was chosen. Then in the days of the Buddha came the "Buddhi Conscious Way".

Then later in the era of Christ it was the "Christ Conscious Way". And all three ways, the Krishna Conscious Way, the Buddhi Conscious Way, and the Christ Conscious Way, are still as relevant today as they were when they were first birthed into humanity's existence.

Paramahansa Yogananda, was the first prominent Indian teacher to settle in America, and the first prominent Indian monk, yogi, and guru to be hosted in the White House by President Calvin Coolidge, after being sent by his lineage to spread the teachings of yoga to the west.

He spoke consistently of a higher consciousness, a **Trinity of God Consciousness** being God the Father, who is Universal Consciousness **beyond creation**, God the Son, who is Christ Consciousness **within creation,** and God the Holy Spirit, which is God's Energy **permeating creation**, vibrating within all conscious life, keeping all conscious life alive and animated.

You see every human being began their life in the same way as every other human being. A group of babies in a maternity ward are all at the same level of consciousness as each other. Then from that moment of physical and psychological animation, a state of awareness kicks in that influences the conscious awareness of each of those babies in a particular behavioural direction, that direction depending on what concepts and experiences each baby is subjected to as it grows physically and develops mentally.

And this continues for the rest of their lives but is more potent in the early stages of the baby's identity formation which is in fact a part of the baby's personal pilgrimage of consciousness.

When it comes to child development, it's been said that the most crucial milestones in a child's life occur by the age of seven. In fact, the Greek Philosopher, Aristotle once said, "give me a child until he is seven, and I will show you the man. Similarly St. Ignatius Loyola the founder of the Catholic tradition of Jesuits said, "give me a child till he is seven years old, and I will show you the man."

But no matter how many influences have come along to change each one's life for better or worse, all those babies, as evolving human beings at different levels of conscious existence still have in their power the self-will to redirect or change their supposed destiny at any stage of their life. It all comes back to the state of mind.

And it can all be done through raising our own "personal level of consciousness" which happens when we harmonise our Soul faculties, our Mind, Emotions and will with the Soul of God, God's, Mind, Emotions, and Will. And how do we know what they are? They are found in the timeless teachings of the Masters of All Ages, Christ, Krishna, and the Buddha.

It is through the harmonisation of our individual Soul, our Mind, Emotions, and Will, with the Soul of Pure Consciousness, God's Mind, Emotions, and Will, that God's love becomes our love, God's forgiveness becomes our forgiveness, God's Compassion becomes our compassion, God's Capacity for Self-Sacrifice becomes ours, God's Kindness becomes our Kindness, God's Creative ability becomes our creative ability. We become in fact imitators of Christ.

Once we understand or recognise our true self as a fragment of God Consciousness setting out on a Personal Pilgrimage of expansion, the harmonisation of our Soul with the Soul of the Supreme Spirit (God) begins. We start possessing a deep desire to live our life experience as an imitator of God's Nature. This is our personal pilgrimage.

At the same time the key components of our Soul, being our Mind impressions, our Emotional expressions, and the Executions of our Will begin to seek a deeper level of harmonisation with the Mind, Emotions and the Expressive Will of the Father. This internal desiring then becomes the platform of our pilgrimage to a higher and higher and higher state of Conscious existence, a state of Ultimate Psychological Oneness with Infinite Intelligence.

Our primary purpose in the first instance is to re-establish that state of connectivity between our spirit and the Supreme Spirit through a simple recognition and acceptance process, known as the process of Self-Realisation in Eastern religions such as Hinduism and Buddhism, and known as Salvation in Western religions such as Christianity. And is that hard? No it isn't. Do we have to search the spiritual and physical world for years as many including the Buddha did? No we don't.

We simply say, "Oh. I get it, that's who I really am. I am not just a body with all these weird goings on all the time. I am a fragment of God's Consciousness that has become localised in a body. I am a spiritual being having a physical experience, not a physical being looking for the ultimate spiritual experience."

When we do this in a sincere way we trigger the synchronisation or harmonisation of the activities of our Soul, our Mind, Emotions, and Will, with the Soul of God, the Mind, Emotions, and Will of the Soul of God, where the desires and pleasures of the flesh are no longer our priority, but the desires of the Spirit are; and thus the combative interaction between the two natures becomes lesser and lesser, and the confusing aspects of our existence are displaced by a quiet confidence.

And as our harmonisation increases so does the actualisation of the character qualities of Divine Intelligence become fully realised in the outward experiences of our life. Others will notice the changes in us but not necessarily know what brought about the change. Consequently the joy and happiness and peace in our outer experience that we have been striving for all our lives doesn't have to be strived for any more or attained through ongoing new pleasurable experiences.

Rather all these things are added unto us automatically as we follow God's Will and God's Way. It's God's Grace freely given. Jesus said, "seek ye first the Kingdom of God within, your True Self, and all those things necessary to successfully navigate an earthly existence will be given to you."

And where can we find God's Will and God's Way? It can be easily found in the timeless teachings of three Master Messengers, Krishna,

Christ, and the Buddha. The Katha Upanishad of Hinduism says the following:

> *"There is the path of joy, and there is the path of pleasure. Both attract the attention of the Soul. (our mind, our emotions, and our will).*
>
> *Who follows the first comes to good; who follows pleasure reaches not the End (of our spiritual pilgrimage).*
>
> *These two paths lie in front of man. Pondering on them, the wise man chooses the path of joy; the fool takes the path of pleasure."*

"There is no wisdom for a man without harmony, and without harmony, there is no contemplation. Without contemplation, there cannot be peace, and without peace, there cannot be joy.

When a mind becomes bound to a passion of the wandering senses, this passion carries off a man's wisdom, even as the wind drives a vessel on the waves; but the Soul that moves in the world of the senses, and yet keeps those senses in harmony, free from attraction and aversion, continually finds rest and quietness."

— Krishna....The Bhagavad Gita 2.

CHAPTER 4

The Harmonisation of Our Human
Soul with The Soul of God

❦

"Go forth in every direction for the happiness, the
harmony, the welfare of the many. Offer your heart,
the seeds of understanding, like a lamp, overturned,
and re-lit, illuminating the darkness."

— GAUTAMA BUDDHA.

O ur consciousness is a fragment of God's Consciousness, the Divine
Essence, and this is the one specific truth we need to firmly grasp
to enable us to navigate this earthly life successfully and peacefully,
regardless of how high or how low we personally rate ourselves physically
and psychologically. The English poet Alfred Lord Tennyson in his epic
poem The Holy Grail wrote the following words:

"For good ye are and bad, and likened to a coin, some true, some light,
but everyone stamped with the image of the King."

In Chapter 2, I spoke of the imprinting factor relating it to a particular
story in the New Testament concerning a denarius, a silver coin used for
tax purposes by the Roman government of the day, and an interaction

Jesus had with the religious people regarding the payment of taxes. In this chapter, I want to take my comments a little further.

When Tennyson wrote these words above, he was reflecting on and thus referencing not only the genetic imprint of the God Personality that has been stamped on each individual human being's life, but he was also referring to the duality of a human being's nature.

He was referencing the truth that, yes, the Divine Genetic Imprint of God's Nature is in fact our true personality or identity, the "I am" of our existence, but accentuating the fact that more often than not we have stifled and smothered its manifestation in our outer existence and experience through our ego driven, pleasure seeking, self-cultivated, survivalist and thus selfish and self-centered attitudes and behaviors in our daily life.

In the story of the Denarius, Jesus was reinforcing the words of the Prophet Moses in the Old Testament's Book of Genesis Chapter 1 which read: "so God created mankind in his own image, in the image of God he created them; male and female he created them," but he was also reminding us how some members of society in their ignorance of this truth have veered away from behaviors that align with that truth.

Remember Jesus at that time was speaking to a gathering of the religious leaders known as the Pharisees, not just his followers and onlookers. Who were the Pharisees? In simple terms the Pharisees were a Jewish social movement and members of a party that believed in resurrection, and in following legal traditions that were ascribed not to the Bible, but to the traditions of the fathers.

Perhaps you could say that that was "the good side" of the coin of their existence that Tennyson spoke of.

But the Pharisees were also a religious sect that opposed Jesus because they wanted to stay in the traditional religion of the past and more importantly to maintain their power base in the religious, political, legal, and social arenas.

Perhaps you could say that that was "the bad side" of the coin of their existence that Tennyson spoke of.

The Pharisees were not obscurantists, those determined to prevent the true facts of something from coming forth. Some were Therapeuts, members of an ancient monastic sect of Egyptian Jews, some were Mystics, being those who see God as transcending all material matter, and who in their spiritual practice and in daily life focus on that which is within, more in a contemplative way, rather than outside practices of ritual and ceremony, that most religions focus on, and some were Essenes, who were members of a Jewish sect or School of Philosophy.

And as such the Pharisees were open to gaining greater understanding of the things of God, even if many were still bound to the religious and philosophical teachings and traditions of their ancestors. And Jesus saw this interaction with them regarding the lawfulness of the tax system, as an opportunity to advance their understanding of the things of God, and not merely as a moment to justify his own existence and teachings.

Jesus in his interactions with the Pharisees was hinting at the truth of "the ultimate non-severability of the nature of the human being with the nature of God", regardless of whether in life one person chooses to pay taxes and one doesn't.

Jesus was saying as was Tennyson, that regardless of whether in life one person has this belief and another a contrary belief, regardless of who appears to hold the greater power and authority in life, regardless of what moral or ethical behaviors we are expressing in our life, regardless of whether or not perhaps through ignorance of the eternal consequences or just through lack of understanding one chooses to prioritize the "bad side of the coin, over the "good side," in their attitudes and behaviors in daily life, regardless of all these things, we are all still a reflection of the Divine Nature, even if we are thinking and behaving as if we aren't in terms of the decisions we take and the choices we make.

When we come to truly understand this, then the Divine Principle of forgiveness becomes readily acceptable to us regardless of how wronged we may feel we have been done by. Jesus understood this which is why he was able to say midst excruciating physical and psychological agony whilst nailed to a cross, "Father forgive them, for they do not know what they are doing."

And as both Jesus and the poet Tennyson emphasised this truth, so too does the Quran, the sacred scripture of the Islamic religion. On the one side the Qur'an says that we are made in the best of moulds, (95:4), fashioned with the Breath of God's Spirit, (38:72), and chosen to be His representative of mercy upon the earth. (2:30).

On the other side of the coin, the Qur'an describes humankind as fragile creatures, made of dust from the same earth they walk upon (23:12); anxious, forgetful, ungrateful, vulnerable to the bite of a fly (22:73), a nothingness in the face of Gods' eternal reality; a mortal that is passing away a breath at a time, inching towards a death that will arrive without warning (31:34).

In terms of a physical coin then, that Tennyson referenced in his poem The Holy Grail and that Jesus was referencing in his discussion with the Pharisees, the point was that no matter how much we or others might attempt to deface the earthly image on the coin, wittingly or unwittingly, consciously or unconsciously, the underlying principle of the eternal image remains firm, and its true value as a currency is never diminished.

And as such in the case of the human being, no matter how much we or others have in attitude and behavior degraded and debased our physical or psychological existence, our true value as a vessel of currency for the Kingdom of God will always remain.

In creating the human being, Infinite Intelligence created an object of form with a unique capacity for both Divine Moral Awareness, the heads side of the coin, and Human Rational Awareness, the tails side of the coin, and that will never change regardless of the many unwise decisions we may make or how many unwise chances we take in our earthly experience.

God made the human being to be inherently different from all other life forms. God has stamped the Divine Image on our being, genetically built into the human being his own character qualities, such as the experience of personality, truth, beauty, meaning, will, and reason, allowing we human beings to relate to God in ways that other life forms such as animal and plant life cannot, and to represent the Divine Essence, to stand as the image of God's righteous authority right now here on the earth.

And as such whilst the Psalms tell us that "the heavens declare the glory of God and the firmament shows his handiwork", it is only the human being, the mental, moral, volitional human being, who can truly declare and manifest the Nature of God and exhibit the personality characteristics of God in their daily life, the key word being volitional, meaning of their own free will. It is our choice if we want to manifest the Nature of God, or if we are content to continue manifesting the self-interested character qualities of our lower nature.

God did not simply create the human being in his image and leave it at that. God perpetually recreates, supports, and sustains the human being in its journey to a higher level of consciousness or conscious existence in accordance with the level of each individual's volition, the degree of willingness and co-operation each individual is prepared to extend, and according to the measure of sacrifice of self-interest that willingness might necessitate.

The human being is distinctly individual from all other life forms who have proceeded from God into matter, in as much as "the image and superscription" of the Creative Sovereign Power, from which it came, remains forever indelibly impressed upon its inmost ego, and must work in it, and will work in it, for its good pleasure until the human being's conscious mind is in full harmonization with the God Mind in all thought, in all intention, and in all behavior.

"For thought sets intention, and intention is the spark plug igniting the engine of behavior".

Humanity is the chosen vehicle for the self-expression of the moral qualities of the Supreme Originating Spirit, but the moral evolution of humanity is not automatic; it is not just going to happen on its own. For according to Kingdom Principle (Divine Law), it is only when two or more agree that something shall or must be done, then in fact it shall be done. The Divine Will waits patiently in the innermost recesses of our being waiting for us to agree with it.

To agree is "to harmonize". In simple terms, when we in our individual thought activity start agreeing with what God says, and in our subsequent intentions and behaviors, we start doing what God would do in the same situation, then it shall be done. A free-flowing, peace filled, functional world is all dependent on the harmonization of the Soul of Humanity with the Soul of God.

Human life is individual, and it is personal. Each one of us is a responsible individual life-center in which the Divine Essence has expressed itself, and we are tasked with individually becoming moral beings willingly, because a moral being is not machine-made, and does not come into existence through good luck or a good upbringing alone.

A child may have the genetic biological imprint of its parents, may have its parents' genes within its being, but that does not mean that that child is going to grow up automatically into the same fine upstanding moral being that its parent is assessed to be.

The moral human being is the product of an evolution of consciousness or awareness to a higher state. And sometimes for that evolution to be progressed, all individuals in the early formation of their identity will be exposed to resisting forces, that attempt to steer that progressive evolution of our individual state of consciousness off its course. And I know this because I have experienced it.

So, for the purpose of ensuring that evolution continues, the human being must emerge triumphant over those resisting forces, those carnal qualities of our lower nature that deliberately and in a calculated way undermine a lack of true wisdom, through exposing us to the carnalities of the flesh and blood existence, and the highs and lows of that existence.

And if this has already happened to you, or is happening to you right now, it is assuredly fixable. But Infinite Intelligence is the only one that can fix it if we are willing. For it is only the power of Infinite Intelligence, the energetic influence of the Kingdom of God within, with our cooperation, our willingness, that can transform the mess of our life into a life message for others, and the one and only power source that can transform our tribulations and trials, real or imagined into triumphs.

For as such as God's Power is revealed in the universe seeing "nature take its course" trying to rectify a human being's unthinking assault on it for its own selfish intention, then God's Nature is able to be revealed in the thinking person to rectify that thinking person's intentional or unintentional assault on themselves or others, occurring through some sort of selfish attachment to some aspects of fleshly desire in thought, attitude, or behaviour.

We must never cease from reminding ourselves that the human being has been put on this planet not for selfish dominion over all things, but rather for selfless and at times self-sacrificial dominion, more importantly for the special sphere of selfless self-manifestation of the Originating Mind, the denying of our will in favour of God's will.

Yes our human existence can be likened to a coin that comes fashioned with two sides. And as such the saying "there are two sides to every coin" rings true. Many countries with their coinage have the image of the ruling monarch on one side, the heads side, and an image of an animal on the other, the tails side.

So with the coin of our life, if we concentrate all our attention on the reverse side of the coin, the animal image, rather than the King's image, if we persist in imagining that our animal nature is our real self, we forget that the King's image is on the primary side, the "heads side", and as such every time we in our decision making flip that coin of choices it will always come up tails.

We can only see one side of the coin at a time, and while we gaze at the reverse side, and the other side with the King's image is hidden, then doubt, depression, pessimism, and an ongoing sense of separateness from the Divine Essence, are the inevitable results.

I would encourage you. Do not always harp upon the worst side of yourself. We are bound to become what we see ourselves ideally to be. The higher your ideal of yourself, the more rapid your growth of consciousness. See yourself ideally as Divine, recognize your True Self, remind yourself that Kingdom Consciousness, the Divine Essence is within you, and this will become your mantra, your primary reality, the heads side of your coin of life.

Remember, you cannot see both sides of the coin of yourself at once. If you keep looking only at the tails side, then the tails side is all you will see. Start turning the coin over, even if hesitantly in the first instance. When you are discouraged by the prominence of the animal nature; when you are prone to give way to appetite or temper, or despondency, or self-detestation, the internal judgement of yourself, instantly force yourself to turn over, as it were, the coin of your thinking life.

The Apostle Paul described this as "casting down all vain imaginings that raise themselves up against our true knowledge of God," our understanding of our True Self, and goes on to say, "and bring every thought into captivity to Christ." The Buddha put it this way:

"We are shaped by our thoughts; we become what we think. When the mind is pure, joy follows like a shadow that never leaves."

Set your goal on "mind stabilization" in the first instant. Begin to get your thinking process aligned with Divine Thought. Harmonize your thoughts with Divine Thought. Krishna in the Bhagavad Gita of the Hindu religion shows us that self-realization, our understanding that our True Self or True Nature on the inside is who we really are, cannot be achieved without the attainment of stability of the mind, or a state of sthitaprajna as it is called.

Sthitaprajna is a Sanskrit term that means contented, calm, and firm in judgement and wisdom. It is a combination of two words: *sthita.* meaning existing, being, and firmly resolved to, and *prajna,* meaning wise, clever, and intelligent. In the Bhagavad Gita, Sthitaprajna refers to a person of steady wisdom.

The Bhagavad Gita of Hinduism Chapters 5 and 6 Krishna speaking say:

> *"When a person gives up all desires in his thoughtful state, and when his inner self is satisfied within itself, at that time he is said to be a sthitaprajna, a master in the stability of mind".*
>
> *"The knower of Brahman (the True Self), being established in the Supreme Brahman (an understanding that the Kingdom of God within is our True Self), shows no need to rejoice when he achieves the objects of his desire, nor a need to embrace agitation when unpleasant things happen to him."*

The last two lines of that passage from the Bhagavad Gita speak of a state of contentment in all circumstances. Contentment is a product of "mind stabilization."

The Apostle Paul in speaking to the people of Philippi said:

> *"I have learned in whatever circumstances I am in, to be content."*

And the well-known Indian philosopher, speaker, and writer Jiddhu Krishnamurti, when once asked what gives you happiness and peace replied:

> *"I simply just don't mind what happens".*

Jiddhu, in his personal life and in his work, continually surrendered to and embraced peace rather than surrendering to circumstance. When we are resisting what takes place, we prolong our confusion, we prolong our pain, and we prolong our suffering. It is only when we submit or surrender our habitual way of thinking and responding to the wisdom of Divine Thought or the Laws of the Spirit, God's way of thinking, that we are truly liberated from the enslavement of our egoic thought patterns. To surrender does not mean to give up or give in, but rather to choose a different path, the Path of our True Nature.

What does that mean in relation to the analogy of the coin. It means that even though at times the tails side of the coin becomes visible, its appearance does not have to immobilize us and disturb our internal peace. And similarly, when the heads side of the coin shines brightly in our life, our ingrained habit of desperately holding on to that happiness or time bound measure of pleasure at all costs, should not become our sole "soul focus", the sole focus of our Mind, Emotions, and Will.

The same two-sided rule applies to our judgments of others. Remember, we cannot see both sides of the human coin at once, and therefore our judgments are literally one-sided.

Sometimes the people we admire are not deserving of all the worship we give them, and sometimes the people we dislike are not as they may have been painted. Some people live with only the reverse side visible, but always there is the other side of the coin, and whilst perhaps not visible in the moment, it is nevertheless ever present.

And as such in moments of disharmony that may occur between us and other human beings, we should always be asking ourselves the question:

"In whose image and likeness has this person been created?"

In relation to our achieving a state of sthitapraina, a state of mind stability, the harmonization of our rational mind with the Divine Mind, the following Divine Principle is something we need to have a firm understanding of to enable us to successfully navigate what are described as the ups and downs of life.

If necessary, read the following a few times and dwell on it in silence. Go over and over it if necessary until it becomes fixated in your mind and ongoing thought processing. It is a key understanding we need to have to enable the achievement of mind stabilization.

The Old Testament Wisdom Book of Proverbs says the following:

"A man's heart devises his way, but the Lord directs his steps."

A profound philosophy underlies that inspired maxim from the Book of Proverbs.

The human being is a threefold being, composed of **Spirit, Soul, and Body**, and this proverb, *"a man's heart devises his way, but the Lord directs his steps,"* indicates what is the true relationship that should exist between these three functioning centers in each individual human being, between their Spirit, their Soul, and their Body.

A human being's stable life progress or unstable life progress is all about "devising and directing". Its success is primarily determined by **"who or what does the devising"** and by **"who or what does the directing."**

And a correct functional relationship between both these things will determine whether in our personal pilgrimage of consciousness we are becoming more Christ-like, or Krishna-like, or Buddha-like, or whether we are becoming less Christ-like, or less Krishna-like, or less Buddha-like. In other words, it will determine whether we are evolving in our level of Divine Consciousness or whether we are devolving in our level of Divine Consciousness. So, to extrapolate this:

Spirit is our innermost being, the primary component of our threefold being. Sometimes referred to as heart, particularly with Evangelical Christians in their salvation experience where they invite Jesus into their heart. It is the Kingdom of God within, it is the Divine Essence within, as opposed to the Divine Essence without. It is the Holy Spirit within us as against the Holy Spirit around us. Remember Jesus said, "I will send you the Holy Spirit who shall be with you, and in you." It is Pure Consciousness, the Divine Essence, differentiated or fragmented into our individual life-center.

Soul is the region of the Mind, Emotions, and Will. It is Intellect, or Mind, where a person does their conscious thinking, it is Emotion where a person experiences their conscious feelings, and it is Will where a person gives attention, sets intention, and subsequently behaves consciously in accordance with what it is thinking (intellect), or feeling (emotion), the moment-by-moment activities of our Mind or our Emotions.

Body is the seat of our sense-consciousness. It is the realm of the senses where our Will or Willingness is expressed consciously in some animated way. It is the vehicle for the manifestation of what our Mind is thinking, or what our Emotions are feeling.

Looking at Spirit, Soul, and Body, individually.

The Spirit is in residence within you. It is what Jesus described as the Kingdom of God within you, and when not grieved, carries out its role of guiding and controlling the Soul. The key proviso here being, "when not grieved."

Our Spirit within is what is described in the Upanishads, the ancient scriptures of the Indian religion of Hinduism as "the Atman within." The term Atman is derived from the Sanskrit term "self-breath". It is the universal self, the innermost essence, identical with the core of the personality that after death either transmigrates to a new life or attains release (moksha) from the bonds of existence.

The Katha Upanishad of Hinduism describes the Atman, this True Self that either transmigrates to a new life (reincarnation) or obtains full release from the bonds of existence, in this way:

"Concealed in the heart of all beings is the Atman, the Spirit, the Self; smaller than the smallest atom, greater than the vast spaces. The man who surrenders his human will, leaves sorrows behind, and beholds the glory of the Atman by the grace of the Creator."

"When the wise realise the presence of this omnipresent Spirit, who rests invisible in the visible and permanent in the impermanent, then they go beyond sorrow."

In Christianity the Atman is described in various ways including our heart, our spirit, Christ in us, the Kingdom of God within, different words than in Hinduism, but with the same meaning. All words or phrases referring to that fragment of Pure Consciousness or God that has become localised or taken up residence within the human body, to give the human body life.

And as the innermost nature of every living being, pure and unchanged, the Atman within is entirely uncontaminated by external influences. Neither birth nor death, nor re-birth can alter Atman. It is the Real, the Unchangeable.

What is the function of the Spirit or Atman?

That Spirit within you is all-powerful, described by the Apostle Paul in the Book of Romans as:

"The Spirit of God, who raised Jesus from the dead, and lives in you."

And Paul goes on to say:

"And just as God raised Christ Jesus from the dead, he will give life to your mortal bodies through this same Spirit living within you."

The Spirit or Atman within is the Holy Breath that first gave us life and its ongoing role is to continue to sustain that life and guide that life. To give life in this scripture means to give **"illumination to the mind"** (intellect), and then **"to bring animation to the body"** and with that enable the right or righteous kind of **"manifestation through one or more of the five bodily senses".** Through vision, hearing, touch, taste, or smell.

The primary function of the Spirit or Atman in its relationship with the human being is to give progressive Divine Illumination of a righteous kind to the mind, resulting in the correct type of righteous animated manifestation to the bodily senses. The primary role of the human being in its relationship with the Spirit is to allow and progress the ongoing Divine Illumination offered by the Spirit, thus enabling the human being's life to be a vehicle for the manifestation of the Nature of God's Spirit continuously.

But it can only do this successfully when it is in harmony with the Spirit in Mind, Emotions and Will. When we disagree with the expressive Nature of God's Spirit in any of these areas, the arena of the Mind, or Emotions, or Will, we grieve the Spirit, we create disharmony, and thus we destabilize the relationship.

The Spirit is grieved when we allow disharmony to enter the picture, when we entertain heart desires (thoughts) that are contrary to Divine Desires or the eternal Divine Will, or project behaviors that are of a carnal nature. And of course, not only does disharmony divide our sense of oneness with the universe in the present, but it also reinforces our sense of psychological alienation from all other life form. We have all I am sure heard the common saying, "he is alienating people with his behavior."

Paul in speaking to the Roman people said that "the same Spirit that raised Jesus from the dead dwells in us now". Meaning that the same Spirit that raised Christ from the dead is living in us now keeping these mortal bodies of ours illuminated, animated, alive, and functioning. But even as in a physical relationship when a grievance occurs it destabilizes the relationship, so in our spiritual life it does too.

However, that psycho-spiritual destabilization does not result in a permanent divorce, rather a trial separation you could call it, giving us opportunity to get the relationship back on track going forward. And in that trial separation we lose not our animation or our potential for illumination, but we do lose our capacity for effective manifestation of the Spirit's energetic influence, its power and authority. We lose our special metaphysical privileges all of which are commonly referred to as Grace.

Later in the twilight of our earthly life, having been given a pre-determined measure of time to evolve our level of consciousness, that Spirit that dwelt in Christ and subsequently raised Christ from the dead, that Holy Breath, that Atman, or individual Fragment of Pure Consciousness within us, that we have lived with harmoniously and per-haps at times unharmoniously, having finished its course permanently departs, and it is at that time our ongoing illumination and animation and thus functionality stops, and we experience what is called death.

Soul on the other hand, being the region of the intellect, is the fac-ulty where a person does their conscious thinking whilst we are alive. Soul or heart as the Book of Proverbs describes it, "devises a person's way", it works out for them the path it believes they should take and plans the details involved in that pathway. To devise is to plan or invent a procedure or mechanism by careful thought.

And as Spirit, our Atman, is the seat of our God-consciousness that fragment of God Consciousness that we been impregnated with that gives us an animated life, so the Soul is the seat of our self-consciousness from which our state of awareness or our state of perception is realized or comes into being. Perception being how we look at things or interpret things in life concepts, and experiences.

"The Soul (mind, emotions, and will) and the Spirit (our Atman or Christ Consciousness) are connected, but separable. So the function of our Spirit is to contact God and receive the thoughts of God and the function of our Soul is to embrace God's thoughts, and express God's Will through the components of our human will."

Which is why Mary the Mother of Jesus as we read in the Book of Luke could say with joy in her heart:

> *"**My Soul** (mind, emotions and, will) doth magnify the Lord, and **my Spirit** (my Atman) doth rejoice in God my Saviour."*

But if that Soul, that individual intellect is wrongly programmed, not in harmony with the God Nature, that pathway might not be the right pathway. In other words, if it is not in harmony with the Divine Laws of the universe a good outcome is not guaranteed.

However, when disharmony raises its mischievous head, to try and derail some aspect of our life, we have been given as a faculty of the Divine Nature within, an intuitive capacity to hear internally, to tap into a circuit breaker, the Divine Guidance of the Spirit within. We have been gifted along with the physical animation it gives us, a capacity for "intellectual illumination", the getting of Wisdom.

Sometimes the Soul is aware that something or someone is speaking to it to give guidance, but often that advice is summarily ignored or dismissed, because the relationship between the two is in a state of grievance or disharmony. We grieve when we lose something.

The more the human Soul is in harmony with the Spirit, what you could call a state of non -grievance, with the Mind, Emotions and Will of God, the more likely the Soul, the mental faculties of the human being, will be tuned into the Voice of the Spirit when it is speaking. There is no grievance preventing them from working cohesively together.

People occasionally refer to that intuitive Voice within as the voice of their conscience, which in fact is true, for it is the voice of their moral state of being, their True Self the God Nature within, as against the voice of their False Self, their carnal state of being, which has been cultivated through life in the absence of Godly awareness or perception.

The words Conscience and Conscious as previously stated are both derived from the Latin roots meaning "to know," and both relate to a state of awareness. The word Conscience relating to a state of moral awareness, and the word Conscious or Consciousness referring to a state of physical or mental wakefulness or aliveness.

> *"The thoughts pertaining to moral awareness emanate from the Kingdom of God within, the thoughts pertaining to self-awareness emanate from the thinking, rationalizing psyche of an individual."*

Sogyal Rinpoche, a Tibetan Dzogchen lama, in his book The Tibetan Book of Living and Dying referred to consciousness, thought pertaining to self or egoic awareness, and conscience, thought pertaining to moral awareness, in the following way:

> *"Two people have been living in you all your life. There is the ego, (the False Self) which is garrulous, demanding, and calculating, and there is the hidden spiritual being, (the True Self) whose still voice of Wisdom, you have only rarely heard or attended to".*

And lastly **Body** is the final component of the threefold continuum of Spirit, Soul, and Body. Body is the seat of our sense-consciousness. It is the realm of the senses where our state of awareness and perception is manifested. In the body all our five bodily senses, our sight, hearing, taste, touch, and smell dwell. And it is one or more of these five senses, which are the catalyst for the manifestation of that which is in our state of awareness or perception.

These five senses, sight, hearing, taste, touch, and smell give us a sense of who or what we are experiencing at a particular moment when we are having an objective experience according to our individual level of awareness or perception.

And here is the point all the above is getting to in relation to that quote from the Book of Proverbs:

> *"A man's heart devises his way, but the Lord directs his steps."*

73

Our Body, the external part of our being, the association of organs clothed in a flesh and blood appearance whereby Pure Consciousness or the Divine Essence experiences for its pleasure the physical universe, ought to obey our "harmonized Soul", and then all is well. But all is well only when the faculties of the human Soul are in harmony with the faculties or Nature of the Spirit within, when there is no grievance occurring.

If the Soul is not in harmony, in other words not on the same wavelength as the Spirit so to speak, then that becomes a problem. But when our human Soul is in harmony with the Divine's Soul, then that is the ideal relationship between the three functioning centers in individual human beings, and as such the key to a successful, peace filled life regardless of prevailing circumstances.

> *"The key to living a life of peace and joy regardless of circumstance, is to have the Body, with its senses, subject to the Soul with its conscious mind, and the Soul, with its conscious mind, subject to the Spirit of Wisdom within us, that fragment of Pure Consciousness empowered with Divine Wisdom that we have been impregnated with to give us an animated and illuminated life."*

And when a human being recognizes this, and lives life in accordance with this understanding, then their functional life automatically becomes one of peace and harmony as both the Soul and the Body doggedly determine even subconsciously not to think, say, or do anything, that would interfere with their harmonious relationship with the Spirit. Determined not to think, say, or do anything that would grieve the Spirit within.

And as previously emphasized, when the Spirit is not grieved and functions in harmony with the Soul, the Soul is not perturbed and functions in co-operation with the body, and the life then lived in the flesh is one that ancient sages and mystics described as "an enlightened state of being."

The process of becoming "enlightened" commences firstly through the initial recognition of the fact that we are all fragments of God's Consciousness, which is an acknowledgement of the Spirit or Essence within. A recognition which is described by both ancient and modern spiritual teachers as "coming to a realization of the True Self".

After this that human being, having recognized its True Self, must then go about conducting itself in a manner that does not create disharmony of any kind and as such does not grieve the Spirit, the True Self within.

> *"In life there is "a becoming" and "a being". The recognition of the True Self is the "becoming", and the complete harmonization of the character qualities of the True Self with our Conscious Self is "the being", the enlightened state of "being."*

To be fully enlightened is not just a matter of understanding the existence of our True Self and leaving it at that. It is about manifesting that True Self, that Krishna, Christ, or Buddha Nature in all we think, say, and do.

> *"The whole purpose of life is liberation. But for complete liberation to occur we must move from salvation or self-realization to soul harmonization."*

The true Christian process of salvation is meant to be twofold, although in many cases it is onefold. In the first instance comes the process of the salvation experience, the acceptance of the Christ within, and then secondly must come the manifestation of the Christ Consciousness in one's life, which Christian theology describes as a "life lived in the Spirit." Unfortunately for some it is also the point in which many Christians stall in their evolution of personal consciousness.

They fail and thus fall simply solely because of the lack of their individual Soul harmonization with the Soul of God, what the Apostle Paul described as "the renewing of the Mind." Their mind, the realm of the individual intellect having not being truly renewed and perhaps showing no inclination to being renewed, simply does not have the spiritual horsepower necessary to transcend life's woes.

> *"True enlightenment is the capacity to go about the business of life without engendering any kind of acrimony or disharmony between yourself and any other life form, whether human, animal, or plant."*

Disharmony of some sort between these three functioning centers, the Spirit, Soul, and Body, has been commonly referred to in religious writings as sin, a misnomer in a way because any act classed as sin can be easily justified as not being sin by the rationalizing egoic self, thus bringing even greater disharmony into the situation as the human being vigorously defends their behavior. Better to call it disharmony.

When disharmony, which manifests as a lack of peace, psychologically or physically, enters our life through our thinking faculties, when mental or emotional disharmony surfaces, it is simply the assertion of the unrealized self, what is described as the egoic or false sense of self, seeking its life and its happiness through human intelligence only. It just wants to leave the Spirit side of our being totally out of the picture. It wants to "devise its own way," and "play out its own step by step rationalized plan."

When bodily disharmony occurs, it is the assertion of the animal appetite or lower nature, seeking its life and its happiness through some pleasure of the senses, through touch, taste, sight, hearing, or smell.

True harmony lies in the Soul Self's alignment with our True Self, Pure Consciousness within, of which the conscious mind is the functioning power, seeking its life and its happiness in obedience to Spirit, thinking itself into conscious oneness with Spirit, the inmost shrine of our complete nature.

Then as Soul will be no longer functioning from the plane of material conditions, our Body obeys our Soul, which is obedient to our Spirit the seat of our True Consciousness. We then thus see the wisdom of the ancient Proverb:

> *"Though a man's conscious mind devises his way, it is the Spirit who directs his steps,"* coming to fruition.

"The great challenge of a person's consciousness has always been to let go of the lesser in order to make way for the greater; to let go of the physical in order to prioritise the meta-physical; to let go of the lower nature to give ascendancy to the higher nature; to let go of the temporal to release the eternal.

Which simply means we no longer entertain the Lower Nature's egoic interpretation of things rather allow our Higher Nature, the Spirit's perception of things, to be the dominant influencer in all our attitudes, thoughts, and behaviours."

CHAPTER 5

Hindrances to Soul Harmonisation
The Psychological Battle for
The Throne of Our Soul

❧

"The mind is very difficult to control. However it can be
controlled by constant practice and detachment."

— KRISHNA, THE BHAGAVAD GITA 6.

"The mind is fickle and flighty, it flies after fancies, wherever it
likes, it is difficult, indeed, to restrain. But it is a great good to
control the mind; mind self-controlled is a source of great joy."

— THE BUDDHA, THE DHAMMAPADA, 3.

We have been gifted the Mind of Christ to be
guided by his thoughts, and purposes."

— THE APOSTLE PAUL, 1 CORINTHIANS 2.

Rene Descartes was a French philosopher, mathematician and scientist, who lived in the 16th century, a man widely regarded as
one of the most important founders of modern philosophy. In his

philosophical and scientific approach, mathematics was central to his method of inquiry, and he connected the previously separate fields of geometry and algebra into analytic geometry. Descartes' Meditations of First Philosophy continues to be a standard text used in most university philosophy departments.

In 1607 he entered the Jesuit College where he was introduced to mathematics and physics, including Galileo's work. Whilst there, Descartes first encountered hermetic mysticism, and then after graduation in 1614, he studied for two years at the University of Poitiers earning a Baccalaureate (Bachelor) Degree in canon and civil law according to his father's wishes that he become a lawyer. From there he moved to Paris.

In his work *Discourse on the Method of Rightly Conducting One's Reason and of Seeking Truth in the Sciences,* Descartes, while addressing some of his predecessors and contemporaries, modified their approach to account for "a truth he found to be incontrovertible". And so started his line of reasoning by doubting everything, so as to assess the world from a fresh perspective, clear of any preconceived notions.

You could say he completely rejected the influence of the seemingly fixed belief systems of his colleagues and predecessors in the field, whilst at the same time respecting them as fellow scientists and philosophers.

Regarding his approach in his writing of Discourse on the Method of Rightly Conducting One's Reason and of Seeking Truth in The Sciences, Descartes recalls:

> *"I entirely abandoned the study of letters. Resolving to seek no knowledge other than that of which could be found "in myself" (intuitively), or else in the "great book of the world". (the scriptures).*
>
> *I spent the rest of my youth travelling, visiting courts and armies, mixing with people of diverse temperaments and rank; gathering various experiences, testing myself in the situations which fortune offered me, and at all times reflecting upon whatever came my way to derive some profit from it."*

In some of his more notable writings in the early 1600's, Descartes presented a formulation for *dualism.* In simple terms *dualism* is the state of something having two main and separate aspects. Perhaps not intentionally but certainly in actuality, Descartes principle gave rise in most parts of the Western world to a philosophical approach to the association of the body and the mind in how they relate to each other.

Dualistic thinking for example is to take the approach when observing a subject matter that it has two separate and different realities to its existence. These realities can be subjective or objective, subjective meaning based on personal interpretation, and objective meaning fact based, measurable, and observable.

They are also usually seen to exist as opposites and in some cases live in an ongoing confrontational mode with each other, or as a minimum, appearing to function in an ongoing state of opposition to each other. You could liken this to the observation of the Apostle Paul when in speaking to the Galatian citizens about the nature of their being he said: "For the desires of the flesh are against the Spirit, and the Spirit against the flesh; for these are contrary one to another."

A prime subject for the exploration of *dualism* with writers over the centuries, has always been that of the inherent nature of humankind, and the perpetual conflict that has always existed between the two sides of that nature, between the good side, and the evil side. I referenced this earlier in the extract from the poem The Holy Grail by Alfred Lord Tennyson where he speaks of the human being as likened to a coin with one good side and one bad side.

In some writings that good side is described as our higher nature and that evil side as our lower nature, and in some spiritual teachings the good side is described as our True Self and the evil side as our False Self. The 'dual' in the word dualism means two. So in dualistic situations we find that two things are set up in opposition and are separate in some essential and irrevocable way. They are not in "harmony with each other in intent or in manifestation".

A religious concept following along the same lines as Descartes formulation, also known as Dualism, is to be found in Eastern Philosophy and Eastern Religion. It is a concept that has been taught throughout the ages in ancient religious cultures. Similarly in Western Religion, in the early formation of the Christian Church and long before Descartes scientific work was published it existed also, but was lost over time, buried out of sight with the introduction of a plethora of institutionalised beliefs and practices.

However here is the most important thing we must understand. That particular concept of Dualism in the pre-Christ and early post-Christ eras only talks about the **'dual operating aspects of the mind'** we possess, whilst still focusing on the "non-dual relationship between our Consciousness and God's Consciousness. So in terms of our composite being you could say that the human being is "a being of one consciousness, but of two minds".

In simple terms it basically teaches that even though our existence or being, the Inner Essence of our life is "at one with God or Infinite Intelligence," remember Jesus said, "I and the Father are one," and "he who has seen me has seen the Father," we have **two different operational aspects of our mind**, two separate minds you could say, both battling for supremacy in our lives. There is the voice of our Kingdom of God Mind and the voice of our Kingdom of Earth or Flesh Mind.

There is the voice of our **"higher mind,"** continually encouraged by our **"higher nature"**, what some would describe as their voice of their moral conscience, the still small corrective voice that whispers within, and there is the voice of our **"lower mind,"** the ever ready coercive inner voice expressing the thoughts of our **"lower nature"** which are all centred on self-aggrandisement, self-desire and attachment to the things of form.

Self-desire and attachment being the two key components of the self-survivalist attitude to life that originated when humankind fell out of a psychological connectedness or one-mindedness with God; when humanity stepped out of a state of God Identification or God Awareness to Self-Identification or Self-Awareness. And with that moved from a state of God Reliance to a state of Self-Reliance.

The Apostle Paul in the New Testament indicated the existence of these two minds with the following words: "But we have the Mind of Christ, to be guided by his thoughts and purposes." (1 Corinthians 2:16). Then in Romans 12:2 we read he said: "Be transformed by the renewal of your mind, that you may discern the will of God."

He was certainly not speaking here of transforming our Christ Mind. He was speaking here of the mind of our lower nature, our mostly irrational mind, that needs to be brought into line or harmonised with the thought processes of the Christ Mind of our higher nature.

We see a perfect example of the assailing nature of the lower mind exemplified in the Bible in a story that has become known as "the temptation of Jesus in the wilderness." Jesus, the highest personification of conscious existence, God in flesh, the one who said, "he who has seen me has seen the Father," was continually tormented in that wilderness experience relentlessly by the thoughts of the lower nature.

The lower nature intensely and sometimes even in a most subtle way, continually tries to widen the gap between the human mind and the God Mind of all human beings, between our way of thinking and God's way of thinking. Life is a continuous battle or Mind Game for the Throne of Our Soul, but life becomes easier to navigate when our Soul is harmonised with the Soul of God.

Life is a battle of two minds. Two minds at psychological war with each other. It is the personal individualisation of a war in the heavenlies being played out on earth. The Kingdom of Darkness waging war against the Kingdom of Light. The flesh without waging war against the Spirit within. Both continually influencing the psychology and physiology of our being.

Two minds that continually seek our attention, one to covertly influence and control our attitudes and subsequent behaviours, and the other seeking to gently guide us in a corrective way along the path of Truth and Wisdom.

Two minds with diametrically opposed thought processes; one pre-birth programmed by God, unchangeable and eternal, the other post-birth programmed according to our life experiences and able to be further programmed according to our whim in the moment. One being birthed from Pure Uncontaminated Consciousness, and the other developed through a contaminated or wrongly programmed Self-Consciousness.

Two minds who if we so choose are capable of living in harmony with each other, but two minds, who, if neglected, morph into a state of ongoing opposition with each other because of the opposite nature of their origin..

And we human beings are the sole decision makers, the arbiters of our eternity, as to who we allow to sit on the Throne of Our Soul. Is the Krishna, Christ, or Buddha Mind seated on the Throne of Our Soul, or have we through ignorance or neglect, accompanied by a long process of attachment and aversion, unknowingly allowed some kind of self-survivalist psychological usurper to ensconce themselves mentally and thus behaviourally in the rulership of our lives.

We must not allow ourselves to forget that we as human beings, as mental, moral, volitional human beings, are the vehicles chosen to declare the Nature of God and manifest the life-enhancing qualities of God's character, characteristics of the Kingdom of Light; in preference to selectively choosing the life-destroying character qualities of the Kingdom of Darkness according to our supposed needs of the moment, and then going about carelessly and indifferently manifesting those.

If we choose wisely, we throw open the Gates of Grace, but if we choose unwisely, if we choose to allow our False Sense of Self to sit alone on the Throne of Our Soul, as so many with a predominate self-survivalist attitude do, we lock down the Gates of Grace. We confine our outer life to an ongoing physical and psychological experience of uneasiness, lack, and pessimism, and an ongoing spiritual experience of wandering aimlessly in the outer courts of our God, searching outside of ourselves for answers, never fully realizing that the answer has been lying in stillness in the Essence Within all the time.

But it is our choice. We are the designated driver of our God given vehicle of life. So do we choose the compassion of the higher nature, or the ill will of the lower nature. Do we choose the love of the higher nature, or the hate of the lower nature. Do we choose the kindness of the higher nature, or the indifference of the lower nature. Do we choose the humility of the higher nature or the pride of the lower nature.

Do we choose the unpretentiousness of the higher nature, or the arrogance of the lower nature. Do we choose the forgiveness of the higher nature, or the vengeance of the lower nature. Do we choose the calm response of the higher nature or the angry outburst of the lower nature. Do we choose peace or disharmony, selflessness or selfishness, fear of the outcome or courage in the moment.

Life is a continuous battle for the Throne of Our Soul and in knowing this one can well understand then how the commonly used phrase "I'm of two minds about this" came into existence, similarly, as did the saying, "should I go with my head, or my heart." So how did this ongoing battle come about, and how does it progressively evolve to the point that for some people their daily life experience becomes one of absolute and continuous confusion and angst?

The mind of our lower nature or false sense of self is described as the lower mind or lower self of the body-mind-intellect persona, and it is a mind that spends all of its functioning time focusing on visible things, seeking out new present moment experiences, activities and achievements. What can I do now? What can I do tomorrow? What will my future look like? What do I like and what don't I like. And this commenced immediately we took our first breath at our birthing into the world.

When we fell out of our mother's womb into the world of form we commenced a relationship of either attachment or aversion to the new things of form or concepts we were progressively exposed to. We set about continuously attaching ourselves psychologically or physically, to present moment desires, and to future hopes and dreams. Focusing on things that now or in the future will bring us a measure of pleasure or some form of happiness.

Or alternately we set about determinedly avoiding things that cause us a measure of displeasure, discomfort, or unhappiness. And in many cases, perhaps unknowingly, whether through attachment or aversion, going against what our higher nature, the Spirit within was prompting us to do.

Over time this lower or false sense of self, entraps our thought processes causing us to continually attach ourselves in our thinking only to things in the present that bring us pleasure, visible things, usually relationships, achievements, and material possessions, or things in the future, mainly dreams and desires that we believe will bring us happiness, peace and contentment. And even at times attaching ourselves to things of the past, things that brought us pleasure at the time and things that may also have brought us pain. All entrapment fodder for a self-determining lower mind.

The consequence of this lower mind's onslaught of activity is that it continually fills in and absorbs all of our thinking time, thus distracting us and diverting us away from any interest or involvement in the will and ways of our higher self, the higher spiritual aspect of our nature, our True Self, which sits in silence waiting to be recognized and acknowledged and wanting to be invited to contribute to our life. The activity of the lower mind keeps us separated from the will and way of our higher mind, the thinking component of our higher nature.

The lower mind in its functional aspect is connected to **Maya,** which is "**a concept of personhood**." Maya in Hindu philosophy meaning illusion. Maya connotes a type of magic show; an illusion where things appear to be real, but things are not what they seem. Maya is "a stage play of the mind", a spiritual concept connoting that life as it exists visibly to the senses is constantly changing and thus is spiritually unreal; it has no eternality attached to it, and consequently it has no relevance to our ability to achieve an ongoing state of peace and happiness.

Similarly the religion of Buddhism uses the word **Mara,** describing humanity as being trapped in the bondage of **Mara**. Mara being "the devil of confusion," where the transient, sorrow filled, and unreal nature of life is not fully recognized for what it is. Mara is described as "the personification of the forces antagonistic to enlightenment."

Thus one becomes totally focused on all the transient things of life, things of form, physical form (possessions) and things of psychological form (relationships). Things that will eventually pass away; things that will rust, rot, and decay because they have no Eternal Essence supporting them.

You see things of form having been conceived and subsequently birthed through human desire or attachment have no eternal principle resident in them, and eventually will rust, decay, and pass away. But things of the Spirit birthed from the highest level of consciousness endure forever. Jesus makes reference to this as seen in the New Testament where he speaks of **"the things born of flesh** that have a temporality attached to them, as against **"the things born of the Spirit"** that have an eternal principle embedded in them."

"Maya or Mara or The Flesh, at work in the "human psyche" is the power or the principle at play in life, "the play of personhood", that conceals from us the true character and nature of our being, by placing a psychological veil between God and us, creating a duality of thought processes."

In the Battle for The Throne of Our Soul, in the play of personhood, the illusionary and confusing life of Maya or Mara or the Flesh separates us psychologically from God, separates our thought processes from the thought processes of God. We are then no longer solely tuned in to the God frequency of energetic influence. We become of two minds about many things. It is a constant distracter, and a constant enabler, and the chief advocate for an illusionary, ever changing, and uncertain type of lifestyle.

This Maya/Mara/Flesh mind principle is like an actor on the life stage of a human drama playing a role and not sticking to the script, but rather adlibbing as they go. It attaches itself to whatever comes its way, whether it is something of matter or of thought. Shakespeare, the

English playwright, poet, and actor, ascribed by many to be an enlightened man, described this illusionary life full of illusionary things in this way in his pastoral comedy As You Like It. He said:

"All the world's a stage, and all the men and women merely players."

However, further to this in opposition with the Maya/Mara/ Flesh Mind we have our ***Mool*** Mind, the thought process of our higher nature, known in Eastern philosophy as the higher mind or higher self. In its functional aspect this upper mind is connected to Mool, "which is a concept centring on the originator of creation, God's Spirit." It is the root and ground of our existence. It is the true stable thought process.

In Christianity this originator is referred to as the Word. We see examples of this in the Old Testament where it is written, "in the beginning was the Word", meaning the Logos, the creative nature of God, the God Mind, "and the Word was with God, and the Word was God." The Apostle Paul in referencing the Mool Mind in the New Testament told the people of the City of Corinth that they had been given "the Mind of Christ", meaning the creative thought processes and perceptive abilities of our Creator God.

When were we all given this Mool Mind or Mind of Christ? We were given it when the genomic imprint of Divine Intelligence was impregnated into our being the moment that a sacrificial fragment of God's Consciousness, the Breath of God, came into our bodies at birth giving us animated life.

Why were we given the Mool Mind or the Mind of Christ? It was given to equip us to successfully navigate the ever changing world of form that we had been suddenly birthed into. We are given the Mind of Christ to support us as we navigate this playground of God that we call our world.

The Old Testament Book of Psalms Chapter 24, with the words "the earth is the Lord's and the fullness thereof," tells us that this earth is God's, and everything in it is Gods'. When David the author of that

Psalm spoke of the "fullness thereof" he was not just saying that everything comes under God's power, he was saying that the Essence of God permeates every aspect of our lives.

The "fullness thereof" is another way of saying that the Consciousness of God, permeates every aspect of conscious existence. Similarly as the Apostle Paul emphasised in the New Testament Book of Acts when he said, "for in Him we live and move and have our being, our very existence," so too in the New Testament's Book of Colossians in speaking of Jesus Paul says, "For in Him all the fullness of Deity (the Godhead) dwells in bodily form completely expressing the Divine Essence of God.

We are all born as children of the Father Consciousness, and as individual fragmented off springs of that Divine Consciousness, each fragment containing all the genetically transferred perfection of that Consciousness, the Divine Fullness. But progressively as we grow physically and psychologically we lose sight of this as the wiles of the Maya, Mara, Flesh Mind ensnare us.

You see in the Battle for The Throne of My Soul, my Maya, Mara, Flesh Mind tells me that I am the creator, that I am the doer. It tells me that I am the principle protagonist on the stage of life, that I play the leading role in the progressive play of God. It tells me that I am the one who can best influence or manipulate things, that I am the one who can move things and shake things and best create my life. It tells me that I am all there is. But the Apostle Paul says, "no you are not, and no you don't have to be, for you have been given the Mind of Christ".

The Christ Mind or Krishna or Buddha Mind represents selflessness, the Maya, Mara, or the Mind of the Flesh represents self-interest. And if you are locked into the carnal or fleshly mind way of thinking and doing in the first instance a switch will require a bit of effort.

For the moment the Maya, Mara, Flesh Mind hears that it is not the doer, it protests, creates doubts, arguments, becomes defensive and storms around, signifying that the battle for the Throne of Your Soul has begun. The Fleshly Mind becomes competitive with Divinity. Some teachers on spirituality describe this as the ego at work.

We will need to remind ourselves continually in the initial stage of our awakening that the Krishna, Christ, or Buddha Mind is the true energetic force that guards our heart and our mind, our emotions and our thoughts, ever seeking to comfort us, correct us, and teach us the will and way of God. We will need to remind ourselves that it alone is the observer of all thought, all matter, and all activity; the observer of all things both Mool and Maya in our lives. So it knows what's going on in our lives.

You could describe the Krishna, Christ or Buddha Mind as the creative influence and watchman of our lives. In its **active or functioning mode** for a Christian it is in fact the person of the Holy Spirit, the active agent of the Christ Consciousness, and for a Hindu it is Shiva the active agent of the Krishna Consciousness. Shiva is called the physician of the world, by those who know the nature of the principles. Shiva is one of the active agents of Brahman, (God), forever endowed with great qualities.

The Maya, Mara, Carnal or Fleshly Mind can be likened in a physical sense to a gun that has the capacity to wound, in this case wound us emotionally or mentally, and even physically, but a gun that only works when the bullets are loaded. The bullets can be likened to unhealthy and unhelpful thoughts. If we choose to load the bullets of unhealthy thinking back into the gun it rearms it.

But the wounding capability of the old way of thinking, the old way of the Maya, Mara, Carnal Mind becomes psychologically emptied once we begin loading the chamber with the bullets of the Krishna Mind, or the Christ Mind, or the Buddha Mind way of thinking and perceiving. If the fleshly mind does try to create discord or disharmony of some kind,, which in this the great battle for the Throne of Our Soul it still will be inclined to do when it finds an opportune time, it will be shooting with blanks.

The Buddha in Chapter 1 of the Dhammapada tells us:

"What we are today comes from our thoughts of yesterday, and our present thoughts build our life of tomorrow; our life is the creation of our mind."

Therefore, said the Buddha:

"If a man speaks or acts with an impure mind, suffering follows him as surely as the wheel of the cart follows the beast that draws the cart."

However, the Buddha continued:

"Since what we are today comes from our thoughts of yesterday, and our present thoughts build our life of tomorrow, and our life is the creation of our mind, then, if a man speaks or acts with a pure mind, joy follows him as his own shadow."

Most people in the early stage of their spiritual pilgrimage, no matter what religious brand they may be attached to are dualistic in their thinking to some greater or lesser degree, meaning they fluctuate between the Maya, Mara, Carnal Mind persona and the Krishna, Christ, Buddha Mind persona, depending on their circumstances.

They fluctuate between personhood and presence, or between non-enlightenment and enlightenment, or between the Flesh and the Spirit, with many leaning more towards a carnal way of thinking as the cares and temptations of life for ego gratification ensnare them. Their Maya / Mara/ Fleshly Mind is always tempting them to either totally ignore or override through logic and reasoning what their inner Krishna, Christ, or Buddha Mind within is trying to tell them.

The Maya Mind in fact chokes off the Voice of Wisdom, silencing it. Jesus references this play of personhood in a parable in the Book of Matthew, where He talks about the good seed in the garden that is choked by the thorns or weeds, a parable being a simple story designed to illustrate a moral or spiritual lesson.

Jesus in that story was once again as he did so many times using parabolic imagery driving home a greater understanding of the great battle for the human soul that is continuously in play as part of the progressive play for the hearts and minds of creation. A great battle for the Throne of Our Soul that is described in the New Testament Books of Romans, Galatians, James, and 1 Peter as "the desires of the flesh warring against the Spirit."

This choking off process could be likened in a physical sense to a person continually talking over the top of you in an attempt to drown out your words. But in our journey of consciousness it is drowning out the voice of the Spirit because **our old nature will always preference logic and reasoning over intuitive thought until we train it not to do so.**

The thought process of the Krishna, Christ, or Buddha Mind within, the way of thinking of the upper mind, is then veiled through a person's deference or bowing to the will and to the reasoning and supposed logic of the lower mind. There is an obedience shift in relation to the things of the spirit.

The Book of Ephesians in the New Testament reminds us that in truth we do not wrestle against literal flesh and blood such as governments, or people, or companies, or circumstances, in as much as they are to us the obvious initiators of our torment. Rather underpinning the visible circumstances that appear as the vehicles for our current woes, are the rulers, the authorities, the cosmic powers (energetic influences) hovering over this present darkness, the spiritual energetic influences of evil in heavenly places." (Ephesians 6).

And where are they hovering? They are hovering over "the Kingdom of God that is within you, your True Self formed from the fragment of God's Breath, God's Divine Essence, that contains the genetic imprint of God that was embedded in you at birth." That is their target.

And why are they hovering over the Kingdom of God within you, why is this metaphysical warfare occurring? Its purpose is to keep the Divine Character Qualities that are within you trapped by "a baffling and perverting carnal mesh which blinds it and makes all error," as the poet Robert Browning described it.

They are hovering as ever present watchmen to attempt to prevent those Divine characteristics of the God Personality from rising to the outer surface of our existence, to prevent that Inner Splendour within from escaping to the outer experience of our life.

> *"Life in its essence is an ongoing battle for who gets control of your progressive personal evolution of consciousness, who gets to sit on the Throne of Your Personal Soul in the Kingdom of God within you."*

In the teachings of Hinduism in ancient scriptures such as the Bhagavad Gita, regarded as the most revered of all Hindu texts, we see war imagery being used in this great struggle for the throne of the Soul; likewise throughout the great Hindu epic the Mahabharata from which the Bhagavad Gita has been extracted.

And similarly as Christians are meant to with the parables of Jesus go beyond the literal meaning of the parable, so too if we desire to understand the true spiritual meaning of the Bhagavad-Gita and the words of Krishna, we must, through contemplation, intuitively go beyond the literal battles of the Mahabharata and focus primarily on all the dialogue between Krishna and Arjuna, the two chief protagonists.

Then in this vast epic a discerning spiritual reader will find contained in its imagery a picture of the great spiritual struggle for the human soul that is occurring in every human being, no matter what religious brand one has attached themselves to, or what philosophical brand. or what ideological brand.

Proof of this can be seen where Krishna in a poem at the end of Chapter 3 of the Bhagavad Gita says:

> *"Be a warrior and kill desire, the powerful enemy of the soul."*

And again at the end of Chapter 4, where it says:

> *"Kill therefore, with the Sword of Wisdom, the doubt born of ignorance that lives in my heart."*

Similarly the Book of Ephesians 6 in the Christian New Testament we see warfare terminology used where says:

"Put on the whole armour of God, that you might resist the devil," and *"Take up the Sword of The Spirit."*

The only thing that enables dualistic thinking to maintain its grip on one's life, the only thing that enables this constant movement or travel back and forth between the higher mind and the lower mind to continue, is in fact us. We are the enablers. It is not some sort of secret spiritual power the lower mind possesses that enables it to distract and divert us away from the thoughts emanating from the higher mind, the Krishna, Christ, or Buddha Mind within.

Regardless of our institutionalised religious status, whether we are a Hindu, Christian, or Buddhist; regardless of our personal status, whether we are a priest or a parishioner, a prince or a pauper, the Kingdom of God is within us all. All human beings have been given the Krishna, Christ, or Buddha Mind, which is the thought pattern and the perception processes of God. All human beings have been given the ability to see life from God's perspective rather than the egos, if we so choose.

How in a practical way does that happen? It happens by our initiating a working relationship with the Krishna, Christ or Buddha Mind. It begins when we as a deliberate act of our will begin to perceive, filter and interpret the happenings of life through the Krishna Mind, the Christ Mind, or the Buddha Mind, rather than solely the Ego Mind.

Midst all the clutter and haste, and midst all the strife and sadness we have in this world, there exists a society of souls desperately needing to know this Supreme Being we refer to as God, rather than just knowing of God, and understand how God works; and in doing so witness the gap of psychological separation closed, witness the veil being lifted, and thus begin experiencing our source of being, the life force within. This is the ongoing plan of God for humanities cosmic consciousness evolution.

You see it is not sufficient that we merely come to a realization of our True Self within as Eastern religion describes it, nor sufficient to merely get saved as evangelical Christians describe it, we must also in our pilgrimage of consciousness come to a restoration of right thought processes, a harmonisation of the faculties of our Soul with the faculties of the Soul of God.

History is littered with examples of spiritually realised teachers or preachers who have come to a realisation of their True Self or had a salvation experience only to eventually become unstuck after a while getting caught up again in the wiles of the enemy of the Soul. Simply because the desires and attachments of the flesh, the ego mind, are continually warring against the Spirit. Neither a salvation experience nor a self-realisation experience is the end of the pilgrimage of our Soul, they are both merely the beginning of that journey.

The Spirit within has been given to us to assist us to change our way of thinking and our way of perceiving or seeing things; She helps us to see life from God's point of view rather than the Ego Mind point of view, until eventually our mind is fully renewed to a new thinking process and thus harmonised with the Mind of God. The gap of psychological separation will be finally closed and the lived experience of being at one with Divine Consciousness, the Divine Essence within and without, becomes our new reality. Then one is indeed a fully enlightened being.

"The weapons of our warfare are not physical weapons of flesh and blood. Our weapons are Divinely powerful for the destruction of fortresses. We are destroying sophisticated arguments and every exalted and proud thing that is raised up against the Knowledge of God, and we "take every thought captive to obey Christ."

— The Apostle Paul 2 Corinthians 10:4

CHAPTER 6

The Weapons of Our Warfare....Divine Revelation Revealed through Chosen Messengers

❦

"The Soul can never be cut into pieces by any weapon, nor
can it be burned by fire, nor moistened by water, nor withered
by the wind. All kinds of physical weapons, swords, flames,
rains, or tornadoes are unable to kill the Spirit Soul."

— KRISHNA.....THE BHAGAVAD GITA 2:23

It is to my mind a self-evident truth, that society, in both Western
and some Eastern cultures, is in many ways degenerating psychologically before our very eyes. Centuries of bad collective karma, born
from the seeds of the unjust and immoral actions of self-interest and
greed, appear more and more to be coming home to roost. The Western
world's longstanding crusade to plunder the wealth of earths' resources
and westernise indigenous cultures through its predatory commercial
schemes, has set off a series of moral and cultural crises that humanity
has rarely seen before.

Whilst many point the finger of blame for certain societal woes such
as floods, fires, and famines, solely at the feet of climate change, many
also tend to casually disregard the other contributing forces that are eating at the heart of modern society, perhaps because these things don't
affect them personally.

Things such as the rampant militarization of the globe, the shocking frequency of mass violent events, the worsening opioid drug epidemic, the sudden rise of militant ideologically driven groups with a particular prejudice against certain elements of society, and the increasing high level of stress related illness. These things must equally be seen as contributing factors to societal degeneration and fragmentation, and cultural isolation, directly linked to the increasing collapse of a collective moral compass.

Our modern world is suffering from mind stress, the dysfunctional attachment in thought to some individuals or groups' immoral, corrupt, and dysfunctional thinking. What the world needs is not a new ideology, not a new cause to hook up with, not a new belief system, not a new movement, not a new religion or a recycled guru, not a new political party, but to simply transcend to a new way of perceiving, thinking, and behaving, and with that a new way of "moral collectivism."

Moral collectivism is the idea that social groups can be moral agents; that we all have moral rights and responsibilities. That groups as well as individuals can take moral action, that the morality of their actions can sensibly be assessed in those terms, and that moral responsibility cannot simply be reduced to the actions of others alone, including the legislature of a country or nation.

Now more than at any other juncture in recent history, the one thing that defines many cultures is the glaring absence of spirit, love, and wisdom. Much of civilization's guiding ethos appears to be that of ego, division, and ignorance.

The illusionary ideologies of consumerism and nihilism have been accepted as natural expressions of our nature, and as such if not arrested can very soon become accepted in a type of mind desensitizing way, which I believe is happening to many in this present day. A true nihilist believes in nothing specific, has no loyalties, and no purpose other than an impulse to destroy that which they don't have, or alternatively take by physical force that which they believe they never will have legitimately.

Many people in modern society, totally focused on their own circumstances, locked up psychologically withing the confines of their own selfish ego, their false sense of self, their self-survivalist lower nature, remain blissfully unaware that behind the outward circumstances of their lives, there are invisible inner forces at work, which sees us all as one human family participating in a metaphysical war between the energetic forces of light and the energetic forces of darkness, the essence of which are spirit and ego.

Now typically, when most people hear the word war, they think of a physically visible war. They picture in their mind a conquering army marching forward, innocent people as well as the enemy being killed, the mass destruction of property, and subsequent awful images of a physically and emotionally broken generation of people. In this current day news images and interviews with victims of Putin's ego driven invasion of Ukraine are sadly a perfect picture of this. That is the physical, visible reality of what we describe as warfare.

However, in terms of the metaphysical reality of this universe, the meaning of war deepens. If we were to adopt a metaphysical understanding of the universe, we would interpret war similarly as with everything else in the world, as specific phenomenon "manifesting from a spiritual plane".

In modern philosophical terminology, metaphysics refers to the study of what cannot be reached through objective study of material reality. In other words it refers to the fact that what you see has a deeper meaning to it than the physicality of the visual.

Metaphysics is the branch of philosophy that examines the fundamental nature of reality, including the relationship between mind and matter, between substance and attribute, and between potentiality and actuality. But if we ignore the metaphysical reality of the universe, if we just throw our hands up into the air and give up, if we just simply ignore the happenings around us, thinking we cannot influence those happenings, and live in some vague vacuum of hope, what potential is there for the ongoing progress of civilization.

For if we don't in a self-exploratory way take active steps to initiate change within ourselves in the first instance, so as to play our part in influencing outer change in the world, then the status quo of the universe will continue, self-interest will continue, wars will continue, famines will continue, droughts will continue, and floods will continue.

Why is this so? Why will these things continue?

Because the Mind of the Universe, having tried in vain but finding no one to help the earth and its inhabitants heal, finding no one to stand in the gap, as the Old Testament Prophet Ezekiel said, to stand in the gap and to play their part, finding few people of both the political and religious persuasion with enough courage and integrity to right wrongs inflicted upon the earth and humanity, will then attempt without partiality, to self-cleanse itself from the evils in society and thus self-heal itself. To self-cleanse itself from those things that are causing its current distress, its progressive physical and mental degeneration.

In other words the Divinely inbuilt nature of the universe, having found no one to help, will take its course, for having found no human helper to heal the land, it will then revert to its original pre-programmed Divine Blueprint to restore peace, balance, and harmony.

This is what we unconsciously refer to as " nature taking its course." Which is Divine Nature taking its pre-programmed course to heal itself, because humanity has failed in its responsibility to express righteous peace filled dominion over the earth.

This is the hidden truth in the teaching of Jesus when he preached to the multitudes, "blessed are the peacemakers." Jesus was not referring only to those who attempt to influence peace between warring nations. He was referring also to those who make peace and harmony with both the metaphysical aspects of the universe and the physical aspects of the universe.

So in the eyes of Kingdom Consciousness, in the eyes of God the Observer, the Oneness that watches, the person who initiates a peace treaty between warring nations in the universe is no more blessed or important than the one who focuses on bringing peace and balance to the earth's climatic situation, or the one who initiates healing and advances the progress of peace in a personal relationship.

We are all called to be instruments of peace, influencers on the inner peace of the individual, which includes ourselves, and influencers on the outer peace of the universe and all it contains.

But in order to be a true instrument of peace, we must first be prepared to accept that the metaphysical reality of the universe is equally as important as the psychical and physical reality of this universe, and thus open ourselves to a greater understanding of what this universe is and how in truth it functions, what it responds to and what it reacts against.

You see when a human being begins to question reality, they may begin to confront borders that an empirical or scientific method by themselves simply cannot transcend, meaning cannot give answers, and then the only choice an individual has in a situation such as that is to give up on their search for answers, or alternately take a leap of faith into the transcendent nature of humankind, the unseen world of metaphysics, using that as a means for finally discovering an authentic existence.

I reference the term Lila in the next chapter, the Hindu concept connoting that the universe and all it contains is simply the stage of a Divine Metaphysical Play, the physical location where the whole drama of this progressive spiritual harmonisation of the Soul of Humankind with the Soul of God is played out.

The place where the forces of Nature and the forces opposing the pre-destined natural occurrence of all things is played out in a type of combined metaphysical, physical, and psychological warfare. The New Testament's Apostle Paul summed this up succinctly with the phrase, "in truth or in reality, we wrestle not primarily against flesh and blood, (physical reality), but against the unseen forces of darkness."(metaphysical reality).

According to this viewpoint the duel between these two opposing energetic forces in the cosmos, the two metaphysical forces underpinning or alternately undermining nature we might call them, that duel, is the underlying factor behind the duelling human forces on the earth that we witness daily in our lives in what we call our physical reality.

In spiritual writings those cosmic forces or energies are termed the "forces of light and the forces of darkness', being good and evil energies, one side Spirit driven (our higher nature) and the other ego driven (our lower nature), continually waging war for the ultimate domination of the inner soul of humanity, the throne of the Kingdom of God within each individual.

In a metaphysical sense then, the many wars and conflicts on earth as imaged on our television screens are not primarily a physical conflict between opposing forces that takes place on the outside of us but more so the product of an inner war that is going on inside us; a contest between the prevailing forces of the lower nature and the higher nature within us, the tails side of the coin and the heads side.

The danger for some spiritual seekers however is to simply pass off all these things as illusionary and then brush them off, giving the lower nature carte blanch to merrily roll along. In other words when we blame the person not the contaminated persona of the person, nothing changes and if anything continues to worsen. The Apostle Paul spoke many times about the flesh waging war against the Spirit. The ego consciousness of the lower nature is continually waging war against the God Consciousness of our higher nature.

And what is the primary weapon the ego consciousness uses against the spiritual pilgrim to defend and maintain its position. In simple terms it uses "the confuse and thus divide principle." It uses doubt and subsequent confusion. And an unflinching attachment to institutionalised religious doctrine has been the lower nature's chief protagonist in cultivating and maintaining individualised confusion.

What did the Buddha say about confusion? He said confusion is the function of attachment, and one of the most essential points in the teachings of Buddhism stresses that confusion is only a temporary thing and as such is not a part of our basic nature so it can be dissolved or transcended through wisdom.

What did Krishna say is the root cause of confusion?
He said, "it is body or mind identification", and used the term Maya.

How did the Buddha describe the energetic force which powers that body mind identification as Krishna described it. He called it Mara, meaning "the devil of confusion".

Our individual responsibility, therefore, in this Lia, the stage play of life, is simply to transcend the onslaught of darkness and confusion through exposing it to the Light. Transcendence is the primary weapon of our warfare in this the battle for our Soul. The role of every individual is to transcend their individual lower nature by veiling it with the attributes of the higher nature, which is the opposite of what is happening in much of the world in this modern day.

More and more so in this modern day we witness the lower nature, in its individualised ego driven insanity, suppress or veil the higher nature. We must be continually aware of exposing the slightest hint of the appearance of an attribute of the lower nature, to the prevailing light of the higher nature within.

In practicality that means as well as exposing our mind to the sacred scriptures of Krishna, Christ, and the Buddha, we must each time we see the ego rising up to take charge in our thinking process conduct ourselves in our thoughts and behaviours exactly as these teachings tell us, until progressively it just becomes a habit to respond to a situation from God's point of view rather than the lower nature's point of view. "We fake it until we make it."

The Apostle Paul in the Book of Corinthians described this as the "casting down of every vain imagination and every high thing that exalts itself against our knowledge of God and bringing every thought into captivity to the thoughts of Christ." But how can we possibly do this if our thinking mind contains limited knowledge of God and God's Way. We can't. And prayer alone, which at times for some can become a type of spiritual buck passing, is simply not enough.

That is what this warfare is all about. It's a war of two minds, the mind of our lower nature and the mind of our higher nature, and our weapons are the Wisdom teachings of God as revealed to messengers such as Krishna, Christ, and the Buddha. But if we have no understandings of these Wisdom teachings we are left weapon less, totally at the mercy of outside forces.

For how can we know if something is exalting itself against the Wisdom of God if we are not familiar with God's Wisdom?

Our priority therefore must be to know and understand the Wisdom of God as exemplified in the sacred Hindu scriptures known as the Upanishads and the Bhagavad Gita, in the sacred Christian teachings of Jesus in the New Testament and in the Gospel of Thomas, and in the sacred writings of the Buddha in The Dhammapada.

In the sacred Bhagavad-Gita of the Hindu religion, the great warrior named Arjuna, instructed by Krishna, his charioteer Guru, God incarnate in disguise, is encouraged to first fight a spiritual war within himself, before even contemplating the hope of victory in a flesh and blood war.

If one merely reads the Bhagavad-Gita as the setting for an actual physical battlefield alone and does not transcend through contemplative reflection in thought to a metaphysical understanding of the story, then one will not see the truth of what this book of scripture is trying to drive home.

What matters not is whether this supposed battle did actually occur, and to debate this matter is unhelpful, what matters most is that this story of the war when viewed metaphorically, as purely metaphorical in nature, is speaking of the war that is going on within the inner being of each and every person, the inner battle for the Throne of the Soul.

Due to society's immaturity or lack of understanding of the metaphysical aspect of the universe and as such ignorance of the world of spirit, much of ancient scripture when trying to bring an understanding of the truth of the spiritual world to a confused generation, has at times used metaphorical language, sometimes even in a mythological context, to get the message across. The ancient sages did it, Krishna did it, the Buddha did it, and Jesus did it.

Iman Ali, the cousin and son-in-law of the Prophet Muhammad, the spiritual leader and founder of the Muslim religion in reference to this said the following:

"Your sickness is coming from within you, but you do not perceive it, and your remedy is within you, but you do not sense it. You presume you are a small entity, but within you is unfolded the entire universe. What you seek is within you if only you reflect".

Simply said:

"If we reflect on Divine Wisdom in a disciplined but relaxed way, over time we psychologically evolve in our attitudes and physically improve our ongoing reactive behaviour, and the world becomes a better place for it."

So humanity is faced with a stark choice. Through refection and understanding, allow or give permission to Divine Wisdom to correct our attitudes and behaviours, or through continued ignorance of Divine Truth progressively die, spiritually, psychologically, and for many undeservingly perhaps physically. For if the structures of the human mind and the subsequent behaviours emanating from these structures remain unchanged, we will always end up recreating the same world, the same evils, the same dysfunction.

And when I speak of Divine Truth I am not talking of institutionalised theological truth, truth that has been contaminated with institutionalised dogma and doctrine. I am referring to reflecting on the teachings of chosen messengers such as Krishna who came to show us the Way of Light, reflecting on the teachings of the Buddha who came to show us the Way of Life, or reflecting on the teachings of Christ who then came to show us the Way of Love. Nothing more is necessary.

The teachings in the Bhagavad-Gita similarly as are many of the teachings of the Christ as seen in the New Testament, are metaphorical in nature, and actually speak of a human being fighting a spiritual war against the ego; seeing Krishna the Divine Being of wisdom and compassion instructing his faithful disciple Arjuna on how to achieve self -realisation, an understanding of who he really is on the inside in the inner depths of his being, as against what he thinks he is, and what appears to be real in the outer circumstances of his environment.

It is abundantly clear that Krishna equates the pursuit of self-realisation or an understanding of the true self with the surrender of one's own ego driven desires to the desires of the Spirit, the Infinite Intelligence that supports and sustains one's very physical and psychological existence.

As with the Christian, Jesus the Christ represents one unique and perfect manifestation of the Divine Spirit in human form, similarly to a Hindu, Krishna represents one unique and perfect manifestation of the Divine Consciousness in form.

Consequently Krishna encourages Arjuna to give up all selfish craving and focus his attention on Krishna's Wisdom. Similarly the Apostle Paul encouraged the people to "be imitators of Christ, as he himself was."

The Bhagavad-Gita Chapter 9 verse 29 says:

"All those who take refuge in me, whatever their birth, race, sex, or caste, will attain the same goal; this realisation can be obtained even by those whom society scorns. Therefore having been born in this transient and forlorn world, give all your love to me. Fill your mind with me; love me; serve me; worship me always. Seeking me in your heart, you will at last be with me."

As a culture, we cling to all the external pleasures of the world that Krishna warned Arjuna about. The world's game of today is a game of wealth, power, and fame. We play the game to enhance our image and our name. Our cultures obsession with pursuing selfish, materialistic desires, just creates more misery for the world. Consequently when you remove a sense of the sacred from life, and assign it a commercial value, what deeper elements remain?

If the worlds rainforests disappear and endangered species go extinct, who cares, as long as logging and mining corporations maximise profits and wealthy businessman grow richer, and shareholders shares increase in value. Who cares if millions of civilians die during senseless wars, as long as the pockets of national leaders, oil investors, and munitions manufacturers grow fatter? Who cares if thousands of young men and women die on the streets from opioid overdoses, as long as there is money to be made off others by unscrupulous drug dealers and cigarette and vape manufacturers.

Divine Consciousness cares, Krishna cares, Christ cares, and the Buddha cares. And we human beings having the Divine Nature within us must care. In what appears to be a never ceasing appearance of all manner of evil in the world, the war on the visible plane of our existence, we must come to understand that societal degeneration can only be dealt a serious blow when each human being in the first instance takes responsibility for dealing with the inner war for the Throne of their Soul.

And to do this we need to become imitators of Krishna, Christ, and the Buddha. We need to volitionally appropriate the weapons of Krishna, Christ, and the Buddha, that we have been so freely given through their teachings, plus all weapons of intuitive Wisdom that lie in stillness in the Kingdom of God within us, waiting patiently to surface to the conscious existence of our lives.

Having merely a form of religion but denying the power of authentic spirituality is no longer an acceptable proposition.

The ancient Chinese General Sun Tzu said:

"Know thy enemy and know yourself; then in a hundred battles, you will never be defeated."

When you are ignorant of the enemy but know yourself, your chances of winning or losing are equal. But if ignorant both of your enemy and of yourself, (your inherent True Self) you are sure to be defeated in every battle".

You see the primitive or unregenerated or unrenewed mind of society in the day of Jesus and even still in this day in western society requires a gospel, good news, something which adapts to the level of consciousness and thus to the mental capacity of the hearer, to their current level of intuitive awareness and thus true understanding. Which is why the Apostle Paul spoke of the responsibility all human beings have for the "renewing of their minds."

The unrenewed minds of society desire something or someone to appear in their lives to give them a measure of hope, and to console them for the evils and trials persistently plaguing their lives, and basically to give them a sense of joy and happiness. But you see what may be for some, whether an individual or a community, or a culture, a gospel of good news, is very far from being good news for all others at that time or even in different eras.

For instance whatever may have been the misguided intent of those early Catholic bishops who oversaw the establishment in which early Christian theology was formulated, from which the Bible's content was the result, we may not know for sure, but we can identify certain parts of their wrong guidance as new revelation is given to us. But still to this day the "indelibly institutionalised mind" continues to hang on every word of that wrong guidance.

For example, and please read this slowly and carefully, and thoughtfully.

The statement taught in most Christian Churches that "the one (Christ) had risen from the dead and become the first fruits of them that slept", which was then extrapolated to teach "that when we die we will sleep for a while, waiting for Jesus to return and take us back to heaven with him," whilst it was part of the Gospel of Good News for early Christianity, it would certainly not be a gospel or good news, for those in possession of the ancient wisdom of the East who were present when the Catholic Church began teaching this..

But when we understand through inner enlightenment the true spiritual meaning of "resurrection from the dead", the true metaphysical and metaphorical meaning, when we understand that the scripture is referring to the deadness of our Soul and not our bodies, we begin to see things in an entirely different way.

And the spiritual misguidance received by us through our institutional brand due to wrongful intellectualised interpretation of the teachings of Christ or the Apostle Paul, is replaced with Truth. The early church fathers in translating the early Christian scriptures did not always get it right, particular if the writings were of a metaphysical or metaphorical nature.

When we understand that it is not physical death that is referred to at all, but the deadness of a human being's spiritual nature, until his Christ's Nature, his Atman has risen again in him and become pre-eminent, when we understand these things, this earthly existence called our life and the circumstances that surround our individual lives take on a whole new meaning.

When we understand that in truth it is speaking about the Soul of the individual having been dead and buried by its descent into matter, desire, attachment, and aversion, whereby also hangs the meaning of "the fall", then we are no longer in mental conflict with a wider and deeper knowledge of these teachings of the ancient masters or the Christian scripture itself that speaks of this, rather we are only in mental conflict with the Church's theological and sometimes institutionally biased interpretation of original scriptural documents.

There are a great many references in the New Testament to the resurrection from the dead which have a deeper spiritual and metaphysical meaning, but they are commonly taught and taken as if they refer to a physical death and resurrection. Why?

Because in the day they were written the evolutionary journey of consciousness of most of society had not evolved to a sufficient enough level to fully comprehend it, or as I previously alluded to, because the hidden political agenda of the church hierarchy was to keep these things to themselves.

And those teachings certainly would not have been good news for Plato or Socrates, not to mention Confucius, Lao Tzu, the Buddha or Adi Shankaracharya, or other sages and mystics who lived and wrote centuries and centuries before Christ.

What sort of good news would it be to ask these teachers and their followers if taken in its crude materialised form to believe that, as Christian theology espouses, when we physically die we lie suspended awaiting the resurrection of our physical bodies. Some of the early church fathers knew better, but their teaching was largely ignored.

Both sleep and death are associated with the spiritual condition of the living not the dead. Romans 15:11 says "now it is high time for you to awaken out of sleep".

The Apostle Paul in this New Testament passage was not speaking to a graveyard of dead people, he was speaking to a living, breathing, functioning group of believers. As there were in the time of Jesus and the Apostle Paul, there are still primitive minds in these matters today who can only be fed with milk in the form of parables, but not with strong meat, the language of metaphysics, the language of the unseen world of spirit.

We must understand that institutionalised religion in its teachings moves within the narrow circle of its own rational mind, limiting the scope of that teaching to ensure it keeps strictly to the doctrinal position it is aligned with.

It has neither the will nor the capacity to enquire into other modes of thought or other religions. Believing that it already has the truth, the whole truth, and nothing but the truth, and indeed believing that it would be a sin to question the basis of those beliefs, it goes on its way perhaps some with a slightly arrogant spiritual swagger, even pitying those whose beliefs and teachings differ from theirs.

I have come to believe that humanity's true evolutionary journey can be likened to a slow awakening of the Soul. And that every intuitive vision creatively expressed, every time a human being sees something Infinite in that which appears finite, and then brings it forth and shares it with the rest of humanity, whether it be through science, art, music, poetry or other forms of literature, that they are contributing to the awakening of the Soul of humanity. and are thus leaving a lasting legacy.

In encouraging the individual to awaken that creative instinct within the Soul the Indian saint and poet Kabir once said:

"O friend, awake, and sleep no more; the night is over and gone; would you lose your day also? You have slept for unnumbered ages; this morning will you not awake?

Similarly in The New Testament we see the Apostle Paul in writing to the people of Ephesus saying:

"Awake, sleeper, and rise from the dead, and Christ will shine as dawn upon you and give you light". (Amplified Version)

Paul is talking about an awakening of a mind that is dead to true Wisdom, not about a physical resurrection from the grave as has long been taught by institutionalised religion. He was talking about the creative instinct coming forth in every individual. That is what he means by "light."

Long before all of this revelatory truth in Biblical scriptures came forth, there were Divine Avatars, messengers and mystics proclaiming the truths of Infinite Intelligence according to the need of the culture or community at that time. Centuries before Christ came forth, a greater understanding of the Divine Self was being messaged to the societies of the day.

One who has discovered truth in the teachings of Christ should not totally discard the ancient Divine Wisdom embedded in the teachings of Divine Messengers such as Krishna and Buddha as seen in scriptures such as the Upanishads, the Bhagavad Gita, and the Dhammapada.

Nor should one who has through cultural inheritance been brought up with the teachings of these ancient scriptures, reject the teachings of Christ that correlate with them. All are beneficial for the ongoing welfare of the soul and its ongoing harmonisation journey with the Soul of God and thus effective weapons in this the Battle for The Throne of Our Soul.

Revelatory truth no matter what era it is birthed in is timeless, and all was given at a particular time in history to assist humanity in its psycho-spiritual evolution and to guide humanity back to a complete recognition of its existing oneness with eternity, and as such is just as effective in this modern day as it was in the day it was first birthed into humanity's understanding.

And all progressive revelation is invaluable as weaponry to be used to navigate life in this the ongoing Battle for The Throne of Our Soul. Whether that be Krishna's Way of Light, or what came later the Buddha's Way of Life, or what came later still the Christ's Way of Love.

Many Christians through ignorance of historical spiritual truth vehemently reject the idea of embracing the ancient sometimes mystical Wisdom of the Hindu and Buddhist religions, equally as much as certain Hindus and Buddhists of Eastern Religion reject the teachings of Christianity. But how many professing Christians who do this actually know of their own Christian mystical literature that is fully in sync with the Hindu and Buddhist teachings.

Ancient masters such as Krishna, Christ, and the Buddha spoke of the True Self, the eternal immortal Divine Self within which is at one with the Consciousness of God. They spoke of a True Self that Jesus simply referred to as the "I Am," and spoke of his own state of harmony with that "I am, " spoke of his own state of "oneness" with the "I am" with the simple words, "I and the Father are one," and "the Kingdom of God is within you."

"Remember, the Kingdom of God (the Oneness that pervades all)) is within you. All the power, all the weapons of spiritual warfare that you can possibly need to navigate life are at your disposal; you need no helper to give them to you, they are yours now."

You don't need to continually rely on a Pastor or Priest, you don't need the supervision of a Shepherd, you don't need continual guidance from a spiritual Guru, although those who are truly led by the Spirit may be helpful to you on occasions in imparting a measure of Wisdom, "you just need the Spirit". Jesus did not say "and I will send you a new Guru", or direct you to another church or another religion, he said, "I will send you the "comforter who shall be **with you and in you"**.

You need no helper in the form of some sort of institutionalised religious ritual to give it to you, you just need to "be still and know that I am (God), that we are all created in the psychological image of God," and as such all the powers of the Godhead dwell in us bodily. And then go about life doing what is necessary to align your daily thoughts, attitudes, and practical behaviours with the principles that govern that Kingdom within, and the nature of the True Self will begin to manifest in your life more and more.

You don't have to keep feeding your inner Spirit, your Atman, with all manner of institutionalised ritual in the hope that this will help. You just need to co-operate with its Wisdom and welcome it into your outer earthly experience. Don't hem the Spirit in with all manner of religious activity, rather be still, meditate on Divine Truth, and thus allow the Spirit to come forth and manifest.

And in the first instance this means we quietly contemplate the Divine messages of chosen messengers such as Krishna, Christ, and the Buddha, and then set about aligning our attitudes and behaviours with these teachings, and progressively we will train our inner ear to hear the Divine Voice ourself in a deeper way.

In speaking of the Battle for The Throne of Our Soul, the Apostle Paul of the Christian religion put it this way; "The weapons of our warfare are not physical." Grace in one's life is not received by aligning oneself with a particular religious institution. Grace is enabled by firstly aligning our attitudes and behaviours with its attitudes and behaviours of God, which are easily identified in the teachings of Krishna, or Christ, or the Buddha.

Jesus tells us that when we seek first the Life Principles of the Kingdom of God, all things necessary to maintain a healthy, happy life will by Grace be given to us.

Those Kingdom Principles metaphysically become our armour and weaponry in the Battle for the Throne of our Soul. They immediately bring the Kingdom Law of Reciprocity into play, the "what you give shall be given unto you" principle into play, releasing the Spirit to come forth into our outer existence, into our practical existence. A play of God referred to in spiritual writings as The Grace of God.

Being open to progressive revelation, means being open to the ongoing revealing of new Divine Truth, truth which is the highest wisdom and that which is above all human wisdom and intelligence. It is the Wisdom that Divine Intelligence is speaking to your heart, in the present moment that progresses the realisation of "the goal of yoga of union or ongoing harmonisation of our consciousness with God's consciousness," as the Bhagavad Gita says, or as the Apostle Paul called it "reaching the stature and fullness of Christ."

You see Yoga is union with the Divine. It is a relaxed realisation of our oneness with all. That is what that weekly yoga class you may attend in your desire to get fitter and to get even unconsciously closer to the spiritual aspect of your being is all about.

That weekly journey to your yoga class is not just about "exercising your body", which of course is helpful, but the original intent of the practice of Yoga, centres on "exorcising your mind of pre-programmed influences". What is "exorcising?" It is a process of complete removal or banishment. Complete removal of all that is not in union or harmony, or you could say "at peace" with God and all other conscious life form.

The potential for the practical expression of the Divine Nature within, the Christos Principle, and all the power it contains runs all through the teachings of Christ, the Buddha, and Krishna. It is freely given waiting to be freely received and voluntarily imprinted into the consciousness of all of humanity, the result being an ongoing state of blessedness. As the Psalms put it:

"Blessed and favoured by God are those who do not follow the advice and example of evil people, nor sit in the company of scoffers, but delight only in the precepts and teachings of God, and in those teachings they dwell.

They shall be like a tree firmly planted and fed by streams of water, which always yields good fruit in its season. Their leaf shall never wither and in everything they do they shall prosper and come to maturity." (A Psalm of David).

"But I am not bound by this vast work of creation, I am, and I watch the drama of works. I watch and in its work of creation "nature" brings forth all that moves and moves not; and thus the revolutions of the world go round.

But the fools of the world know not me when they see me in my own human body (my creation). They know not my Spirit Supreme the Infinite God of this all.

Their hope is in vain, their works are in vain, their learning is vain, their thoughts are vain. They fall down to the nature of demons, towards the darkness of the delusion of hell.

But there are some great souls who know me: their refuge is my own Divine Nature. They love me with a one-ness of love: they know that **"I am the source of all."**

— Krishna.....The Bhagavad Gita 9:9 to 13.

CHAPTER 7

The Progressive Play of Kingdom Consciousness Under the Watchful Eye of the Oneness that Watches

❦

At the end of the night of time all things return to my
nature; and when the new day of time begins I bring them
again into Light. Thus through my nature I bring forth
all creation, and this rolls round in the circles of time."

— KRISHNA......THE BHAGAVAD GITA 9:7,8.

The basic recurring theme in Hindu theology and mythology is the creation of the world by the self-sacrifice of God, "sacrifice" in the original sense being the "creating of something sacred", whereby God (Infinite Intelligence) sacrificed a small portion of its Divine Essence which became localised into a body, creating a world of conscious form.

An act which, in the end, then sees the souls of those created forms with a measure of consciousness having maintained their sacredness, having honoured God's sacrifice, once again returning unto God, their source, to be re-harmonised with God for eternity; the key being to maintain that sacredness or righteous state of being, no matter what things, circumstances or people assail them in life.

And having maintained that sacredness, they return to their source, that from which their consciousness first came forth, witnessing the ultimate realization of the harmonisation of their being with the God Being, and thus the final complete remerging of the individualised Soul back with the Soul of God from whence it first emerged.

In other words that small portion of his own Pure Consciousness that God sacrificed to give life and thus animation with a capacity for Divine illumination, to an individual life form, to create a living breathing Soul, if its initial sacredness is maintained in the manifested body, will then depart from that life form it was embedded in and return to God having successfully completed its act of service.

Otherwise that "fragment of Pure Consciousness," if its sacredness is not welcomed and embraced and harmonised with by the form to which it has been assigned, is reassigned to another body to complete another cycle of earthly manifestation, and the original body in which it was contained is relegated to the dust of the earth.

This whole process, no matter what outcome is achieved, is all part of the Divine Stage play of life, initiated by the Divine Essence of the universe, the Oneness that Watches.

The Old Testament's Book of Genesis Chapter 2 Amplified tells us:

> "And God formed, that is created, the body of man, from the dust of the ground, and God breathed into his nostrils, the Breath of Life; (the Holy Breath), and the man became a living being, an individual, complete in Body and Spirit, and thus the man became a "living Soul".

This creative activity of the Divine in Hinduism is called **"Lila, the play of God", and the universe and all it contains is seen as the stage of that Divine Play**, the place where the whole drama of this progressive psycho-spiritual harmonisation of the Soul of Humankind (humanity's mind, emotions, and will) with the Soul of God (God's mind, emotions, and will) begins, is played out, and concludes with the individualised

Soul's departure back to the Source from whence it came, the Holy Breath.

The Bhagavad Gita 9 Krishna speaking says:

"I watch and in its work of creation nature brings forth all that moves and moves not: and thus the revolutions of the world go round. But the fools of the world know not me when they see me in my own human body. They know not my Spirit Supreme, the Infinite God of this all."

We are all "primary players" in this Lila the progressive stage play of life as Nature takes its course, and because of this at various times during our physical life, our ongoing involvement will necessitate some sort of sacrifice or surrender, perhaps material, perhaps psychological or perhaps emotional.

William Shakespeare, the English playwright, poet, and actor, widely regarded as the greatest writer in the English language and the world's greatest creative dramatist ever, in the phrase that begins a monologue from his pastoral comedy As You Like It, spoken by a melancholy, disillusioned and satirical observer of life named Jacques, describes the concept of Lila in this simple way:

"All the worlds a stage, and all the men and women merely players."

In this play Shakespeare through his character Jacques divides the life of a human being into seven stages. The baby or infant stage, a child of school age, a lover, a soldier, a justice or judge, an old aged or elderly person, and finally an extremely elderly person likened again to a child.

The main theme of Shakespeare's play being that every human being has seven specific stages during their lifetime and every human being performs seven different types of roles in their lifetime, and then finally after all this drama called life is completed, the human being takes a bow and exits from this worldly stage of life.

The theme of this Shakespearian message and the concept of Lila is that at the end of life it is the "human form", the physical form of the human being that is the ultimate loser in this game, in Lila, the ongoing play of God, seeing the curtain drop on its role of being and becoming, thus witnessing the conclusion of its individual part in the overall play.

The human being's material form and the accompanying physical and emotional lifestyle it so rigorously pursued, defended, and attached itself to, is mandatorily relinquished. From dust this human form was originally created and to dust it will return. The Soul that gave it life returns to its source, and with that the body that it gave life to begins decaying into dust.

The Book of Genesis in the Old Testament quoting God speaking puts it this way. "By the sweat of your face you shall eat bread, till you return to the ground, for out of it you were taken; for you are dust and to dust you shall return."(Genesis 3:19 ESV).

That is the ultimate destination for this body and mind that most people spend the majority of their lives trying to enhance or exploit in some way. This is Infinite Intelligence reminding us of the place of this human body in the greater cosmic scheme of things. But if we human beings will allow it, and not resist it, but rather seek to co-operate with it, then Lila, that "play of life" will work itself out through this earthly body in the most enjoyable and fulfilling way.

Then life supported and sustained by the guiding Light of that which set it in place in the beginning and supports and sustains it in its transition and transmigration, "the Divine Gamemaster of this universe", need not be one of ongoing drama and confusion, but rather a life lived in joyous wonder and amazement, no longer bound by the demands of the body or mind.

That gamemaster of this universe, is Infinite Intelligence or Pure Consciousness, the Oneness that watches over us, which having sacrificially given us our first conscious breath, then continues as the guiding Light that watches, sustains, supports and manages the dramas that continuously manifest as the universe unfolds and evolves, as new things are brought into our conscious awareness and our circumstantial existence, and as old things change from their current form and structure.

Krishna as seen in The Bhagavad Gita, which many seekers of the East and the West regard as among the most important and best known of the religious texts of Hinduism says the following:

"But I am not bound by this vast work of creation, I am, and I watch the drama of works. I watch and in its work of creation Nature brings forth all that moves and moves not."(Bhagavad Gita 9).

The phrase "I am" is speaking of "the Oneness or Essence within and without that watches." The Oneness that Watches is that which many people refer to as nature, and it is in a way, but rather the Divine Nature, the creative arm of the Universal Intelligence set in place in the beginning and given specific instructions on how this universe and all it contains will operate. Instructions that I refer to as Divine Principle, (Law), the same instructions that others might unknowingly commonly refer to as the Laws of Nature.

How did Jesus describe to his disciples the presence of this "Oneness or Essence that watches" that is invisible, omnipotent, omniscient, omnipresent, and omnibenevolent? How did he describe this Infinite Intelligence, this creative gamemaster of the universe that watches and observes the creative work of the Divine Nature in progress?

In the Gospel of Thomas we read when questioned on this subject Jesus said the following words:

"It is I who am the Light that presides over all. It is I who am the entirety: it is from me that the entirety has come, and to me that the entirety goes. Split a piece of wood I am there. Lift a stone and you will find me there."

The Bhagavad Gita in describing "this oneness that watches" says in Chapter 15, Krishna speaking:

"And he watches over the mind, and it's senses, it's ears it's eyes, it's touch, it's taste, and it's smell, and his consciousness enjoys their world, and with the powers of his nature enjoys life, whilst those in delusion see him not; but he who has the eye of Wisdom sees."

The Bhagavad Gita in describing the visible and non-visible character-istics of this Oneness, this all-encompassing power or Oneness that per-vades all and watches the drama of men's works, enjoying all works that are aligned with its Nature, says the following:

"**I am** the Soul, prince victorious, which dwells in the heart of all things. Among the sons of light **I am** Vishnu, the radiant sun. **I am** the Lord of the winds and storms, and of the lights in the night. **I am** the moon. Above man's senses **I am** the mind, and in all living beings **I am** the Light of Consciousness. **I am** the vast ocean; **I am** the prayer of silence.

I am the season of flowers; **I am** the beauty of all things beau-tiful. **I am** the goodness of those who are good, **I am** the wisdom of those who seek victory. **I am** the silence of hidden mysteries; **I am** the knowledge of those who know. **I am** the seed of all things that are, of all knowledge. **I am** the knowledge of the Soul, and of the many paths of reason. **I am** the one that leads to truth. **I am** the beginning, the middle, and the end of all that lives. **I am** OM, the word of eternity.

And what is this **I am** in the Bible?

I am is an identifying name of the Oneness or Divine Essence that pervades all and contains all. In the New Testament's Gospel of John we see recorded that Jesus made seven profound **I am** statements. He said: **I am** the bread of life, **I am** the Light of the world, **I am** the gate, **I am** the Good Shepherd, **I am** the resur-rection and the life, **I am** the way the truth and the life, and **I am** the true vine.

In speaking of this "oneness that watches over this Lila the play of life," the philosophical tradition called Vedanta in the religion of Hinduism, shows "the way that this Oneness, Brahman, God, the Word, is expressed in every aspect of the empirical world and explains how it is both the source and the goal of all conscious existence. The two key words here being **"source"** and **"goal."** Vedanta says:

"Seek to know him from whom all beings have come, by whom they all live, and unto whom they all return. He is Brahman."

Krishna in the Bhagavad Gita 7:5,6,7, puts it this way;

"Beyond my visible nature is my invisible Spirit. This is the fountain of life whereby this universe has its being. All things have their life in this Life, and I am their beginning and end. In this whole vast universe there is nothing higher than I. All the worlds have their rest in me, as many pearls upon a string."

The Apostle John similarly in the Book of Revelation wrote:

"I am the Alpha and the Omega, the First, and the Last, the Beginning, and the End, the Eternal One."

You see all things that exist have a source and then a journey to complete, a life cycle or pilgrimage to undertake, the end result being that a goal is reached. The term source meaning "that from which something emerges or comes forth out of," and the term goal referring to "the ultimate end of the journey."

Whether it be something of matter for example a river, or something with conscious life such as the Soul of a human being, all things have a source and an end goal. It's what I would describe as the "ashes to ashes, dust to dust principle." It's the birth and death principle and the intermediatory journey in between. Every human being has a purposeful pilgrimage to complete, regulated only by their present level of consciousness.

The Book of Genesis in the Old Testament tells us that God breathed into the first human, Adam, the Breath of Life (Divine Consciousness), and Adam became a living Soul, " a body with a mind, with emotions, and a will, and as such came alive and animated.

Infinite Intelligence you could say then is the source of all sources, the Alpha of existence, the ultimate Being or Presence from which all things emerge into some sort of life-form, and at that moment come alive, having been gifted with "God's Breath of Consciousness".

And as Infinite Intelligence is the Alpha of all life form, the source from which all individual conscious breath emerged, so Infinite Intelligence is the Omega the destination to which all those fragments of the Holy Breath distributed equally to give animated life individually shall return.

The 15th century Indian mystic, saint, and poet Kabir in speaking of the Holy Breath, God's Breath of Consciousness said:

Are you looking for me?
I am in the next seat; my shoulder is against yours.
You will not find me in stupas, not in Indian shrine rooms,
Nor in synagogues, nor in cathedrals: not in masses, nor in kirtans.
Not in legs winding around your own neck,
Nor in eating nothing but vegetables.
When you really look for me, you will see me instantly,
You will find me in the tiniest house of time.
You ask me "what is God?"
"God is the Breath inside my breath."

Jesus in speaking of this Breath, this Oneness that pervades all said: "If those who lead you say to you, see, the Kingdom is in the sky, (heaven), then the birds of the sky will precede you. If they say to you, it is in the sea, then the fish will precede you. Rather, the Kingdom of God is inside of you, and it is outside of you. When you come to know your-selves, (your True Self) then you will become known, and you will realise that it is in you, and you are the sons of the living Father." (The Gospel of Thomas).

For all things that come into existence there is "a time to be born, a progressive pilgrimage of experiences to complete that manifest as the contents of our individual life, and then a time to die." And at times we will all get a little side tracked on our personal pilgrimage as the cares of life, those primary protagonists in this the play of life surface to distract and confuse us, causing us to embrace specific self-survivalist attitudes and behaviours, that throw us off course.

Nevertheless life will continue, and nature will continue to take its course, and the Divine Essence will continue to watch it taking its course. For our confused way of interpreting life and subsequent manner of resistance to its outworking does not deter it from its course, it just stalls its journey in the present moment in the individual being who is surrendering to confusion.

However, if rather than surrendering to confusion, we are willing to "surrender to circumstance or co-operate with circumstance," which is Lila at Play, then Divine Grace, the "oneness that watches these events" is every ready to guide us back onto the straight path giving us greater knowledge and understanding of the many ways that Divine Principle works to safely steer our ship of life through the turbulent waters that are rising up.

The Old Testament Wisdom Book of Ecclesiastes in describing "nature taking its course" put it this way:

> *"There is a season, a time appointed for everything, and a time for every delight and event or purpose under heaven. A time to be born and a time to die; a time to plant and a time to uproot what is planted. A time to kill and a time to heal; a time to tear down and a time to build up. A time to weep and a time to laugh; a time to mourn and a time to dance.*
>
> *A time to throw away stones and a time to gather stones; a time to embrace and a time to refrain from embracing. A time to search and a time to give up as lost; a time to keep and a time to throw away. A time to tear apart and a time to sew together; a time to keep silent and a time to speak. A time to love and a time to hate; a time for war and a time for peace."*

All conscious beings are made alive through the Breath of God. All conscious beings have a pilgrimage to complete, and all human beings are sustained and supported by that Breath of God during their journey as they hasten towards God's ultimate goal for them. And what is God's ultimate goal for each individual?

It is the full realisation of the Light of Ultimate Truth. And what is that Ultimate Truth? It is an unshakeable realisation of the existence of "the Oneness that Watches," and with that the manifestation of a life of unified peace with all. The Bhagavad Gita Chapter 13 says:

> *"He who sees that the Lord of all is ever the same in all that is, immortal in the field of mortality...he sees the Truth. And when a man sees that the God in himself is the same God in all that is, he hurts not himself by hurting others: then he goes indeed to the highest path."*

That is the Ultimate Truth. The realisation of our oneness with The Oneness, (God) and with all sentient beings. This teaching also explains and complements the teaching of Jesus where we read in the Book of Matthew Jesus telling those around to "love thy neighbour as thyself."

Why did Jesus emphasise this?

Because our Atman, (Sanskrit word in Hinduism translated in English as our Soul), our higher self, our true self, the self-existent fragment of the Divine Essence in all human beings, our true nature distinct from our ego and intelligence, not only dwells in us but simultaneously is fragmented in our neighbour, and if we love our neighbour we love this God Essence who is in us all, and in whom we all are. But conversely if we hate our neighbour, we are hating a container of God.

And what is the result of our "loving our neighbour" in a practical way (deeds) and in a psychological way (our thoughts)? The Bhagavad Gita Chapter 6 Verse 9 tells us that it is the gaining of "peace," a state of peace and inner joy that will enable us to behold all relatives, all companions, all friends, and all those who are impartial or indifferent to us, or even hate us, with the same inner peace that Christ possessed.

We hear the expression quite often used to justify a particular course of negative interaction against another human being, "aw this is just who I am". No it isn't. It is who you choose as an act of your own volition, to be in the moment. But it is not who you truly are in your innermost being. If we acknowledge and love our true self, and cultivate this love, then we will have no desire to hurt our neighbour and as such we will not offend God.

But by contrast if we hurt our neighbour, in thought or in word or in deed, we hurt ourselves and we hurt or offend not only the conscious person whoever that might be, but also the Christ or Atman Consciousness within that person. We grieve the Spirit within.

The life cycle of our body and our mind is a transient one, a stage play in progress, and the great truths underlying the teachings of Krishna, Christ, and the Buddha all deal with this transitory nature of our lives and the self-will we have been gifted to influence the path our being will take. Our Souls are sojourners in a foreign land, taking up temporary residence in a transient body, all under the watchful eye of "the Oneness that Watches."

And the Katha Upanishad of Hinduism, and the Old Testament teaching in the Book of Deuteronomy, and the New Testament teaching in the Book of Revelation, all reference the paths we can choose to take in this transient life. The Book of Revelation describing them as open doors set before us, and we can choose which one we want to walk through. There is the path of joy and peace (spiritual Life) and there is the path of pleasure and pain (spiritual Death). But here is the thing.

The reason we must choose wisely is because **both the path of spiritual life, and the path of spiritual death "attract the attention of the Soul"**, and as such we need to choose wisely which path we take in every aspect of this transient life. For the spiritual Law of Reciprocity (a law of nature) is ever watchful to return to us what we project into the universe in thought and deed, good or bad. It does not differentiate. You give out good and it will be returned to you, you give out bad and it will be returned to you in some way at some time.

The Buddha in referencing this transient life we are living in, described it as a life of self-interest that is vanity or all in vain, and this can be evidenced in the many unwise choices we make in life through the influence of this vanity, the primary characteristic of the egoic mind. The Old Testament preacher in the Book of Ecclesiastes said, "vanity of vanities, all (of life) is vanity."

What is this vanity of vanities that the Old Testament preacher and the Buddha spoke of? It is "the pointlessness of human activity in the name of egoic self-interest, and the pointlessness of temporary self-pleasure in our feeble attempts to self-create momentary happiness." Why is the physical life in many ways seemingly pointless? Because it will all eventually become as dust lost in the progressive decay of a thousand todays that will so quickly pass and morph into a thousand yesterdays. When your pleasure seeking body dies, sorry, it is gone.

But the Buddha also makes it clear that those beautiful moments of life that we can catch glimpses of as we triumph over this vain transient life can be very enjoyable. We just always need to be alert to the fact that, as Sigmund Freud put it; " it's a fine line between (current) pleasure and (future) pain."

Lila, the Divine Stage Play of Life, will continue, until our earthly pilgrimage ends, and there will be ups and downs in the process. But Divine Intelligence has given us the psychological and behavioural keys to use to guide us through the ongoing myriad of madness that is present in this world we sojourn in.

What did Jesus say about these keys?

He said as we read in the Book of Matthew:

"I will give you the Keys of the Kingdom, and whatever you bind on earth, (declare to be improper) shall be bound in heaven (by me).

You see we have not been left defenceless or comfortless, we have been given the keys to defend ourselves from the wiles of the enemy. And where are these keys that set us free from all the horrors of the world around us to be found? They are already in us, lying in stillness in the Kingdom within, our Atman, waiting to be activated, waiting to be set free from the shackles of their confinement.

We just have to allow them to come to the transient surface of our lives. This is why Jesus encouraged us to above all else, "seek first the Kingdom of God." He was not telling us to hunger after heaven. He was encouraging us to find "the pearl of great price" hidden within.

There are two worlds involved in our life that create our reality as we see it. There is the external world where our body moves and lives and has its being, a world that we must navigate carefully with our five senses. However it is a world that limits our freedom at times, and the ego will remind us of this, which is why we must obey the laws of nature, the Divine Principle set in place in the beginning, otherwise we suffer. The current crisis of climate change is visible evidence of this.

And it is the task of our intellect intuitively guided to gradually discover those laws and cooperate with them to remain free from the chaos that can ensue when we disobey these laws, these Laws of Nature.

But there is also the world of our inner life. In our inner world there is something which is not affected by the goings on in our outer visible existence. It is in a sense the eye of the cyclone. In the innermost part of our being, the temple of our Soul, our Atman; there abides the world of spirit, and the world of spirit or oneness is free. And as the Apostle Paul said, "where the Spirit of the Lord is there is liberty." But the more we deny the existence of the Spirit of the Lord within, our true self, our Atman, the more we are bound.

In this Lila the play of life, in this our personal pilgrimage of Consciousness, if we choose to we could live entirely in the centre of our Soul and thus feel the infinite joy of Brahman or the Oneness or the Word, that pervades and permeates all things continually.

But instead of yearning and desiring to stay in that centre we make infinite centres of selfishness and self-interest that loiter in the outer physical circumference and in the inner psychological machinations of our programmed mind, that programmed mind in most cases being the initiator of the chaos.

Which is why the Apostle Paul in the New Testament Book of Romans stressed that the only way to transform our life in the first instance is to set about "transforming our mind to a new way of thinking."

What does all this that I have spoken about mean? It means that in Lila the progressive play of life, we human beings all have access to the creative power of God, and it matters not what you call yourself or which religion you have identified yourself with.

You can call yourself a Catholic, you can call yourself a Protestant, you can call yourself a Hindu, a Sikh, or a Buddhist. You can call yourself a saint or a sinner, you can call yourself a Communist or a Conservative, you can call yourself a philosopher, a poet, a pastor, a priest, a pope, a poor man, a president, a prince or a princess, but it matters not to God. God sees each and every life form as individual fragments of his own Divine Breath, each a pilgrim in their own personal journey of consciousness.

All human beings and all other life form with a measure of consciousness are equal in God's heart. And all human beings have access to the character qualities and life sustaining, life supporting powers of a Kingdom Life, that emanate from that fragment of God Consciousness, the Breath of God within us.

Our physically animated and psychologically illuminated self has been gifted through the Holy Breath all the necessary awareness needed to navigate our earthly sojourn successfully, seeing our Soul return to its source triumphantly. Which includes progressive revelation in Divine Wisdom as seen in the teachings of Krishna, the Buddha, and then Christ. Revelation is unique. It comes from the Mind of God directly into our personal consciousness.

It is not something that is rationally figured out rather it is a gift to us from the Divine Storehouse, the Kingdom of God within, for our well-being. It is the Krishna, Christ, or Buddha Mind speaking to our mind showing us the Way.

And regardless of all the time we are wasting, needlessly cultivating cultural, political, religious, ideological, and social differences according to our identified brand, whilst perhaps at the same time languishing in our current circumstances no matter how they came about whether fortuitously or self- intentionally, all beings with a measure of conscious life will go on until an appointed time, so what we do in between matters.

Lila this progressive play of God, the Divine Nature at work, will continue going about doing its ordained work of watching, of observing, of sustaining, supporting, and re-creating, continuously attempting to progressively with an individual's volition, restore the Soul of Man into complete harmonization with the Soul of God, regardless of all the pointless activity we engage in and subsequently attach ourselves to.

However the more we hunger after those loitering and tempting centres of attachment, the further we detach ourselves or move away from communion with the True Self within our innermost being, and the further we distance ourselves both psychologically and physically from the Light of Oneness that lies within sent to guide our personal pilgrimage.

The three great masters of the spiritual life, Krishna, Christ, and the Buddha, have all given us practical ways, to discover that Light of Oneness, tools, to facilitate the harmonisation of our Soul with the Soul of God. Practical ways that lead to a joyous and peace filled existence as our Soul embarks on its "sacred and at times sacrificial pilgrimage" through this earthly life back to its Source.

"When the Divine Essence manifests creation, it does it as a threefold Trinity of Consciousness; that Trinity described as the Father, Son, and Holy Spirit, in Christianity, and described as Sat, Tat, and Aum in Hinduism.

The Father (Sat) is God as the Creator, existing "beyond creation". (Pure Consciousness).

The Son (Tat) is God's omnipresent intelligence, existing "in creation". (Christ or Krishna Consciousness).

The Holy Spirit (Aum) is the vibratory energy of God that objectifies and becomes a created life form."

CHAPTER 8

The Energetic Influence of Soul Harmonisation on Body and Mind

∞

"All the great masters who have ever existed lived their faith in different forms, but the one thing that they all perfectly aligned on with each other, was the belief that there are two fundamental and irrevocable truths that govern this universe."

Truth number one pertains to the existence of Pure Consciousness, a Supreme Creative Energetic Essence and Influence that exists beyond the visual sense realm. It is an Energetic Essence which is the true reality of our existence, that we are meant to know, understand, psychologically harmonise with, and feed from in this our earthly experience.

Truth number two speaks of the Divine Energetic Principles or Divine Laws, pertaining to the Natural Order of Things, that this Supreme Being has set in place, that you could say power that Natural Order of Things, and maintain harmony. Principles which when agreed with and acted on, enable this transitionary earthly pilgrimage of consciousness back to our source, to be a blessed one, lived in power, love, joy and unity, and a peace filled successful co-existence with all of humanity.

133

"Every individual body perseveres in its state of being at rest or of moving uniformly straight forward, except insofar as it is compelled to change its state by forces impressed on it." So said Sir Isaac Newton, mathematician, physicist, astronomer, and theologian.

As Newton's Law of Motion sees outside invisible forces impacting on visible present circumstances, so similarly in both ancient spiritual teachings and in the philosophy of metaphysics, from which many secular teachings on mindfulness are based, we have come to understand that our thoughts, our individual thoughts are themselves waves of energetic force, impacted on by two opposing energetic forces.

The importance of us coming to at least a basic understanding of the contents of this chapter cannot be underestimated. For whilst we see much written and taught on the subject of right thinking to create right outcomes, most people are not familiar with the scientific and physiological evidence behind this important truth.

Yes, thought does impact on the internal makeup of our being, (our psychological makeup) and on the activity of our being, (our behaviour), and in doing so does effect some sort of change or transformation of current circumstance now or in the future.

Much emphasis has been given in this book on the importance of the harmonisation of the Human Soul with the Soul of God, the creation of a harmonious working relationship between the human mind, emotions, and will, and the God mind, emotions, and will. And this is simply because in our everyday lives the energetic influence of rational thought (human initiated thought) does not by itself have sufficient energy to transform that negative energy which is currently in existence.

When the Old Testament Prophet Isaiah said in referencing God: "My thoughts are not your thoughts, neither are your ways, my ways," he was not just talking about the God Mind being at times of a different viewpoint from the human mind, because of course it is. He was talking about God's Thoughts being more energetically dynamic and thus more life changing than human thought.

In the 20th. and 21st. centuries scientists have been exploring what is known as the HEF, the human energy field. The HEF is defined as a luminous field of energy that comprises a person, extends beyond the physical body, and is in continuous mutual process with the environmental energy field. It is vital energy that is a continuous, whole, and is recognized by its unique pattern; it is dynamic, creative, non-linear, unpredictable, and flows in lower and higher frequencies.

A HEF in balance is characterised by flow, rhythm, symmetry, and gentle vibration. You could if you chose to liken it to the musical instruments of an orchestra totally in sync with each other creating a wonderful experience for the senses. The most disturbing thing in an orchestral concert is when one of the instruments in not in sync with the flow and rhythm of all the other instruments. And to the trained ear the vibrational disturbance that occurs can be jarring to the senses.

However hundreds of centuries ago, ancient teaching had referenced this "new current scientific discovery" on HEF also, referring to it as the existence of "the human aura." Sacred images from ancient Egypt, India, Greece, and Rome used this convention in diagnosing and healing sickness of body and mind.

That human aura was identified as a field of energy that surrounds every living thing. It was believed to reflect one's mind, emotions, and physical health, indicating disturbances in the natural order of things that were leading to the manifestation of a particular type of psychological or physical sickness. And it was a "human aura or force field" that the ancients believed was capable of not being displaced or removed, but rather transformed so as to treat sickness of body or mind.

So in other words if the HEF, was dysfunctional, evidenced in the appearance of some sort of physical or mental illness, whilst the overall HEF couldn't be removed, those parts of it causing some sort of dysfunction could be displaced by a stronger energetic influence, thus transforming the overall aura or the overall human energy field of the individual..

Auras or our personal energy fields are our life force, best explained as an electromagnetic field of the individual that can send, receive, or store information. It does this with both positive and negative energies and uses our physical body and our mental body to store both positive and negative energy.

When something is stored it is retained into the future, and as such from the moment after it is stored it has an energetically influenced past, and so too it has an ongoing influential future, as energy cannot be destroyed only transformed. This is a scientifically proven principle or law.

Both Sir Isaac Newton and Albert Einstein said the following:

"Energy can neither be created nor destroyed; rather, it can only be transformed from one form to another."

For example if your car rolls down your long driveway and hits your garage wall, the potential energy contained in it is transformed into what is termed kinetic energy. Now a brief lesson on the subject of these two forms of energy to give greater understanding on how "the energy principle" impacts on our life in terms of our thoughts, attitudes, and subsequent behaviours will be helpful.

Energy is everywhere and comes in many forms, with the two most common forms known as **potential energy and kinetic energy.** Although they are very different in terms of how they interact with the physical world, they have certain aspects that make them complementary to one another. But to understand how they both work, you first need to understand what they are and the definition of energy itself.

In the simplest of terms, energy is "the ability to do work", which is when a force is applied to an object, and it moves. We have all heard people use the term when confronted with a problem or a project that needs attention, "I can't be bothered. I just don't have the energy (force) to deal with it," meaning I have neither the mental or physical strength needed to address it, "to do the work.

Potential energy is one of the two main types of energy in the universe. It's straightforward, although slightly difficult to grasp intuitively. It is a form of energy that has the potential to do work but is not actively doing work or applying any force on any other objects. Potential energy of an object is found in its position, not its motion. It is the energy of position. From a psychological perspective you could liken it to "intention" that has not yet been realized into some sort of activity or movement.

When objects are displaced from positions of equilibrium, they gain energy that was stored in the objects before being knocked out of equilibrium by elastic rebound, gravity, or chemical reactions. This is best demonstrated in an object like an archer's bow, which stores the energy that is created from pulling back the bowstring. And that **potential energy** that is stored in the pullback is responsible for the energy that occurs upon release, which is known as **kinetic energy.**

Kinetic energy is created when potential energy is released, spurred into motion by gravity or elastic forces, among other catalysts. It is the energy of motion. When work is done on an object and it accelerates, it increases the kinetic energy of an object.

There are three subcategories of kinetic energy: **vibrational, rotational, and translational.**

Vibrational kinetic energy is, unsurprisingly, caused by objects vibrating. Rotational kinetic energy is created by moving objects, while translational kinetic energy is caused by objects colliding with one another. These three subcategories of kinetic energy comprise nearly all the energy in motion throughout the known universe.

The main difference between potential and kinetic energy is that:

"One is the energy of "what can be," and the other one is the energy of "what is".

In other words, potential energy is stationary, with stored energy waiting to be released, waiting to go to work; kinetic energy is energy in motion, actively using that previously potential energy for movement.

And although these primary forms of energy are very different, they are complementary to one another. Potential energy always leads to kinetic energy when it is released and kinetic energy is needed to allow an object to store energy as potential, in one way or another.

For example, a rock on the edge of a cliff does not directly need kinetic energy to store the potential energy that will send it down the eroding cliff face. But the act of erosion to get the rock to the edge requires kinetic energy. Therefore, the rock requires the kinetic energy of erosion for its potential energy to be converted into kinetic energy that it transforms to in the act of falling down the cliff face.

Given that these are the two main forms of energy in the world, especially on the human scale, there's a constant push and pull between potential energy and kinetic energy in everyday life. How are these principles of both potential and kinetic energetic influence witnessed in this universe we live in and in our everyday experience of this universe we live in?

The movement of planets around the sun and other stars in the galaxy is kinetic energy at work. As they are drawn towards the large objects at the center of their respective orbits, due to the strong gravitational pull, they fall towards the center of the mass. This results in an orbiting motion, and all motion is a form of kinetic energy.

Rubber bands can be classified as having both potential and kinetic energy, depending on the state of the band. When an elastic is stretched, it's loaded with potential energy; when released there is a shift to kinetic energy. This is especially true if the elastic is transporting another object, such as with a stone being flung from a slingshot.

Rivers are strictly kinetic energy at work. The water is constantly moving, and all that motion is constantly creating kinetic energy. The only time a river could be seen to have potential energy is if it is dammed, with the artificial reservoir storing energy to be used when needed along a hydroelectric dam, or perhaps when a calm river becomes flooded and overflows its banks due to heavy rains.

Now as I said previously, when something is stored it is retained into the future, and as such from the moment after it is stored it has an energetically influential past, and so too it has an ongoing "potential energetic future", as energy cannot be destroyed only transformed. So once stored it still contains the energetic ability to affect us in some way in the future, unless it is transformed before some particular catalyst transforms it into kinetic energy.

If it helps relate this to the energy contained in a particular sad memory, say an adverse relationship memory that even though we believe it is stored away, it still has the capacity to affect us when we recall it in the present moment. You see this dramatized in movies where people get drawn back into a previous relationship that caused them distress.

Past energy keeps old patterns going and pulls us back into old habits, whilst future energy determines our life in this lifetime and if you believe in reincarnation, where you will end up in your ongoing future life when your Personal Consciousness leaves your physical body and moves on. This is the ancient Eastern principle of karma in play.

Ancient religions taught that when we think, speak, or behave or act in a certain way, we either align our personal energetic vibrational frequency with a universally present energetic vibrational force of either the positive or negative kind, either helpful or unhelpful to our Personal Consciousness, and in that specific moment when we broadcast it into the universe, the universe will respond or react according to what is broadcast.

Basically it means we can transform existing energy into the more powerful energetic force of our Divine Nature within, if we so choose, or alternately stay in the energetic realm of the lower nature and manifest the consequences of that.

Our higher or lower nature always responds and recreates something in the physical or psychical world according to what the energy level of that thought or spoken word that has been presented to the universe specifically is. It is the "like produces like principle", the Divine Law of Reciprocity in action.

Our higher nature will only respond to those thoughts, words, or deeds of a higher vibrational wave frequency, whilst our lower nature greedily grasps those of a lower vibrational frequency, or you could say those that align with the egoic side of our nature. This overall creative concept of energetic influence, alive and hovering, within us and around us, having potential but dormant until activated, is spoken of in many ancient teachings, and it is recorded that it became activated in the first instance in the creation of the world.

The Old Testament reads, "the earth was formless and void, and darkness was over the surface of the deep. And the Spirit of God (an energetic force) was hovering over the surface of the waters. (as potential or stored energy). And God said, "let there be light, and there was light". (potential energy transformed into kinetic energy). And the Old Testament then goes on to give detail of the physical properties and various life forms of this earth that were created when that kinetic energy came into play through the Voice of God.

This was the original creative principle at work. God had a thought, God spoke that thought, and in the first instance physical light overcame the physical darkness that was present and thus the visible existence of this material world, what we call the universe, and all it contains was created in accordance with that God thought. Physical darkness did not go away for all time. It was temporarily transformed into light, by the extension of the energetic influence of Divine Thought and action.

God saw the darkness, God had a thought to make his creation visible, so as the world could witness a Divine Manifesting Principle, God took action and spoke "let there be light", and light came into existence and as such Divine Thought combined with Divine Principle made manifest a new state of being.

All things with a measure of conscious life, including human beings, were created by extensions of that thought of the Spirit, like spiritual arms, Divine tenacles, extensions of that primary energetic force with the same energetic DNA. All life forms at birth become containers of the Divine Breath and with that storehouses of the Divine DNA and the potential energy frequencies it contains.

So the human being that was created was a living, breathing, vibrational, creative, energetic field of pure potential ready to be transformed into kinetic energy. This has in fact been proven in modern centuries to be a scientific fact. Which means that the human being also has unlimited potential to create or displace, meaning change or transform the energetic structure. Jesus referenced this with the following words as seen in the Book of Matthew:

> *"I will give you the Keys of the Kingdom of Heaven; whatever you bind on earth will be bound in heaven, and whatever you loose on earth will be loosed in heaven."*

Jesus is not talking about giving us the front door key to a magical place called heaven in the afterlife. He is talking about giving us the ability to tap into Christ's energetic influence in the present life that currently lies dormant in our Soul (as potential energy), waiting to be released. In its normal usage the phrase "to bind and to loose" simply means "to forbid" (bind) by an indisputable authority, and "to permit" (loose), by an indisputable authority.

The science of Quantum Physics has discovered the following. Our body is composed of energy-producing particles each of which is in constant motion, vibrating, dancing together, creating something, or creatively changing something. Sometimes for the better and at other times for the worse, depending on the instruction it receives from our thoughts.

When these particles or molecules vibrate, they can move back and forth or up and down. Sound energy causes the molecules to move back and forth in the same direction that the sound is travelling. This is known as longitudinal wave, so named because the energy travels along the direction of the particle's vibration. For a vibration to occur, an object must repeat a movement during a specific time interval. A wave then occurs which is a disturbance that extends from one place to another through space and time.

This is the energetic principle behind the mostly Hindu or Buddhist practice of chanting a specific mantra over and over.

I recall when I was on the road travelling, quite often sitting on a park bench in a beachside town where I was living in my motorhome at the time and observing quietly a group of Hare Krishna devotees joyously chanting their mantra of hope as they bore witness to their faith in the Divine Essence.

It is believed that when one chants the Hare Krishna mantra, as well as certain other mantras, they start to clear the impure consciousness that keeps them separated from the energetic influence of their true self, or higher nature. The vibrational sound frequency of this mantra aligns or harmonises with that higher vibrational energy and helps one to break away from that endless cycle of attachment to the physical world.

Vibrational wave frequency is measured in what is known as hertz. (Hz), named after Heinrich Rudolph Hertz (1857 to 1894), the first person to provide conclusive proof of the existence of electromagnetic waves. Hertz in the International System of measuring is defined as one cycle per second. One Hertz equals one vibration per second. The number of cycles, or times that a wave repeats in a second, is called frequency. Frequency is measured in the unit hertz referring to the number of cycles per second.

Light and sound are vibrations that move through space. Sound waves, visible light waves, radio waves, microwaves, water waves, (the ridge of the wave as opposed to the waters that oscillate), sine waves (waves of a pure sound, all sounds in nature), cosine waves (similar to sine wave except they occur earlier), stadium waves, (synchronised or mechanical), earthquake waves, waves on a string, and slinky waves (back and forth), are just a few of the examples of our daily encounters with waves.

Vibrations are energetic waves all having specific rhythms and happen on a grand scale in many things such as seasonal changes, but in a less obvious and more subtle way in terms of how and when they occur and can be recognized and categorized in our bodies and life events. To explain this in the terminology of Simple Awareness you could say:

"As vibrational rhythmic wavelengths are broadcast to the universe in our thoughts and behaviours, including in our silent attitudes and expectations, then our inner bodies or outer physical circumstances, will respond accordingly and creatively change to align with those specific thoughts or behaviours that we have broadcast into the universe".

So yes, "thoughts through energetic influence produce our reality", but it is not random reality. It is reality energetically aligned with those thoughts. In other words, like produces like. Habits, which are really manifested thoughts that we have repeatedly entertained, when consistently applied to our experience produce what is to us reality, and through continuous repetition cement that reality into our being into our state of conscious awareness. And thus what is termed a habit is formed and remains until it can be transformed energetically.

Similarly, "attitudes produce our reality", because attitudes are simply thoughts (potential energy) that have been consistently held onto for so long, that they have also become embedded in our consciousness and as such have "potential" to automatically come alive as kinetic energy in specific situations as they are triggered. All attitudes and all thoughts have their own specific vibrational frequency, which in turn energetically induces a specific behavioural response.

A perfect example of this can be seen in the emotion inducing thought pattern of fear. Fearful thoughts (potential energy), or the memory of a fear filled experience, will induce a psychological and physical response of either aggression, meaning a compulsion to fight back, known as the "fight syndrome", or produce an anxiousness to escape, known as the "flight syndrome". (kinetic energy).

Our heartbeats, breathing rates and circadian rhythms, are all commonly known functions of our everyday existence and are also examples of physiological vibrational wave rhythms that we can see, feel, and measure, and that are open to influence and change.

Circadian rhythms are 24-hour cycles that are part of the body's internal clock, running in the background to carry out essential functions and processes. One of the most important and well-known circadian rhythms is the sleep wake cycle. But there are much smaller and less obvious vibrations happening in our bodies too, inside each one of our cells, cells being the basic building blocks of all living things.

The latest scientific research estimates the total number of cells in the human body to be around 30 trillion, with about 30 billions of them dying and being renewed daily. All these cells work in harmony to carry out all the basic functions for human beings to survive and potentially thrive, but most human beings just take them for granted.

Researchers have found that vibrations and the electromagnetic energy associated with them causes changes in our cells which can affect how our bodies function psychologically and physically, and thus emotionally.

Researchers have also known for a long time how certain thoughts and behaviours affect the vibrational rhythms in the body. Anxious thoughts trigger the release of stress hormones that stimulate the heart rate. Likewise, the sound vibrations of music, affect our thoughts and emotions. That's why some people use certain types of music to relax, and others use certain types of music to perhaps vent, or to mentally escape from their current emotional state, or to enhance their current emotional state.

This change of vibrational wave frequency in our cells through music, thus influencing our physical and emotional responses, is all about the vibrational wave frequency of the specific music and specific lyrics we are listening to, which alters our existing individual energetic wave frequency status, and converts it to the higher vibrational frequency that our cells are absorbing through the music.

Depending on the type of music we are listening to, we are either vibrationally energised, and as a consequence experience an emotional state of happiness or peace, or vibrationally deenergised, and as a consequence experience an emotional state of melancholy or sadness.

You see everyone's individual wave frequency hungers to operate at a higher vibrational level. Why? Simply because it makes us feel better. It gives us a specific emotional vibrational stimulus that our being is hungering after in that moment. What is our being really doing from a spiritual perspective? It is hungering for "a higher or deeper level of consciousness" or spiritual presence. King David we read in the Book of Psalms cried out, " my Soul thirsts for God."

Our Soul wants to get closer to "the God frequency". How do we know what vibrational frequency God is? We don't, it can't be measured. But what we do know is that God is love, the scriptures tell us this, and love has one of the highest vibrational frequencies and this has been proven scientifically.

Research conducted by Dr. Leonard Horowitz, an internationally recognized authority on public health in his study of brain waves, has ascertained that the emotion of love generates a vibrational frequency of 528 Hertz; which becomes very desirable to our emotions, considering the average human body functions at a vibrational frequency of 3 Hertz to 17 Hertz.

It is important for us to understand that every cell in our body has the vibration of life in it, whether we are fully aware of it or not. Every cell in our bodies is comprised of energy that has the potential of fully resonating with and ascending to the highest vibrational frequency it possibly can. And at the same time, every cell in our bodies has the potential to descend to the lowest level of vibrational frequency.

"And the catalyst for this is the existing emotional vibrational frequency that we manifest at a particular time, which is intrinsically linked with our thoughts and subsequent behaviours at that time."

Emotions have voltage. The vibrational frequency of emotions are always on either an ascending and expanding vertical dimension of some sort, or alternately on a descending and contracting vertical dimension, all relative to the vibrational voltage of a particular emotion we are experiencing at a specific time. This is a scientific fact.

Remember, "like produces like". Emotions resonate with the vibrational frequency that they generate. The higher the vibrational frequency, then the higher the expansion, and the greater life force in our cells. The lower the vibrational frequency, then the greater contraction, and the lesser life force is in our cells. The brainwaves of a fully enlightened person have been proven to vibrate at the highest frequency of 700 Hz and at what is considered by researchers to be the greatest potential degree of energy expansion.

Scientific research measuring brainwave activity with the use of an electroencephalograph, has shown that the vibrational frequency of joy is 540 Hz and is expansive, meaning it can be increased and increased indefinitely in the right circumstance.

Jesus said as we read in John 15:11, "I have told you these things so that my joy and delight may be in you, and that your joy may be made full and complete and overflowing". What things had Jesus told them? All things pertaining to the Way of Light, the Way of Love, and the Ways on how to live Life. In other words, Jesus was saying, "I have given you these Kingdom Principles, these Keys, so that you can put them into practice, and in doing so change your vibratory energy to its highest possible level."

On the other side of the coin research has found that the brainwave vibrational frequency of fear is 4 Hz. Not far off zero. No vibration, no consciousness, no life. Perhaps this is where the common saying "scared to death" came from.

And fear is the emotional feeling that the ego mind uses over and over again to interfere with and stall our evolutionary journey through consciousness. Which is probably why Jesus said, "God has not given to us a spirit of fear, but of power." Which indicates that when fear grips us it is emanating from an energetic force (Spirit of Fear) that opposes God's energetic power and influence.

If you likened the whole vibrational expansion contraction thing to say a day out on the river canoeing, a ripple on the river does not necessarily affect us emotionally or behaviourally in a major way if we are out paddling our canoe up a gently flowing river; we feel at peace.

But if a sudden rainstorm hits, the kinetic energy vibration of a torrent of water that comes down on us can dramatically affect our emotional well-being and behavioural instincts, when that emotional state of panic or fear emerges. Emotionally induced energy vibration in extremely fearful situations can become an intensifying charged current like a psychological tsunami that hits us with its full force.

We see this with the emotion of grief pulling some people down psychologically to despairing levels, and likewise the emotional energy of depression and loneliness can cause a person to feel so heavy and lifeless to a point that if it is severe enough, lifelessness is all that person can see in their future. Which then leads some to contemplate suicide as the only solution and a preferable option. Fear causes the energetic life to drain out of us.

Research has shown that higher frequency vibrations are associated with things like gratitude, love, joy, spending time in nature, sunshine, yoga, raw whole foods, beautiful music, and lower vibrations can come from things like envy, jealousy, toxic people, toxic relationships, electronics, arguments, violence, junk food, drugs and alcohol, and resentment, anger, unforgiveness, and guilt.

The higher the frequency of your overall energy or vibration, the lighter you feel in your physical, emotional, and mental bodies. You experience greater personal power, clarity, peace, love, and joy. You have little, if any, discomfort or pain in your physical body, and your emotions are easily dealt with.

It is important we understand that over time the above scientific truths about vibrational influence and the impacts they have on our wellbeing both physical and psychological, have in fact been evidenced in the teachings of a variety of faiths. All simply referring to the same thing, Creative Vibrational Energy Centres in our body and mind that we need to be aware of, and completely understand the role they can play in influencing our life for the better or for the worse, regardless of our "religious brand."

Even if most have not realised it, there is a distinct correlation of understanding and belief between the major religious institutions of the world on the existence of a singular creative energetic force, a Holy Breath, involved in the affairs of humankind, albeit taught and practiced in different ways according to different hereditary influenced religious teachings.

In Hinduism, the word used to describe the overall concept of energetic forces flowing through the body is termed prana. What exactly is prana?

Prana is the Indian Sanskrit word for "**breath**". Prana is energy, vitality, power. Prana is the foundation and essence of all life; the energy and vitality that permeates the entire universe. Prana flows in everything that exists. Furthermore, prana is the connecting link between the material world, consciousness, and the mind.

The different locations in the body and mind that that energy collects, or groups together are called the chakras. This word chakra is a widely used concept in Indian religion that underpins many spiritual practices and philosophical systems. Within some forms of yoga, the chakras refer to energy or vibrational centres found in the body, located at major branching's of a human being's nervous system, beginning at the base of the spinal column, and moving upwards to the top of the skull.

Chakras are points of metaphysical and or biophysical energy in the human body, which provide a nexus, one or more connections for the linking and flow of energy.

Chakras are also considered to be graduations of consciousness that reflects states of the soul, with chakras seen as energy centres wherein subtle electromagnetic forces connect to the physical, emotional, mental, and spiritual aspects of a person, vital force, material force, matter energy, organic material energy, or pneuma, describing the psycho-spiritual energies that permeate the universe.

The word chakra itself is the Sanskrit word for wheel because chakras are said to be the spinning forces of energy in the body. In the Hindu teaching on this subject it is said that sometimes certain energy centres become blocked, and the process of clearing the blockage happens through specific yoga postures, breathing practices, or meditation.

From India, the notion of chakras as separate energy centres was taken to China, where it was introduced into the religion of Taoism, absorbed, and harmonised with Chinese concepts of the flow of energy known as Qi.

The word Qi means "**air or breath**". In Chinese medicine, traditional Indian chakra locations correspond to Chinese acupuncture points. So, we see many people of no particular religion, who, understanding this, turning to regular Tai Chi practices to get a subtle taste of this energetic force. Similarly some people of no religious affiliation may turn to acupuncture treatment for bodily ailments. What are they doing? They are raising their vibrational frequencies and subsequently their sense of wellbeing. Qi is breath, vital energy.

In Taoism, Chi is the force that animates the universe. Chi is the force that sets the world and everything in it into motion. Chi is also the force that sustains all things once they are created. Chinese Taoist influences made their way to Japan and were absorbed into Shintoism, Japan's native belief system, and a religion which around 80 percent of Japanese citizens follow. In Shintoism Chi is known as Ki.

In the Islamic religion of Sufism there is a process called Sufi Healing. Sufi healing is an advanced ancient spiritual healing method resolving trapped emotional, physical, and spiritual energies. It uses the process of chanting sounds of erratic prayers for deep healing of ingrained patterns and trauma. These ancient sounds are said to carry a powerful healing vibration into the cells and energy fields of the person, to deliver healing at a profound level, well beyond the reach of the human mind.

In Sufiism, the mystical branch of the Islamic religion, the goal is awakening and self-realisation. It is taught in Sufism that each one of us possesses an energy field or an aura that surrounds and penetrates the physical body, in a way you could say, guarding it. It is a psychological and physical creative influence associated with the physical and mental wellbeing of a human being.

It is also taught that the more we are optimistic in our thoughts the more we generate positive energy or higher vibrational frequencies you could call them, while the more pessimistic we are in thoughts the more we generate negative energy, lower vibrational wave frequencies.

In terms of the early Christian writings, **pneuma** was the ancient Greek word used for **breath**, similarly as Qi is in Taoism, and Prana is in Hinduism, and Ki in Shintoism. Pneuma in both ancient philosophy and religion, refers to the vital spirit, soul, or creative energetic life force of a person.

We see in the Christian religion, in translating the word pneuma into English in the Greek New Testament there are 254 instances where the word pneuma, meaning breath, was used in the original ancient writings to refer clearly to what has been normally translated in the Christian Bible as the Holy Spirit or more simply spirit.

What is the Holy Spirit? It is the Divine Breath or Spirit, an energetic creative force. It is Infinite Intelligence, the God Mind, in spirit form. An example of the use of pneuma in the New Testament Book of John, is where we read that Jesus **"breathed"** on His disciples and said, "receive the Holy Spirit". Meaning receive the vital spirit or creative force. John was transferring the spirit that he had received over to the disciples to empower them.

Quantum physicists believe it's possible to speed up or slow down the vibrations that occur at the cellular level by changing our thoughts, behaviours, and even our surroundings. Scientists agree with this, psycho-analysts agree with this, and the ancient spiritual masters who spoke of the use of mantras to change our vibrational structure agreed with this.

It's all about the vibrational electromagnetic waves changing the cells in our bodies and brain structure, which then influence the physical and emotional energetic levels of our body and mind .

Other researchers of both the psychological, spiritual, and medical kind have discovered that certain thought patterns such as gratitude, joy, peace, love, and acceptance create high vibrational frequencies, while other mindsets such as anger, despair and fear vibrate at a much lower rate. We all vibrate energetically at a particular frequency, and this determines how we feel about our circumstances and how we react to our circumstances.

The lower the frequency, the denser your energy, and the heavier your problems seem, and the more exhausted you can become physically. Here you may experience pain and discomfort in your physical body, and experience heavy emotions and mental confusion, or just plain old tiredness. Psychically your energy is darker. Overall your life takes on a negative quality. And it all comes back to our state of mind in the moment, our thoughts.

Vibrational change is the key component of consciousness change, through promoting an evolutionary change in consciousness (our state of being), that takes us to a higher level of conscious awareness of our inherent Divinity and the power within, or conversely moving us to an even lower level of conscious awareness and alienating us even further from an awareness of the Divine presence, thus lessening our potential for psychological and circumstantial change.

Synchronisation or harmonisation of the vibrations of different elements in our human character with the vibrations of the different elements of God's Divine character is the key to living a dynamic purpose filled life.

Jesus spoke of this synchronisation or harmonization in a mystery in the Book of John when he said, "if you abide in me and my word abides in you," meaning if we are energetically united because his thoughts which contain his vibrational energetic life are in our thoughts, "you can ask what you will, and it shall be done for you."

He was speaking of the power of Divine Principle at work if we synchronise our thoughts with his thoughts. The same principle applies to our synchronisation of our thoughts with the thoughts of chosen messengers such as Krishna and the Buddha.

How do we know the thoughts of Jesus. We contemplate specific teachings of his, particularly those relating to life and love in the New Testament such as are seen in the Sermon on the Mount and those hidden in the mystery of his parables. They all align with specific teachings of Krishna on light and life in the Upanishads and more specifically in the Bhagavad Gita, and with specific teachings of the Buddha on life and love in the Dhammapada.

And synchronization or harmonization is what we all unconsciously hunger after. Our soul desires oneness with the universe and all it contains. Many Christian people would never entertain the idea of embracing any ancient "religious concepts" in their health regime and daily practices.

Yet we do see for example some Christians in their unconscious search for an understanding of this hidden vibrational influence, turning to various forms of yoga or mindfulness disciplines or things such as Tai Chi, because they have found that these things help them cope with the everyday circumstances and stresses of life, both physically and psychologically.

What many people don't completely understand is that the spiritual concept of vibrational influence lies at the heart of yoga and certain other popular new age teachings. If they did, they would be less likely to find that weekly trip to a yoga class or a meditation session tedious, but rather see it for what it truly is, a magnificent tool given to us by our Creator as a psychological Support System, given to us by Infinite Intelligence, to eliminate those things that interfere with our Personal Pilgrimage of Consciousness.

Life is all about vibrational influence, but it's also about the type of vibrations that we release in our life, and most importantly about synchronised or shared or harmonised vibrations that have the power to transform or recreate.

Ervin Laszlo, a Hungarian philosopher of science, systems theorist, integral theorist, originally a classical pianist, and an advocate for the theory of quantum consciousness, twice nominated for the Nobel Peace Prize, said the following:

> *"Vibration is the language of consciousness, and we can control and thus consciously use vibration to make changes in our states of consciousness".*

By working on our thoughts and behaviours, which means harmonising those thoughts and behaviours with the auras of past spiritual masters such as Krishna, Christ, and the Buddha, we in fact begin transforming our personal auras, our personal energy centres.

And through clearing or transforming those energy centres through right thinking, right speaking, and right behaving, we will find that the negativity we hold onto will become less and less and with that we will begin to see concrete movement forward in our physical, psychological, and spiritual life.

"The Kingdom of God is within us. That temple of peace and stillness where truth abides in fullness, is within us. It is unperturbed by the chaos on the outside of our being brought about by the self-survivalist attitudes and behaviours of ourselves and others, nor the mental murmurings on the inside of our being, emanating from our false sense of self, our cultivated identity.

But we have lowered a psychological veil between Kingdom Consciousness, the Divine's Awareness of the universe, and our own Personal Consciousness, our personal state of awareness. We have allowed our self-programmed awareness and understanding of the universe and all the goings on in us and around us, to be the dominant influencer in our lives.

Thus not only have we have not recognized or understood or acknowledged the truth of that Divine Essence within, and its sovereignty over all things, more importantly we have not fully embraced the myriad of remedies it contains to treat our earthly woes.

It is like having a free, at no cost to the consumer, Divine Pharmacy right at our doorstep, that we in our own ignorance or indifference, never bother to shop at in our psychological or physical distress."

CHAPTER 9

Krishna, Christ, and The Buddha. Divine Messengers of Light, Life, Love, Peace and Harmony

❧

He who drinks of the waters of Truth, he rests in joy with mind serene. For he whose mind is well trained in the ways that lead to Light, who surrenders the bondage of attachments and finds joy in the freedom from bondage, who free from the darkness of passions shines pure in the radiance of that Light, even in this mortal life he enjoys the immortal Nirvana."

— THE BUDDHA.....THE DHAMMAPADA 6.

Divine Wisdom, no matter in what era or through whom it is birthed into the universe is eternal. Divine Wisdom does not divide but rather unifies. No matter when it was revealed, it never fades nor wearies, never rusts, nor decays. If a purported spiritual truth divides rather than unifies, it is not of the Divine Nature rather of the nature of the lower mind. Institutionalised theologised dogma and doctrine that supposedly complements Divine Truth and Wisdom, if it divides, is not truly Divine.

However the kernel of eternal Truth that is embedded in that original Wisdom will always remain waiting for a more opportune time to become a catalyst for the unifying principle. Godly Wisdom and Revelatory Truth no matter when or to whom it was originally revealed, no matter in what culture it surfaces, or perhaps resurfaces due to an earlier rejection, is everlasting.

It's light continues to shine brightly, its message continues to inspire and open up a pathway for the good, and when acted on its energetic influence continues to support, sustain, and bring about change.

Progressive Divine Truth, call it spiritual truth if it sits better, coming forth through personal intuitive means or through a spiritual teacher, in any era, and yes even in this modern era, is in fact a movement from Divine Truth to more Divine Truth, but the original truth filled intent of the original kernel of Wisdom from which it first sprouted is not negated, simply expanded to appeal to the culture and understanding of the current era. That intent always centred on the re-establishing of harmony or union between the Soul of God and the Soul of Humanity.

Progressive revelation can also be the movement from truth to truth, the lesser truth to the greater truth, the provisional to the permanent, the inadequate to the perfect. Whereas institutionalised dogma and doctrine, in existing religions, or in new emerging religions, whilst perhaps in some cases having a truthful intent, has always been a catalyst for division and disharmony between different religious cultures throughout the world.

From a Christian perspective the Old Testament is the beginning of God's "progressive revelation of Himself", but it is not a full revelation. It does not necessarily reference the Truth that came before the emergence of the primary prophets of the Old Testament. And in the Islamic religion whilst the Qur'an is said to be a progressive revelation of God as revealed to the Prophet Muhammad, it is not a beginning and an end of the Islamic culture's understanding of God and God's revealed purposes regarding humanity.

For hundreds of centuries before Muhammad and Christ made their appearance, the sages, mystics, and philosophers of old, had discovered the way to relate to God, to comprehend who this God Being is, to understand the ways of God, the ways of Light, of Life, and of Love, and to know the life changing power of that Divine Wisdom and Truth.

Hundreds of centuries before religion became institutionalised, Mystics, Monks, Initiates, Seers, and Divine Avatars had declared these truths for those with an inner ear to hear. This is the one great fact that our modern interest in and knowledge of ancient literature, practically unknown for centuries and centuries, has brought to light.

Over the decades I have come to clearly realize that neither the Christian scriptures, nor the scriptures of Hinduism, nor the teachings of the Buddhist religion, nor the teachings of the Muslim religion, can in their isolation claim to be unique, and certainly can no longer individually claim to be the sole guide for a distracted humanity in its effort to discover Divine Truth and thus successfully navigate life in peace, happiness, and harmony.

Modern day teachers of truth have emerged into societal existence since the times of Krishna, the Buddha, Christ, and Muhammad, and using the original kernel of Wisdom embedded in the teachings of those masters, taken those teachings to even greater levels of understanding, able to be readily digested by modern cultures. The subject of "Presence," being one.

Yes without doubt those four primary teachers can individually claim to be the sole guide for those particular societies who then and now know of no other. However the danger for any spiritual pilgrim with an institutionalised religious attachment, is that an egoic institutionalised arrogance can quickly come forth with a determined prejudice towards that attachment. Which then causes them to reject all other revelatory truth not birthed in their own religion, to reject it outrightly or even as in some cases, label it as being the work of the devil or of some heathen origin.

You see ever since primitive person first walked upon the earth, Infinite Intelligence or Kingdom Consciousness has been progressively revealing more and more of itself, more of its eternal nature, according to the particular level or state of consciousness that the primitive person of that era had attained, and in line with the cultural experience that each individual person had been birthed into.

Specific Divine revelation that was necessary to guide the spiritual journey of the Jew was not similarly necessary for the spiritual journey of the Arab, or the Gentile, those nations of non-Hebrew heritage.

A culture that has not evolved in its level of conscious awareness past the baby stage, regardless of what religious branding it is immersed in, can only be fed the milk of Divine Thought not the meat, until it has evolved spiritually enough to be able to be weaned off the milk of Divine Thought, and thus able to comfortably digest the "meat of God's Truth," without psychologically gagging in confusion.

The Apostle Paul in the New Testament said to the people of Corinth, "I fed you with milk, not solid food; for you were not yet able to receive it," and in describing this principle of the progressive revelation of Divine Wisdom, the New Testament's Book of Hebrews 1:1-2 says: "Long ago, 'at many times and in many ways', God spoke to our fathers by the prophets, but in these last days he has spoken to us by his son, whom he appointed the heir of all things, and through him also he created the world".

So in relation to the Christian religion Adam received a little understanding of God's True Self, and Noah also received some understanding of God's True Self. And God spoke more fully to Abraham, unveiling more of his True Self and his purposes, and to Moses and then later through various other Old Testament Prophets and New Testament Prophets and Apostles.

Similarly in other religions, progressive revelation is a part of God's plan. For progressive revelation is a movement from truth to more truth, and so eventually to full truth.

The sacred Scriptures of the Muslim religion recorded in the Quran's 114 chapters and more than 6,200 versus, took 23 years to be revealed in the practical sense. And since much of the Quran, similarly as with the Buddha's teachings, and Christ's teachings, and Krishna's teachings were revealed in response to questions people asked and circumstances they were facing, then it only made sense that the revelation would be revealed after, rather than before the question was asked or conflict was faced.

When once asked why the Quran did not unveil itself all at once the Quran replies by saying "so that your heart may be strengthened at that particular time."

You see it can be said that the silence or space between revelations time wise, era wise, was part of the revelation, because without that silence we would not be able to integrate the message fully. Just as the space between words gives a sentence meaning, or the silence between notes creates rhythm, God is telling us that even in the silence, his truth and mercy is present. Just because there is a moment of silence, does not mean that God's Eternal Symphony is completed.

In describing the meditative or contemplative state in which sometimes Divine Revelation will occur, with regards to that silent space or gap between deep breaths the Buddha said: "Whilst sitting silently, just watching your breath, there is an inhalation, then a gap (a silent space) and then an exhalation; then an inhalation, a gap, and then an exhalation. That gap is the most mysterious phenomenon inside you. When the breath comes in and stops and there is no movement, (inner and outer stillness), that is the point where one can meet God".

So for a Christian to believe that before Christ existed humankind had no understanding of the God of the Universe, is the height of religious institutionalised arrogance. There is ready evidence to show that there has always existed since the beginning of recorded time an understanding of the underlying metaphysical reality of the universe and with that some sort of understanding of the spiritual nature of humanity.

And yes whilst the many theological propositions about God as witnessed in differing religions may be found on analysis to be self-contradictory, it is essential to remember that every teacher of Divine Wisdom and Truth had to adapt their teaching to the level of intuitive understanding of their hearers, and the general notions of the time and the community culture to which they belonged.

The teachings of Jesus, the founder of Christianity, as witnessed in the New Testament scriptures and the Gospel of Thomas, had to be adapted to the crude Jewish conceptions of a personal and patriarchal God, who required above all things to be propitiated and worshipped. And as such it would appear that for Jesus to even hope to reach the hearts of his hearers, his presentation of God had to include words describing God as a "heavenly father figure," because that was the most reformative one that his hearers were capable of understanding.

The Buddha, the founder of the religion of Buddhism, on the other hand we see had to deal with a cultural mindset of quite another order, and accordingly we find that he refused to personify not only the gender of God nor in any other way define the Absolute. When regularly questioned as to the nature of this Absolute Principle by certain questioners seeking to enter into some divisive discourse, he was always silent, occasionally commenting on that type of questioning as simply being "unhelpful."

So also with the religion of Hinduism. In Hinduism there is a term, "neti neti", seen in the Upanishads, the religion's sacred scriptures. It is a Sanskrit expression that translates in English to "neither this, nor that " or "not this not that." The first neti means "I am not this thought" and the second neti means "I am not the thought thinking this thought."

So if a Hindu teacher is confronted with an "unhelpful" question, a question that has nothing to do with the true nature of Brahman (God), a question trying to give some sort of attribute to the Absolute (God), the Absolute being the omnipresent, eternal and spiritual source of the universe, an attribute that may divide, the teacher simply replies, "neti neti," simply negating everything that the nature of God "is not" without entering into any divisive discourse on the matter.

The moment Divine Truth is breathed into the hearts of humanity by the Divine Breath it remains eternal, it endures forever. And once reverently ingested into one's personal consciousness, a human being will discover that nothing can separate us from it, nothing circumstantially, nor anything psychologically; if we respond to it and harmonise it into being, its energetic influence will continue to sustain and support us.

In the words of the Apostle Paul, "neither death, nor life, nor angels, nor principalities, nor powers, nor things present, nor things to come, nor height, nor depth, nor any other creature, shall be able to separate us from it" and the loving intent from which it first came forth.

History shows us that the ancient sages and mystics of various eras received some of God's revelatory truth as seen in the writings of the Bhagavad Gita and the Upanishads, which teach that **"God is Light,"** that teach the Path of Light, the meta-physicality of our existence, and as such this teaching at that time began influencing people's attitudes and behaviours and understanding of the world and workings of the Eternal Spirit, similarly as they still do today.

The Buddha came centuries later, and through him society received some more of God's revelatory truth, appropriate to the correct time and in the appropriate cultural setting, as we see in the writings of the Tripitaka or Tipitaka and the Dhammapada, which teach that **"God is Life,"** that teach the Path of Life, and as such this teaching began influencing society's attitudes and behaviours in relation to virtuous and ethical behaviour.

And then Jesus came centuries later and taught that not only is God the **"God of Light and of Life, but in addition that God is a God of Love"**. Jesus taught that whilst the human being must have an understanding of the spiritual/metaphysical world, the Way of Light, and a deeper understanding on how to navigate this earthly world, the Way of Life, these things individually or together are not sufficient if one has no understanding that primarily God is a God of Love.

Jesus was the bearer of progressive revelation, coming to primarily reveal that **"God is Love"**, and then in his departure handed over that responsibility to the Holy Spirit who he said, "will teach you all things". What are these "all things" that he spoke of? They are all things not only pertaining to the Way of Love, but all things pertaining also to the Way of Light, and the Way of Life.

So does that mean that an understanding of this Divine Spirit called the Holy Spirit never existed in ancient cultures before Christ? No it doesn't. The Holy Spirit, the third member of the Christian Trinity has always been there albeit described differently in differing cultures in various eras.

We are told that "in the beginning was the Word, and the Word was with God, and the Word was God." What was the Word? It was and is the Trinity of Pure Consciousness. And just as in Christianity the Holy Spirit is the third member of the Christian Trinity of God or Pure Consciousness, so in Hinduism Shiva is the third member of the Hindu Trinity of Pure Consciousness, and being part of the Param Atma, of God or Brahman, Shiva is thus defined as the Holy Spirit.

And such as in Islam, the Holy Spirit acts as an agent of Divine Action and Communication, so in Mahayana Buddhism, the Sambhogakaya is the intercessor for Ultimate Reality, performing the same work as the Holy Spirit.

The Holy Spirit or Shiva or the Sambhogakaya came to share with us deeper truths, things relating to Light, the metaphysical aspect of God's Existence, and to give us physical and psychological navigation principles relating to a harmonious experience of life lived in the flesh. Teaching us those Godly Personality qualities that are necessary to successfully navigate this earthly life in our evolutionary personal and collective journey of Consciousness.

When Christ came to teach that God is Love, all the teachings of the Buddha still remained relevant, and when the Buddha came to teach us the Way of Life, all the teachings of Krishna on Light still remained relevant. Their energetic influence continued.

Throughout the ages Divine Truth for the edification and uplifting and guidance of humanity has been revealed to us through many messengers and in many ways in many different eras of humanity's known existence, and with regards to Krishna, Christ, and the Buddha, all of their teachings are still as relevant today in our pilgrimage of consciousness as they were in yesteryears past.

For all are truths that address God's Eternal Intent, to show or reveal a way or pathway for all human beings to harmonise their level of conscious existence or awareness with God's Consciousness, and then having done this eventually return to the same source from where their personal fragment of God consciousness first emerged, the Supreme Consciousness. The key word in relation to this process being "harmonise."

> *"You see we think our earthly life is all about making a comfortable living. God knows that our earthly life is primarily about our personal pilgrimage of consciousness, and with that through his Grace setting free our earthly life from those things which bind us, enabling it to be both comfortably liveable and comfortably lovable."*

Jesus was described as the Prince of Peace. Peace or harmony is a basic pre-requisite to making life liveable and lovable. Peace or harmony is an ideal path. Peace or harmony means dealing with disputes and resolving conflicts fairly, properly, ethically, and virtuously, so as to psychologically and then visibly support or neutralize a negatively energised situation that may be arising.

The Buddha describes this as choosing the Middle Way. To choose the Middle Way is to walk the path that furthers both the welfare of the individual and the wellbeing of humanity as a whole. It means loving our neighbour as ourself, and thus waking and walking with them in complete harmony, properly, fairly, ethically, and virtuously, at all times.

To wake and walk in harmony means that at all times all thoughts, all feelings, all speech, and all deeds are all of the same will and thus willing the same result, and not contradicting each other. The expression Middle Way refers to the Buddhist understanding of practical life, avoiding the extremes of self-denial, and self-indulgence, as well as the view of reality that avoids the extreme positions of externalism and annihilationism.

In the Buddha's transcendent state, in his search for True Wisdom, he went beyond the constraints of the egoic thought process, the "what's in it for me" way of thinking. He believed that he was made aware of the fact that true happiness or contentment can only be found in a life of moderation in which one chooses to walk a "middle path," not the way of extreme indulgence and not the way of extreme self-deprivation. With this mindset his teaching on the Middle Way to happiness and peace was conceived.

To take the middle path is also the essence of the teachings of Krishna in the Bhagavad Gita scriptures. Krishna said, "One who works too much and one who is lazy, both cannot reach the height of yoga," meaning "harmony of body and mind".

Paul the Christian Apostle spoke of "living a life of moderation, a middle way, of freedom from all excesses." And the ancient Greek Philosopher and Scientist Aristotle listed moderation as one of the primary moral virtues, and defined virtue as "the means between extremes", implying that moderation plays a vital role in all forms of moral excellence.

Those things, extreme indulgence and its opposite self-deprivation, are things of the flesh, things that happen in time and space. They are those things of the flesh, those thought things or material things that we, through our own ignorance of Divine Truth, have allowed to veil the Christ presence from our psychological sight.

However once we psychologically ingest the thoughts of God as expressed in the teachings of messengers such as Krishna, Christ, and the Buddha, through imprinting the Christ, Krishna, or Buddha ways into our own nature, our own personality profile, and then begin practically applying these teachings in our lives, we draw nearer to that energetic centre which is beyond time and space. This is the meaning of the words of the Apostle James: "Draw near to God, and God will draw near to you."

And in that personal chosen act of drawing nearer, the negative energetic veil blocking the positive energetic influence of Infinite Intelligence dissipates, energy blockages to understanding are unblocked, thus releasing the Divine Breath, the Divine Essence, to freely roam the inner sanctums of our minds and bodies.

This is how God, Divine Intelligence, transforms the useless into the useful, the meaningless into the meaningful, the purposeless into the purpose filled, and the temporal into the timeless. You could liken it to the grand velvet curtain on the Broadway stage being slowly lifted to begin revealing to the conscious awareness of the audience the stage play of life in progress behind it.

All the Divine Wisdom and Divine Principles relating to Light, Life, and Love, for navigating this earthly life can be discovered in the time-less teachings of Krishna in the Bhagavad Gita and the Upanishads, of Christ in the New Testament and the Gospel of Thomas, and of the Buddha in the Dhammapada.

It is my intention in the following pages to impart to you the reader a basic understanding of who those chosen messengers Krishna, Christ, and the Buddha were, and a further basic understanding of the religious institutions that were birthed through their teachings, as well as the scriptural context of their Messages of Light, of Life, and of Love. But it is only a basic understanding.

It is we as individuals who must do the work in imprinting their teachings into our conscious existence in this the pilgrimage of our Soul to a higher level of consciousness, and thus bring about through the Law of Reciprocity. a deeper and more meaningful conscious experience of life for ourselves and others on earth.

⌒∞⌒

KRISHNA AND HINDUISM

Krishna is a major deity in the religion of Hinduism. A deity or God is an avatar, a supernatural being, who is considered Divine or Sacred. A deity has been commonly defined as a Being with powers greater than those of ordinary humans, but a Being who interacts with humans, positively or negatively, in ways that carry humans to new levels of consciousness, beyond the grounded or habitual preoccupations of ordinary thought and perception or awareness.

The term avatar in the ancient Sanskrit language literally means "descent." It signifies the material appearance or incarnation of a powerful God, Goddess, or Spirit on earth. Hindu scriptures state that Krishna appeared "in all the fullness of his glory", and as such Krishna is worshipped as the Supreme God in his own right similarly as is Jesus.

An avatar is a manifestation of a deity or released soul in bodily form on earth. Krishna is worshipped as the eighth Avatar of Vishnu., an incarnate Divine Teacher, similarly as Jesus is worshipped in the Christian religion as the Christ or God in flesh, a Divine Teacher, and a Supreme God in his own right.

The Hindu religion speaks of Vishnu from whom Krishna incarnated as "the preserver and protector of the universe", one of the triple deities of Supreme Divinity that include Brahman and Shiva, whose role is to return to the earth in troubled times and restore the balance between good and evil, to bring harmony to two conflicting things, whether of thought or form, to restore the natural order of things.

Krishna then as an incarnation of Vishnu is the God of protection, compassion, tenderness, and love, and is one of the most popular and widely revered amongst Indian deities. Hinduism teaches that so far in the history of the world Vishnu has been incarnated nine times, and also believe that he will be reincarnated one last time close to the end of the world.

Incarnation concepts of the avatar kind, that are in some respects similar, are also found in Buddhism, Christianity, and other religions. The Buddha is considered the ninth avatar according to the Vaishnava tradition of Hinduism, and Jesus has been described as an avatar of God, the New Testament telling us that Jesus was God appearing "in flesh as to dwell amongst the people, with the fullness of God dwelling in him bodily".

Born into the Yadava clan of Mathura to Queen Devaki and her husband King Vasudeva on July 21, 3228 B.C., the first known depiction of the life of Krishna himself comes relatively late, with a relief found in Mathura, and dated to the 1st-2nd century CE.

A relief is a sculptural method in which the sculptured pieces are bonded to a solid background of the same material. This creates a sculpture to give the impression that the sculptured material has been raised above the background plane. The term relief is from the Latin verb *relevo*, which means "to raise".

This particular fragment of what is believed to have originally been a much larger relief, seems to show Vasudeva, Krishna's father, carrying baby Krishna in a basket across a river, where at one end of the relief a makara crocodile is thrashing about and at the other end a person seemingly holding a basket over his head.

The earliest textual reference containing detailed descriptions of Krishna as a personality is the epic Mahabharata, which depicts Krishna as an incarnation of Vishnu. That Mahabharata is the national scriptural epic of India, and it encapsulates ideas about morality, law, family, relationships, class, structure, and reincarnation. References to Lord Krishna can also be found in several Hindu mythological scriptural books.

It is in the Mahabharata however that we see detailed descriptions of the personality of Krishna, narrating various stories that teach us various life lessons. The most important one being that no matter what trials or tribulations beset us, life always goes on. No matter how much you have been wronged or feel you have been wronged, no matter how many difficulties you are currently experiencing or have in the past experienced, life will and must still go on. The only alternative is death.

Krishna is central to many of the main stories of the epic. The 18th chapter of the sixth book of that epic constitutes what is known as the Bhagavad-Gita, which is basically a dialogue between Krishna and his friend Arjuna, seeing Krishna giving advice to Arjuna his dearest friend and disciple on how to not only navigate the physical battle that Arjuna was engaged in, but also the psychological battles that were troubling him causing him much distress.

The anecdotes and narratives of Krishna's life are generally titled as Krishna Lila. He is a central character in the Mahabharata, the Bhagavata Purana, the Brahmavaivarta, and the Bhagavad-Gita, and is mentioned in many Hindu philosophical, theological, and important to note, in many texts of a seeming "mythological nature."

The outcome you could say of all mythology is "to put a face to story." Stories emerged in ancient writings about Gods and Goddesses and because human nature is always looking to find that which is visible hidden behind something invisible, a myth was seen as the easiest way to promulgate understanding.

The renowned psychoanalyst Carl Jung was in his time very interested in the way societies and different cultures for hundreds of centuries have used myths to enable a culture or tradition or religion to be easily passed down in digestible form, almost in storybook mode, from generation to generation. The definitive meaning of a myth is that it is a traditional story mostly centred on the early history of a people or society, explaining a natural or social phenomenon typically involving supernatural beings or events.

Krishna is portrayed in various perspectives of both spiritual and mythological form in all the known records we have of his life and teachings. For instance in terms of spiritual and theological writings he is portrayed as a Universal Supreme Being, an avatar of Divine status, what you could call a Divine Child, similarly as Jesus was portrayed as a Divine Child, conceived by the Holy Spirit, described in the New Testament as God in flesh.

The presence of Krishna as a child held a fascination for all people of all ages. It is told that even as a child he had everyone wrapped around his finger. Similarly Jesus as a child is said to have amazed those around him.

The story recorded in the New Testament tells of Mary and Joseph heading home after a day of travel and, on discovering that Jesus was missing, they then returned to Jerusalem finding him three days later. It is said he was found in the Temple in discussion with the elders listening to them and asking them questions and that the elders were amazed at his learning at such a very young age. He was twelve years old.

But Krishna is also portrayed as a prankster, a lover, and a divine hero. His iconography reflects these legends, and shows him in different stages of his life, such as an infant eating butter, or as a young boy playing a flute.

It also makes mention of Radha or Radhika, a Hindu Goddess and the chief consort of Krishna, regarded as the goddess of love, tenderness, compassion, and devotion. Not dissimilar from what we see with Jesus and Mary Magdalene in the New Testament; Mary being depicted as a loving Consort of the King of Kings, the first person who Jesus chose to appear to, after his crucifixion and resurrection as she wept in the garden outside his tomb.

Many Muslim scholars of the Islamic religion consider Lord Krishna of the Hindu religion as a Prophet of God, similarly as they believe were the prophets Moses and Christ of the Christian religion. The teachings of Krishna and Christ are as important to sincere non-radicalised Muslims as are the teachings of all the great prophets of God, for they see them all as they see their own Prophet Muhammad, as messengers of Divine Truth.

It is recorded that Krishna lived 125 years, eight months, and seven days. His date of death being 18 February 3102 BC when he was 89 years of age.

⎯⎯∞⎯⎯

CHRIST AND CHRISTIANITY

Christ, also referred to as Jesus of Nazareth or Jesus Christ, was a first century Jewish preacher and religious leader who historical records tell us was born in a lowly manger in 4 BC, and who passed AD. 30/33. A manger or trough is a rack for fodder, or a structure or feeder used to hold food for animals. Mangers are mostly used in livestock raising and generally found in stables and farmhouses, but they are also used to feed wild animals in nature reserves.

Since the earliest days of Christianity, Christians have commonly referred to Jesus as Jesus Christ. The word Christ was a title or office, not a given name. It is derived from the Greek *Christos,* a translation of the Hebrew *mashiak*h, meaning "anointed", and is usually transliterated into English as Messiah. Christians of that time designated Jesus as the Christ, because they believed him to be the Messiah, whose arrival is prophesised in the Hebrew Bible and in the Old Testament. In post biblical usage Christ became viewed as a name, one part of the name Jesus Christ.

References to Christ can be found in the writings of both the Old and New Testaments of the Bible, the word testament meaning covenant. Jesus became the central figure in the religion of Christianity, the world's largest religion. He is believed by most Christians to be the Son of God, the human incarnation of God and the awaited Messiah, the Christ, as prophesised in the Hebrew Bible, the Tanakh, and as recorded in the Old Testament.

Christianity is an Abrahamic, monotheistic religion, a religion that teaches that there is only one God, and the Christian faith is based on the history, life, and teachings of this man Jesus of Nazareth and of those who followed Him.

By comparison whilst the religion of Hinduism is considered by some to be a polytheistic religion, (more than one God), it may also be considered in some ways to be a monotheistic religion, as most Hindus believe in one Supreme God, whose qualities and forms might be represented by a multitude of deities, all of which emanate from him.

Whilst Buddhism is a religion, lacking the idea of a unique creator God. It is a kind of trans-polytheistic religion that accepts many long lived gods, but sees ultimate reality, Nirvana, as being beyond all of these.

Christian theology includes the beliefs that Jesus was conceived by the Holy Spirit, was born of a virgin named Mary, performed miracles, founded the Christian church, died by crucifixion as a sacrifice to atone for the sins of humanity, and subsequently rose from the dead, and ascended into heaven, from where he will return in what is described as the second coming. Commonly Christians believe Jesus enables people to be reconciled to God. The great majority of Christians worship Jesus as the incarnation of God, the second of three persons of the Christian Trinity.

In the Islamic religion Jesus, often referred to by his Quranic name Isa, is considered the penultimate Prophet of God, and the Messiah, who will return before the Day of Judgement. Muslims believe Jesus was born of the Virgin Mary but was neither God, nor a son of God, and it is this that has over the centuries created the great divide and subsequent disharmony between institutionalised Christianity and institutionalised Islam.

Some early Christian groups had separate descriptions of Jesus's life and teachings that are not in the New Testament. These include the Gospel of Thomas, the Gospel of Peter, the Gospel of Judas, and the Apocryphon of James. These teachings were unearthed archeologically in 1945 in Egypt and are known as the Nag Hammadi texts.

The crucifixion and death of Jesus occurred in first century Judaea. The crucifixion and subsequent resurrection and life experiences, attitudes and behaviours of Jesus are described in detail in the four Gospels, Matthew, Mark, Luke, and John, and also in what are called the New Testament Epistles of which there are twenty-one. Most of the Epistles are believed to have been written by the Apostle Paul.

Over the centuries, as the Christ story penetrated various corners of the globe, most people came to believe that the original Jesus event, the birth, life, and death of Jesus was purely a westernised phenomenon. And whilst this is the current unconscious perception due to Christianity being the predominant religion in Western society, what we need to keep reminding ourselves of is this. The Jesus event in the first instance was a "near Eastern event."

When Christ first emerged in physical form on this earth that first appearance, according to historical records was in Palestine, not in lands of English heritage. And of course we understand that from Palestine the Christ story radiated out in all directions. In one case it was exported to the west where the message was carried by the Apostle Paul through Turkey, and into the Greco-Roman territories.

But the life changing, energetic influence of Christ birthed in the East did not cease to spread there. That energetic influence also went south west to Africa, travelled up the West Coast of France, to the Celtic strongholds of Britain, and Ireland, and radiated to the east into Persia, India, and even China.

And from Persia, now known as Iran, that same energetic influence traversed through Iraq, Syria, and Turkey, in many cases, complimenting existing spiritual teachings in various traditions regarding the energetic influence of the spirit. For example, the Chinese Christians of Zian have a distinctly Buddhist flavoured version of their teachings of Jesus.

However over time as the message of Christ spread, divisive differences came to the surface in the way different cultures interpreted both the man and the message he brought. In particular the following.

The Christianity of the West favoured the concept of *"soteriology"* which is a word derived from the Greek *soteria* meaning "salvation." Soteriology is the branch of theology dealing with the study of salvation. The term is also related to the Greek *soter,* meaning Saviour.

And as such the majority of westernised Christianity agreed that salvation and with that eternal life, was and is made possible only through the crucifixion, death, and resurrection of Jesus the Christ. Westernised Christianity believed that salvation was the true message that Christ was sent to deliver. That the "giving of salvation" was the gospel of Christ, the good news he brought to the world.

But the original Christianity of the East, the birthplace of Christ, saw things radically different from the Christianity that evolved in the West.

"The West saw Christ through God as "a giver", (of salvation) but the East saw Christ through God as an "expressor," (of God's Nature).

The Christianity that was birthed in the East, the birthplace of Christ, was not one of *soteriology*, but rather a religion of *sophiology*. The word *sophiology* having its root meaning in the word Wisdom, Sophia being the Greek word for Wisdom.

So whilst western society primarily saw Jesus as "the giver of God's gift of eternal life," eastern society with their own established religious and cultural beliefs, saw Jesus primarily as "the expressor of Divine Energetic Life," and as such the Master Teacher of a Divinely Energetic lifestyle, a "Spirit Led" life. In the original Aramaic story of Jesus, his followers saw his life as a living expression of Divine Energy as were the lives of Krishna and the Buddha.

You could say that for the earliest Christians of an Eastern ethnic, cultural, and religious hereditary background, Jesus did not come as the Saviour, but as the energetic life giver and the dispenser of Divine Wisdom.

What much of the religious culture of the West and the religious culture of the East must come to understand is this:

"The soteriology of the West, and the sophiology of the East can, and are meant to harmoniously co-exist. You can still believe in the concept of salvation and at the same time be a seeker of Divine Wisdom, how to apply the salvation experience to your daily life to increase your level of conscious awareness."

In the 1870's, Ramakrishna, the Indian Hindu mystic and spiritual leader, embraced Jesus as an Avatar and placed him within the Hindu pantheon, a group of the most prominent deities of contemporary Hinduism. Known as the Trimurti, those most prominent deities are Brahma the Creator, Vishnu the Preserver, and Shiva the Destroyer.

In the original Aramaic records of the story of Jesus and his followers, there was no use of the word salvation it was all about being "made alive," it was all about the enabling of ourselves to become expressions of God's Image through the indwelling Christ and thus expressors of Divine Wisdom.

In the early Christianity of the East salvation was understood to be a bestowal of the Energetic Consciousness of Christ, and to be saved was to be made alive through him in the present moment, not to be saved from hell and gain entrance to heaven in a future moment after physical death.

You could say that the East believed that what the West termed salvation through Christ, was in fact an impartation of God Consciousness that saved people not from the place termed hell, but rather from a hellish experience on earth, substituting in its place a heavenly experience on earth, a heavenly, happiness filled, pleasurable experience, whilst they were in the land of the living.

The Apostle Paul expressed this to the people of Ephesus with the following words:

"Even when we were spiritually dead and separated from Him because of our sins, He made us spiritually alive together with Christ." (Ephesians 2:5)

When Jesus entered the waters and was baptised by John the Baptist, it signified the process of "one coming alive". Jesus emerged from the waters as the Mahyana, the expressor of Divine Wisdom alone. The Buddhist concept of Mahyana refers to the doctrine of the absence of "the false sense of self" to all elements of existence, releasing the "True Self" the inner container of True Wisdom, Kingdom Consciousness, to function unhindered.

And when he emerged from the waters he came forth as a "fully enlightened one," a man whose life was fully integrated into the will and way of Divine Wisdom. Now life was different. Jesus had now become:

"The Master of his own conscious awareness and not merely the servant."

As such Jesus's disciples, seeing him now to be a "master of his own consciousness", realised that he was offering them a path on which they too could walk. Jesus emerged from his baptism in the waters as the Ihidaya, (Aramaic), an early title given to him, most often translated as the "single or unified one". It was a title given to the second person of the Trinity of Consciousness.

You see there were two primary streams of teaching that flowed out of the life and teachings of the Jesus of the East. One of these was adopted by the Roman Empire and subsequently exported to the West, to replace pagan traditions, to become their state religion. That stream focused mainly on salvation from sin through Jesus's sacrificial death. It was almost what you might call a safe, non-inquisitive path. A path that says, "okay now you are saved you are going to heaven so nothing else is needed; just obey your church elders and the Roman government.

The other stream, which went east, south, and into the Celtic lands via North Africa, took with it, the "wisdom tradition", the ways of the wise, and these teachings are expressed in those lost Gospels that emerged at Nag Hammadi in 1945. In those lost Gospels as they are termed, Jesus is speaking as the life giver, or the single one, or the Unified One, being referred to in the East as the Ihidaya.

Ihidaya is the word for "Single One" or "Singleness" in the Syriac-Aramaic language and is used to describe souls that enter into mystical oneness. One becomes a fully integrated being, psychologically and hence attitudinally and behaviourally. One becomes a person who has fully integrated his or her being around the principle of non-dual consciousness, a state of unification or harmonisation between personal consciousness and Divine Consciousness, Kingdom Consciousness.

When we begin looking at the world from a point of non-duality, it does not mean we lose our sense of individuality, it means that our individuality seeks at all times to find the common or non-dual approach to all life situations. When we observe life from the perspective of non-duality, it does not mean that we lose our sense of binary perception, it means we are able to move as our intuitive heart directs without prejudice or animosity.

And sometimes we will be directed to choose a different path from that which we first thought to be the right path, because we now understand that at all times we are all manifestations of the One Source, but at varying levels of Consciousness or Awareness evolution and as such our binary thinking differs from human being to human being.

You see a non-conscious person, one who has not come to an understanding of the non-duality of our existence, one who is torn between the false self and the True Self, embraces "binary bias" in all their thoughts and rationalisations. This binary bias defines a deviation of thought that makes us process all information received in a dichotomous way: good or bad, black or white.

How did this illusionary self come into being?

Without going into the metaphysical and mythological background to its existence, let's just say that it commenced its own pilgrimage to "devolve our state of consciousness" from the moment we came into conscious life.

And it did this by relentlessly bombarding our as yet immature level of consciousness with a multitude of forms and concepts and experiences, good and bad, which grouped together and became pillars for our own personal identity, our understanding or in most cases false understanding of who this person me really is. Let me simply say this:

"The illusionary self is who we think we are, but the True Self is who God or Pure Consciousness knows we are."

Examples of binary thinking are: "If I am right, then you are wrong". Or "you are either a conservative or a liberal or a democrat or a republican". Or "women are emotional and men are rational". Or "being rational is better than being emotional or vice versa". Or "you are either for me or against me". Or "if I don't win, I lose." Or "if you don't get an A on your test you have failed." That's binary thinking.

When we process life from a perspective of non-duality, as did Jesus Christ, we are able to easily embrace the non-binary way of processing thought born out of perception, and as such we become "messengers and expressors of peace" at all times, in all situations, we become, as Jesus was deemed to be in the East and still is, "the master of our own individual consciousness" and "the Prince of Peace."

⌘

THE BUDDHA AND BUDDHISM

Siddhartha Gautama, also known as Gautama Buddha, also known as the Buddha, was a philosopher, spiritual teacher of meditation and a religious leader, who lived in ancient India around the 4th century B.C.E.

Whilst the Buddha was born into an aristocratic family, he eventually gave up that type of lifestyle in favour of travelling throughout India, teaching that the goal of life should not be just to ascend to a state of extreme materialistic success, nor to just attain a state of extreme spiritual self-discipline, known as asceticism, but rather to achieve a state of balance between the two. He taught this as walking "the Middle Way."

In Pali which is the language of the Buddhist scriptures in Ceylon, Indochina and Burma, the word Buddha comes out of the root *budh* which means "to be awake, or to be conscious of and to know." From that same root *budh* comes the word Buddhi. That same word Buddhi is also found in Hinduism's Bhagavad Gita, which in different contexts can be taken to mean, "true intelligence, right reason, progressive vision, and true wisdom". All non-binary ways of processing thought.

The Buddha taught what was termed this Middle Way of obtaining happiness and peace, a way that would result in one achieving what is known in Buddhism as a state of Nirvana, a transcendent state of mind in which there is neither suffering nor desire, nor a sense of the ego self. A state in which a person is released from the "karmic cycle" of birth, death and rebirth, and moves into a higher state of consciousness or conscious awareness, commonly known as enlightenment.

In Buddhism Karma or the karmic cycle could be simply described as the debt we owe and have to pay back for any untoward actions we commit in life against ourselves, against a fellow human being, or against society; offences for which according to karmic law we must make restitution. With Buddhism if we fail to make restitution in this life, another opportunity to pay back our karmic debt if we die still owing it, is made possible through the process of reincarnation.

Buddhism teaches that if we physically die having a karmic debt, whilst our physical body dies, our personal fragment of consciousness or Holy Breath which has given us life and animation, being imperishable does not die, and so returns in a new body to start a new life in order to make restitution, in order to make amends for the outstanding debt of the previous body, in order to pay back our karmic debt.

It may be a debt to an individual of the physical or psychological kind, or it may be a debt to society, but it is with certainty a debt flowing from some sort of attack or offense or non-virtuous behaviour against a fellow human being or life form. The level of conscious awareness that we commence our new journey of life in, in our new body, will be in accordance with the final level of conscious awareness we possessed prior to the moment our individualised Holy Breath departed its existing physical life encasement.

Nirvana you could say is the final goal of Buddhism. It is the state that all Buddhists strive to attain to, and centres on achieving a new state of mind, where the thinking processes and resulting behaviours are no longer controlled by the Ego Mind, and consequently we no longer sin against our fellow man or against ourselves; and we maintain our sense of harmony with all life form, which by implication means we no longer incur karmic debt.

This spiritual principle of paying back a karmic debt is very similar to the principle of forgiveness as spoken of in the Bible, both designed to clear the slate of our mind, to remove all aspects of guilt from it, and to restore our spiritual standing and Soul Harmonisation with God. But mere faith in the forgiveness principle alone without actions to back it up is not true forgiveness, it is faith without works and as such it is dead faith.

The major difference in this area of life and death between Christianity and Buddhism is that Buddhism teaches that if you don't get it right in this lifetime you will have another lifetime to try again, and Christianity teaches that you need to get it right in this lifetime otherwise you are done, there are no second chances, it's judgement time and off to heaven or hell with you. This is why the Catholic religious leadership places such great importance of a priest administering the last rites to a dying person, which is basically supposed absolution from karmic debt through priestly power of attorney.

However it must be noted that in the traditional selective scriptures of the New Testament as given to the masses by the early church fathers, while we see that Jesus was most emphatic about the power and principle of forgiveness and restitution to clear a debt owing, he neither confirmed nor denied in any way whether a second opportunity to escape the cycle of birth, death, and rebirth is made available to us if we don't get it right in this lifetime.

But as previously mentioned it is interesting to note that the karmic cycle of humanity was still a belief held in the day of Jesus as we read in the Book of Matthew Chapter 16 the following: "Now, when Jesus went into the region of Caesarea Philippi, he asked his disciples, "who do people say that the Son of Man is?" And they answered, "some say, John, the Baptist; others Elijah; and still others, Jeremiah, or just one of the past Prophets.""

There are parallels between this Buddhist process of enlightenment and the Atonement process in Christianity, in that the end result desired by both religions is that a person fully transcends out of a life lived through their lower nature and thus ego mind into a life lived through their God Nature and thus their God or Christ Mind. Whilst in Buddhism this is referred to as a life lived in Nirvana, in Christianity it is referred to as a life lived in the Spirit.

Similar to Buddhism the final goal of Christianity's Atonement process, is a transcendent state of mind, a new state of mind, where through the technique of mind renewal, our thinking processes and resultant actions are no longer controlled by the Ego Mind but aligned with the Mind of Christ.

Consequently we no longer sin against our fellow man, and we no longer continue to incur karmic debt. Unfortunately much of Christian teaching focuses very little on the subject of mind renewal after the salvation experience has occurred, which results in producing Christians who whilst attending church on Sunday have no problem attending a White Supremacist rally or something similar over the weekend.

The simple practicality of both journeys to a deeper level of consciousness, the journey to Nirvana in Buddhism and the Atonement journey in Christianity can be described as an individual's movement from a dualistic mental lifestyle to a non-dualistic one, from an ego driven existence to an intuitive way of life.

In the dualistic mental lifestyle, which is an inherited state of being that everyone shares from the moment of birth, two spiritual forces, or you could say two cosmic energy forces jockey for supremacy, both desiring to govern and control a human being's thought processes, and subsequent intentions, which in turn then influences and directs a person's behaviours and actions. These forces are referred to in spiritual writings as the lower nature and the higher nature, the lower nature being primarily the dominant and most active one in most human beings.

After six years of strenuous spiritual struggle, as the Buddha's life was exposed to the continuous oppositional facets of his lower nature, the Buddha awoke into the Infinite Light. In the radiance of this Light, he gave us The Way of Life, guiding principles we are meant to live by, words of wisdom and love, words that have helped spiritual pilgrims in times past, that help us now, and wisdom that will help the world in times to come.

Because whatever an unimaginable future may bring to humanity in ages yet unborn, the great words of this spiritual leader shall be forever. His Light of Wisdom and Truth that lights our way of life, and that which has been a light for a few in past times shall continue to be a light for all in future times, giving voice to the words of Jesus concerning Divine Truth, "heaven and earth shall pass away, but my words shall not pass away."

It is said that the Buddha lived for 80 years, but there is considerable uncertainty concerning the date of his death. According to the Buddhist Chronicles, when the Buddha died near the city of Kushalnagara in northern India, he broke free from the cycle of rebirth and attained Nirvana, absolute release from karmic rebirth.

"When the mind leaves behind its dark forest of delusion, thou shalt go beyond the Scriptures of times past and still to come. When thy mind, that may be wavering in the contradictions of many Scriptures, shall rest unshaken in Divine Contemplation, then the goal of yoga, of union or harmony with all things is thine. He whose mind is untroubled by sorrows, and for pleasure he has no longing, beyond passion, and fear, and anger, he is the sage of unwavering mind."

— KRISHNA....THE BHAGAVAD GITA 2.

CHAPTER 10

The Teachings of Krishna, Christ, and the Buddha

❧

"To truly unlock the treasures of Divine Wisdom, the eternal
truths of the universe, one must first be persuaded to set
aside temporarily all religious dogma and doctrine. For it
is only when those shadowy influences of institutionalised
religious thought, that loiter at the gates of our minds
and hearts causing hesitancy, are set aside, that an open
pathway to the realisation and subsequent internalisation
of Truth and Divine Wisdom will be revealed."

THE TEACHINGS OF KRISHNA
THE UPANISHADS AND THE BHAGAVAD GITA

Sanskrit is the sacred language of Hinduism, the language of classical
Hindu philosophy, and of historical texts of Buddhism. It is an ancient
Indo-European language of India, in which the Hindu Scriptures and
classical Indian epic poems are written, and from which many northern
Indian languages are derived.

The Sanskrit word **Upanishad**, *Upa-ni-shad,* contains several morphemes. In breaking down this Sanskrit word Upanishad into its respective morphemes we find *upa* from the Latin meaning *under, ni* found
in English meaning *beneath or nether,* and *shad* which in Sanskrit means
to sit down, to lie down, to settle. If I could take a little literary licence
here, you could say that the whole of the word Upanishad references

instruction being given in the way of happiness and blessedness, whilst sitting at the feet of the Master.

Similarly we read in the New Testament Gospels that Jesus went up into a mountain: and when he was set, or settled, his disciples came to him, and sitting at his feet, the feet of the Master of Divine Consciousness, they attentively listened whilst Jesus gave instruction in the ways of living a virtuous life and thus a blessed life. Jesus in that moment gave an oration that has been commonly termed in Christianity as the Sermon on the Mount. Consequently the Sermon on the Mount might be considered to be an Upanishad according to the true meaning of that word.

The Upanishads are spiritual treaties of different lengths, the oldest of which it is believed were composed between 800 and 400 BC, and the youngest as late as the fifteenth century A.D. Scholars believe that if all the Upanishads were collected in one volume, they would make up an anthology about the same length as the total Bible. Each Upanishad is noticeably of different length, the longest one covering around 100 pages and the shortest only having around eighteen verses.

The composers of the Upanishads were thinkers and poets, they had the vision of the poet; and the poet knows well, that if poetry takes us away from a lower reality of daily life, it is only to lead us to the vision of a higher reality where the melancholy of limitation gives way to the joy of liberation.

These Upanishads of ancient India are as much above the mere archaeological curiosity of some scholars, as light is above its definition. Scholarship is necessary to bring us the fruits of ancient wisdom, but only an elevation of thought, and emotion can help us to enjoy them and transform them into life. And one of the primary messages of the Upanishads, is that the Spirit can only be known through union or harmony, not through mere learning, not purely through intellectualism.

The Upanishads teach us that no amount of learning can make us feel or impart love, or see the beauty of all life form, or hear the unheard melodies of the symphonies. Unfortunately many have only seen the variety of thought in the Upanishads, not their underlying principle of unity. The Spirit underpinning the Upanishads is the Spirit of Brahman, God himself is their underlying Spirit.

Arthur Schopenhauer was a German Philosopher,(1788-1860), whose primary philosophical belief was that all things with life, both nature and human, are the expressors of an insatiable will, and that it is because of that unbridled will that human beings attract and find suffering, their desire for more being what empowers that insatiable will. Upon contemplating the Upanishads Schopenhauer said the following: *"Their reading has been the consolation of my life and will be of my death."*

The Upanishads are very comprehensive and extensively written. It thus can become hard to draw lines of what some are really all about, but the central theme is always philosophical, and hence we can say that they are books on spiritual philosophy. The first mention of Krishna, as early as the 6th. century BCE, in the Chandogya Upanishad, refers to him as a sage and a preacher.

The Upanishads narrate how the God Rama took birth as Krishna, and how various divinities and virtues became people or objects in Krishna's life. Most impactful in my own life have been the teachings of Krishna as recorded in the Bhagavad Gita, which is basically a dialogue between Krishna and his friend Arjuna.

Adherents to Krishnaism believe that Krishna is the Supreme Lord, and that humans are eternal, spiritual beings trapped in a cycle of reincarnation. The nature of the cycle for individual beings is determined by Karma, that I spoke of previously, the law of the consequences of past actions, which returns beings to physical existence, if past karma has not been atoned for.

That Evolutionary Law called Karma, explains the apparent injustice in the world with the following sublime simplicity. There is a law of cause and effect continuously in play in the moral world of humanity. We are the builders of our own destiny, and the results are not limited to one life, since our spirit is the same spirit that dwells in all, and it has an Eternal Principle embedded in it.

And since the Eternal Spirit that was never born, and will never die, is within us, a sacrificial fragment of God's Consciousness embedded in us, referenced in the words of Jesus as "the Kingdom of God within", when its current earthly vessel dies, when our physical body dies, it has two choices of destiny, one pertaining to ascent and the other to descent.

If it has successfully completed its Karmic cycle it will ascend back to its source to be re-absorbed into Pure Consciousness or having been deemed unsuccessful due to outstanding Karma in its vehicle of manifestation, the human being, it must once again take to itself a body, that the lower self may have the reward of its works. Good shall lead to good, and evil to evil. From God, joy shall come, and from evil shall come suffering. Thus the great evolution of consciousness flows on towards perfection.

There are however two points that seem to have puzzled many readers of these sacred texts: the problem of personality, and of the final union with Brahman. It has been thought that because matter, and the lower personality have only a relative reality, later on to be called Maya, illusion, something that passes away, since it is not eternal reality, our personality, that personality so dear to us, with whom we continually identify with has been considered unimportant and neglected.

This has led in this current day to many seekers, once self-realisation has occurred, once an understanding of the non-duality of our existence is realised, adopting an attitude of "well life is just an illusion, it's not real, and since I know that I am Consciousness, since I know that Divine Consciousness is my True Self, I might as well just ignore life, and when life gets away from me just remind myself occasionally that life is just an illusion so all will be well".

It's a type of blind faith approach to life. It is the opposite to what the Apostle Paul was speaking of when he told the people of Philippi to "work out your salvation," where Paul is speaking of continuously confronting and dealing with any barriers to an increased level of consciousness. Paul was saying, okay you have had your soteriology experience, now its time to start your sophiological journey.

As such we must remember this. As the visions of the Upanishads, are based on the consciousness of our own being, in relation to the being of the universe, whatever may be the mental progress of the human being upon this earth, one can never go beyond the visions of the Upanishads: one can never go beyond themselves, their own consciousness, their own life. Could a human being think if they were not alive?

So to that end we must always remind ourselves that life is a visible manifestation of creative consciousness, not just something trivial to be simply labelled illusionary when the going gets tough.

Life is consciousness at work in the present, and as such that level of consciousness that is expressing life in various forms in each and every present moment must be of the highest energetic vibration possible. We don't have to live life as a continual struggle of psychological and physical survival, and we cannot afford in terms of our eternal destiny to just rationalise the bad things in life away, for life won't go away.

Every human being is a lone centre (individual) centre but not an alone centre of life. Every person is a unique and individual component of the cosmology of the universe, each an individual fragment of consciousness and together a part of Universal Consciousness, and as such our individual circumstances and experiences will always be different, because our consciousness is being progressively programmed and re-programmed differently according to our current experiences.

The answer of the Upanishads is quite definite: Atman, the Spirit within us is with us to guide us into all truth regardless of our current life experience. We might be a lone individual, but we are not alone as we traverse the earth. So how can we be lonely. Atman, the comforter is with us, Kingdom Consciousness, the light of our soul, the love, which is the source of infinite joy, is within us. And that source, the Atman within, is something which is above reason and binary perception, and therefore it can never be attained by reason alone.

As in Christianity the indwelling Spirit of God is defined as the Holy Spirit, who Jesus said, "is with you, but shall be in you," so too, the monumental message in the Upanishads is that God must not be sought as something far away, as a Divine Being separate from us, but rather be understood to be the very inmost part of us, residing as the highest self in us, and thus reflecting that higher self far above the limitations of our little self.

And as such, we hear the following words of the Upanishads speaking to us: "not through much learning is the Atman reached". These words are saying that it is not through the intellect alone, that we touch God, for whilst scholarship is necessary to bring to our existence the fruits of these ancient teachings, only an elevation of thought and emotion, a moving beyond binary thinking can help us enjoy them and transfer them into the practical experiences of our lives.

One of the central messages of the Upanishads is that the spirit can only be known through union with him, and not through mere learning. For those of us, who have at times, experienced the joy of a particular poem, or a particular song, or a particular sound of nature, can any amount of learning about those lyrics or melodies or sounds cause us to feel love, or peace, or see beauty, or hear the unheard melodies. That joy comes to those who know and feel the poem or song beyond thought.

The Mundaka Upanishad says, "who knows God becomes God." Similarly as the Psalms tell us, "ye are gods, and all of you are children of the highest," or as the Apostle Paul said, "for you all are Sons of God." To be a son denotes a hereditary oneness. A person of the same hereditary and thus genetic origin, what the Bible speaks of as "being created in God's image."

When, through contemplation, one comes to truly understand that the transient has been left behind, when final liberation has been attained, when our little self is lost in the greater self in us, and in all, as a drop of water is lost in the sea, does it mean that all consciousness is lost?

And after the death of the lower self, when the small drop of human consciousness, that fragment of consciousness that supports and sustains us has become fully one with the ocean of Universal Consciousness, when, in the suggestive words of the Brihad-aranyaka Upanishad "the seer is alone in that ocean", is our personal identity lost? No of course it isn't.

What it means is that the little self, call it our old self if you like, has then become fully immersed in the Self Supreme, and not only has in its possession the consciousness or conscious awareness of its long experience, the ups and downs of personal life, and the learnings obtained from them, but and more importantly has in its possession access to the consciousness of the Divine full of all wisdom and knowledge. It is the "fullness of God that dwelt in Christ."

Not only does that person understand the book of its own past, but is also in possession of the Wisdom Book of the universe. What does that mean? In the words of Saint Teresa it means that, "the silkworm has died and has become a beautiful butterfly, free from its limitations". So then for the little self, life becomes not a continuing struggle towards death, but a victory over death, a rising and a resurrection, a spiritual resurrection of the soul, whilst we are still alive on earth.

Humanity in many religious teachings in particular Christianity has placed greater emphasis on our physical resurrection after death because of the cross of Christ, rather than on our psychological resurrection during this our present life, because of the indwelling Christ, or Atman, the Kingdom Consciousness within. It has placed greater importance on the afterlife rather than the present life. Placing emphasis on ritual rather than righteousness, but not so the ancient sages of the Upanishads.

So important is this present life, that in the Katha Upanishad, it is stated that the spirit can only be seen in this life, or in the highest heaven, but not in the regions of the departed, or in the lower heavens.

How disappointing would it be I say, tongue in cheek, to arrive in "heaven" after death, having hung our hope on our future heavenly experience, open the door, and find God's not home. The importance given to this earthly life is clear beyond the symbolism. The joy of the final union was felt by St John of the Cross in the present when he described the Beloved within as the "silent music" and "the sound of solitude".

Similarly Saint Teresa with the following words that remind us of the joy of final union as described in the Upanishads said:

"It is like water falling from heaven into a river or fountain, when all becomes water, and it is not possible to divide or separate the water of the river, from that which fell from the heaven; or when a little stream enters the sea, so that henceforth, there shall be no means of separation."

The path of the Upanishad is essentially a Path of Light. The Katha Upanishad speaks of two paths we are able to choose from, and we can't take both. It says:

"There is the path of joy, and there is the path of pleasure. Both attract the attention of the soul. The two paths lie in front of man. Pondering on them, the wise chooses the path of joy: the fool takes the path of pleasure."

Those spiritual messengers who found light, life, and love all speak of paths we are able to take all leading to a realization of ultimate joy and happiness and peace in our present lifetime. And in speaking of their own paths the sage of the Katha Upanishad of Hinduism spoke of the path as being "narrow as the edge of a razor" whilst Christ of Christianity spoke of the path as being narrow when he said, "narrow is the way which leadeth unto life."

⚬

One of the primary Upanishads that has had a magnificent impact on my own life has been the **Bhagavad Gita**. The Bhagavad Gita, a Upanishad in its own right, is the Essence of the Upanishads and brings the essential teachings of the Upanishads into our own life, into the quality of our character. It is believed that to possess those character qualities and personality traits helps humanity to distinguish between the good, the bad, and the ugly of the universe we live in.

To be able to, in a confident and ready manner, mentally separate what is beautiful and good from what is ugly and evil, what is truth from what is falsity, helps a human being walk on the path where the great prayer of the Upanishad's finds its fulfilment;

"From delusion lead me to truth, from darkness lead me to light, from death lead me to immortality."

It enables humankind to step out from embedded mental delusion to the Light of Truth, and to separate psychologically and thus transcend behaviourally from those delusions of darkness to behaviours that truly reflect the Truth of Light and Love in our daily lives.

The Bhagavad Gita was included in the Mahabharata, which is a vast epic, one of the two major Sanskrit epics of ancient India, the other being the Ramayana. It narrates the struggle between two groups of cousins in a war, and the fates of those princes and their successors. The Mahabharata also contains philosophical and devotional material, such as a discussion of the four goals of life.

The main story of the Mahabharata centres around a war between the opposing forces of good and evil, represented on the whole as the armies of the Pandavas and the Kuravas. Scholars have compared the importance of the Mahabharata in the context of world civilization to that of the Bible, to the Quran, and to the works of Homer and the works of William Shakespeare.

The Bhagavad-Gita often referred to simply as the Gita, is a 700 verse scripture, having eighteen chapters, as against the total Mahabharata which has 200,000 individual verse lines and is considered to be the longest poem ever written. Hence the presence of the Bhagavad Gita nestled in the pages of the vast Mahabharata can be likened to a beautiful flower nestled in a vast jungle of greenery.

Whilst scholars believe that the war as recorded in the Mahabharata is meant to be a real war, it is obvious that the war as depicted in the Bhagavad-Gita has more of a symbolic meaning, because in the two main protagonists of Arjuna and Krishna in the Mahabharata we find two different beings from the Krishna and Arjuna of the Bhagavad Gita. Symbolic of what?

The war in the Gita is symbolic of a great battle for the Throne of Our Soul, a great battle being raged between the forces of good and evil for the dominion of our Soul, our mind, our emotions, and our will, and as such complete dominion over our circumstantial existence and subsequent life experience. The Gita symbolically depicts the eternal battle for the throne of the Kingdom of God within us, for the rule of the Kingdom, and with that battle for the rule of our Personal Consciousness or Conscious Awareness..

Who will we volitionally allow to win the Battle for The Throne of Our Soul is the underlying premise in the Bhagavad Gita? Will we allow the forces of Light and Love lying in stillness within us waiting to come to the surface of our lives to defend us, or will we allow the forces of Darkness and Hate, the noisy energetic forces primarily those of desire and attachment to, through binary appeasement, cause us to capitulate, for how easy it is to find reasons to avoid a righteous battle.

This war imagery can be seen significantly throughout the book. For example, it is used by Krishna at the end of Chapter 3 where he says, "be a warrior and kill desire, a powerful enemy of the soul, and then, at the end of Chapter 4 where he says, "kill therefore with the sword of wisdom, the doubt born of ignorance that lies in the heart."

In the storyline of the Bhagavad-Gita, Arjuna is represented, as the Soul of man, and Krishna is represented as the charioteer of the Soul. The use of external images to press forward a spiritual argument is quite common in literature. St John of the cross used the imagery of marriage to describe the supreme communion of love. Similarly the Song of Songs was incorporated into the Bible and spiritual meaning given to it.

And in the Hitopadesha, an Indian text in the Sanskrit language consisting of fables with both animal and human characters, the following imagery is given to describe the interpretation of the Hindu ritual of bathing in the Ganges:

> *"The Spirit in thee is a river. Its sacred bathing place is contemplation; its waters are truth; its banks are holiness; its waves are love. Go to that river for purification. Thy Soul cannot be made pure by mere water."*

Jesus also often spoke using imagery, in the form of parables, using them for spiritual symbols. When Jesus spoke in parables, he was not meaning them to be true stories, but stories representing the Truth, Divine Truth, symbols leading to a deeper understanding of a specific Divine Truth.

Similarly in Buddhist Scriptures, a chariot is used, which is called "he that runs in silence". The wheels of the chariot are right effort: the driver is Dhamma, or Truth. The chariot leads to Nirvana, the Kingdom of Heaven. The end of the journey is the land which is free from fear.

The Bhagavad-Gita is primarily what you could describe as a spiritual poem, and as such it must be read as one reads a poem, not as a document that needs an analytical approach, but quietly and reverently to reveal the beauty and truth hidden in each phrase. It should be read in a meditative and contemplative manner, for as the wonder of the stars in heaven only reveal themselves in the silence of the night, the wonder of this poem the Bhagavad-Gita only reveals itself in the silence of the soul.

When the restless ramblings of unreasonable reason are quenched in the solitude of silence, then the interfering thought process is subsequently stilled even in just that moment of silent reflection.

Unreasonable reasoning is a hindrance, but right reasoning is a great helpmate. The importance, given to right reason in the Bhagavad-Gita is very noticeable. Arjuna is told by Krishna that he must seek salvation in reason, and that the first condition for a man to be worthy of God, is that his reason should be a pure reason.

Reason is a component of virtuous behaviour. Reason is the faculty given to a human being to enable them to distinguish true emotion from false emotionalism, faith from fanaticism, imagination from fancy, and true vision from visionary illusion. As such self-harmony or self-control is praised again and again in the Bhagavad-Gita.

The Bhagavad-Gita wants us to transform our whole life into an act of creation not one of destruction, and as such the destruction of our false sense of self becomes a priority. In Hinduism Shiva, known as the destroyer, is the God responsible for the destruction of the false self similarly as in Christianity the Holy Spirit is. Thus right or righteous thinking is able to feely roam the inner sanctums of our minds unhindered.

Only self-control and right or righteous reasoning makes it possible for us to live in harmony with other people. Virtuous behaviour and self -control are inextricably linked. Virtuous behaviour must be at the centre of our creative existence, but all virtue depends on the power of self-control.

Regarded as one of the most widely respected Hindu Scriptures, the Bhagavad Gita has been a source of inspiration and comfort for many people of times past and times present, including well-known personalities, some of who I have listed below. All who have come to believe that the Gita has been the guiding force of their lives, more than just a scripture, but a God given light that has guided their way.

Henry David Thoreau, the notable American poet, author, and philosopher, who was deeply influenced by Indian philosophy, and spiritual thought, said of the Bhagavad-Gita, "how much more admirable is the Bhagavad-Gita than all the ruins of the East."

Sunita Williams, the American astronaut, with Indian roots, holds the record for the longest spacewalk time for a woman. When she was heading out on her expedition as a member of the International Space Station, she carried a Ganesh idol and a copy of the Bhagavad-Gita, with her into space. In explaining why in her words she said: "They are spiritual things to reflect upon; yourself, life, the world around you, you begin to see things from a different perspective. I thought they were quite appropriate."

Ralph Waldo Emerson, the popular American essayist, lecturer, and poet, of the mid 19th century, who was introduced to Indian philosophy earlier in life, while reading the works of the Bhagavad-Gita commented: "I owed a magnificent day to the Bhagavad-Gita. It was as if an empire spoke to me, nothing small or unworthy, large, serene, and consistent, the voice of an old intelligence which in another age and climate had pondered and thus disposed of the same questions which exercise us."

Albert Einstein, the theoretical physicist who developed the "theory of relativity "one of the two pillars of modern physics, and who received the 1921 Nobel Prize in Physics for his services to theoretical physics in developing the photelectric effect said of Krishna and the Bhagavad Gita: "I was very impressed with the teachings of Krishna, and when I read the Bhagavad Gita and reflected about how God created this universe, everything else I understood seemed superfluous."

Thomas Merton, an American monk of the ascetic Roman Catholic Order of Cistercians, a writer, theologian, poet, mystic, social activist and scholar of comparative religion, who pioneered inter-religious dialogue and travelled with prominent Asian spiritual figures such as the Dalai Lama and Thich Nhat Hanh wrote about the Gita:

> "The word Gita means song. Just as in the Bible, the Song of Solomon has traditionally been known as the Song of Songs, because it was interpreted to symbolise the ultimate union of Israel with God in terms of human married love, so the Bhagavad-Gita is, for Hinduism, the great and unsurpassed song that finds the secret of human life in the unquestioning surrender to awareness of Krishna within."

He continued, "the Bhagavad-Gita can be seen as the great treatise on the active life. But it is really something more, for it tends to fuse worship, action, and contemplation, and a fulfilment of daily duty that transcends all three by virtue of a higher consciousness: a consciousness of acting passively, of being an obedient instrument of an all transcendent will."

Aldous Huxley, the English writer and philosopher, who wrote nearly 50 books, both novels and non-fiction works, as well as wide-ranging, essays, narratives, and poems, including his most famous novel Brave New World, and his final novel Island, which presented his vision of dystopia and utopia respectively, said of the Bhagavad-Gita:

"It is the most systematic statement of spiritual evolution of endowing value to mankind. One of the most clear and comprehensive summaries of perennial philosophy ever revealed; hence it's enduring value is subject not indeed to India alone, but to all of humanity."

Hugh Jackman, the Hollywood superstar known for playing lead roles in award winning movies, a man who was born a Christian, is now deeply soaked in Hinduism in his personal life. In many interviews, he has accepted that mysticism attracts him. He dedicatedly follows the teachings of the Upanishads and the Bhagavad-Gita Scriptures the fundamental teachings in Hinduism.

T.S. Eliot, the poet, essayist, publisher, and playwright, and Anglican convert, considered to be one of the 20th century's major poets, a man influenced by both the teachings of Hinduism and Buddhism, described the Bhagavad Gita as one of the greatest spiritually philosophical poems ever written.

The Bhagavad Gita in its essence could be likened to a spiritual symphony having many themes but three central themes; the themes of Jnana, Bhakti, and Karma, being Light, Love, and Life. It has been translated into more than 80 different languages, and its influence spans across spiritual boundaries and physical countries, causing it to become a staple in religious, philosophical and personal growth discussions.

I spoke in the Preface about the "letter of the law and the spirit of the law," for with regards to rules or laws, there are two possible ways to approach them. There is "the letter of the law" and there is " the spirit of the law." To obey the letter of the law is to follow the literal reading of the words of the law as did religious leaders in the Old Testament days and for some still in this present day. Which means that the element of forgiveness and the involvement of mercy does not enter the picture at all.

Unlike when we follow the letter of the law, to follow the spirit of the law we have to make room for the components of forgiveness and the dispensation of mercy. The Essence or Spirit must not be left behind in our understanding of how to implement practical wisdom into our everyday experiences.

The Spirit behind and embedded in what you could term "the life laws of the Upanishads and the Bhagavad Gita can be compared with that same Spirit that is behind and embedded in the "laws of a life of blessedness" outlined in Jesus's Sermon on the Mount, it being summed up with the words "I and my Father are one," and "the Kingdom of God is within you."

THE TEACHINGS OF CHRIST
THE NEW TESTAMENT GOSPELS

Much historical information concerning the life of Jesus can be found in the first four chapters of the Bible's New Testament. The first three chapters Matthew, Mark, and Luke are known as the synoptic gospels, so known because they are similar in content, narrative arrangement, language, paragraph, and structure, and are set out so that they can easily be compared with one another.

The Gospel of Matthew emphasises that Jesus is the fulfilment of God's will as revealed in the Old Testament. The Gospel of Mark speaks of Jesus as the Son of God, who is mighty in works, and who demonstrates the presence of the Kingdom of God within him, and the Gospel of Luke presents Jesus as the Divine human saviour, who shows compassion to the needy, is the friend of sinners and outcasts, and who has come to seek and save the lost.

The prologue to the Gospel of John, which immediately follows the Gospel of Luke, differs in as much that whilst the previous three Gospels accentuate the different aspects of Jesus's life and work, the Gospel of John deals more or delves more into the metaphysical aspects of Jesus's life. It identifies him as an incarnation of the Divine Logos, or the Divine Breath of God, Pure Consciousness, going on to say that as part of the Divine Breath, all the power and might of the Divine Logos was eternally present and active in his being.

Many scholars believe that the first gospel to be written was the Gospel of Mark, written around AD. 60–75, followed by the Gospel of Matthew, written around AD 65–85, followed by the Gospel of Luke, written around AD. 65 to 95, and followed then by the Gospel of John written around A.D. 75 to 100. Most scholars agree that the authors of Matthew and Luke used the writings of the Gospel of Mark as a source for their respective Gospel.

In my thirties and forties I spent many hours meditating in the writings of the New Testament. I was not aware of the existence of the Gospel of Thomas and so the Christian New Testament scriptures were my primary source of reference in my attempt to come to a greater understanding of the life and teachings of Jesus.

In order to gain a deeper understanding of the things of God, and of the Christian faith, as a regular disciplined routine, I would retire to bed at 9 p.m. and arise at 3 a.m. to read, study, and contemplate the scriptures, and to meditate for a few hours in the quiet and solitude of early morning. Then it would be back to bed for an hour or two before it was time to get up and ready myself for my day job.

My reasoning for doing this was based on the Hindu philosophy that speaks of the Amrit Vela or the ambrosial hours just before dawn as being the best time to wake up and to practice things of the spirit in order to maximize the potential for spiritual awakening. This time of day is said to be the time when the veil of the ego is thinnest, offering fewer of the distractions that are present through the rest of the day.

After being sufficiently satisfied with my understanding of the historical aspect of Christ's life and mission on earth, I spent much time contemplating specific passages of the New Testament relating to the preaching and teaching side of the ministry of Jesus, lengthier sermons such as the Sermon on The Mount in the Book of Matthew as it became known, and specific homilies of a parabolic nature in certain passages of scripture.

Now whilst sprinkled throughout the Gospels there are verses pertaining to the Wisdom of Christ and the metaphysical and Divine aspects of Christ's Nature, there are also numerous homilies, mostly of a parabolic nature. A homily is a sermon or religious speech offering encouragement or moral correction.

In our more recent times you could say the late Dr. Martin Luther King Jnr., the renowned civil rights activist and preacher, was a master of the homily. A parable or teaching of a parabolic nature is a simple story that teaches a spiritual or moral lesson. They are short tales that illustrate a universal spiritual or moral truth.

Unfortunately in this modern day these homilies or parables are not given as much attention to by the believer as they should be, hence the fact that the majority of those of the Christian faith are unaware of their existence, except for odd ones such as The Prodigal Son, and far less able to grasp the depth of Divine Wisdom they contain.

To put some context into my statement above I have listed the following parables that I am aware of, but there may be more. They are all contained in the Gospels of Matthew, Mark, and Luke, some short and others much longer.

In the Books of Matthew and Mark, with some of these in the Book of Luke we see the parables of The Sheep and the Goats, The Talent, 10 Virgins, The Faithful and Wise Servant, The Fig Tree, The Marriage Feast, The Vineyard Owner, The Two Sons, The Vineyard Workers, The Unforgiving Servant, The Lost Sheep, The Owner of A

House, The Casting of The Net into The Sea, The Pearl, The Concealed Treasure, The Yeast, The Seed, The Weeds, The Sower, New Wine in Old Wineskins, New Cloth on an Old Coat, The Wise and Foolish Builders, The Lamp Under a Bowl, and the Salt of the Earth.

And in the Book of Luke we see The Two Debtors, The Good Samaritan, The Friend, at Midnight, The Rich Fool, The Unfruitful Fig Tree, The Lowest Seat at The Feast, The Great Feast, The Cost of Discipleship, The Lost Coin, The Prodigal Son, The Shrewd Manager, The Rich Man and Lazarus, The Master and His Servant, The Persistent Widow, and The Pharisee and The Tax Collector.

In terms of lengthier sermons, in my contemplative times, the one titled The Sermon on The Mount became the most significant for me. The Sermon on the Mount, a group of short sayings, commonly referred to as The Beatitudes, because they all begin with the words, "Blessed are...", goes to the heart of the Christ Nature in a wonderfully compelling way.

These Beatitudes were the scriptures that most kids who attended a Christian Sunday School were exposed to, the Christian Sunday School being the Sunday Morning teaching classes designed to introduce children to the teachings of Christianity in a non-threatening and enjoyable way. Unfortunately in most Christian Church preaching that I have witnessed over the years, the Beatitudes are sadly missing, appearing to be the most neglected of the teachings of Jesus.

There are eight Beatitudes in total, and in the original King James Version of the New Testament, which was the version that was taught in my Sunday School class, they read as follows:

1. Blessed are the poor in spirit, for theirs is the kingdom of heaven.
2. Blessed are those who mourn, for they shall be comforted.
3. Blessed are the meek, for they shall possess the land.
4. Blessed are they that hunger and thirst after justice, for they shall have their fill.
5. Blessed are the merciful, for they shall obtain mercy.

6. Blessed are the clean of heart, for they shall see God.
7. Blessed are the peacemakers, for they shall be called the children of God.
8. Blessed are they that suffer persecution for justice sake for theirs is the Kingdom of Heaven.

However it was not until, as an adult, I came to contemplate the Amplified Version of the Beatitudes, that I came to fully understand the magnitude of their meaning as a means of understanding the nature of Christ and how the actions of Christ's Living Expressive Nature should be applied to one's daily life, because of the depth of blessings their application return in the form of psychological peace of mind, and absolute contentment with one's circumstances no matter what assails one in daily life.

The Amplified version reads as follows:

1. Blessed, spiritually prosperous, happy, and to be admired, are the poor in spirit, those devoid of spiritual arrogance, those who regard themselves as insignificant, for theirs is the Kingdom of Heaven," both now and forever."
2. Blessed, forgiven, refreshed by God's grace, are those who mourn over their sins and repent, for they will be comforted when the burden of sin is lifted.
3. Blessed, inwardly peaceful, spiritually secure, worthy of respect, are the gentle, the kind-hearted, the sweet spirited, the self-controlled, for they will inherit the earth.
4. Blessed, joyful, nourished by God's goodness, are those who hunger and thirst for righteousness, those who actively seek right standing with God, for they will be completely satisfied.
5. Blessed, content, sheltered by God's promises, are the merciful, for they will receive mercy.
6. Blessed, anticipating God's presence, spiritually mature, are the pure in spirit, those with integrity, moral courage, and godly character, for they will see God.

7. Blessed, spiritually calm, with life joy in God's favour, are the makers and maintainers of peace, for they will express his character, and be called the sons of God.
8. Blessed, comforted by inner peace and God's love, are those who are persecuted for doing that which is morally right, for theirs is the Kingdom of Heaven, "both now and forever."

Whilst the Hebrew word for blessed centres more on the consecration, the Greek word for blessed, as used in the Beatitudes and as translated into our English bible, is Makarios. In ancient Greek times, Makarios referred to the gods.

The blessed ones were those who were likened as gods. These were beings who had achieved a state of happiness and contentment in life that was beyond the normal human being. They lived psychologically in some other world, away from the cares and problems and worries of ordinary people. The Buddha would say they were in a state of Nirvana.

To be in a state of Nirvana, to be in a "state of Makarios", is to have extinguished all desire, all hatred, all ignorance, and as such eliminated the resulting suffering in life, and rebirth in the afterlife. Literally it speaks of a blowing out, or becoming extinguished, as when a flame is blown out, or when a fire burns out. A state of Nirvana then is "a state of being" where the life of attachment and aversion that all human beings are trapped in is burnt away.

That is what is the state of Nirvana, that is what is the state of Makarios or Blessedness. Those who achieve Nirvana have joined God, through the merging of their Atman, their pure self within, in perfect communion with their life activities. And how can that be achieved. It can be achieved simply by living and breathing the Beatitudes in every aspect of our existence.

As such, in this state, the state of Nirvana, or Makarios, or Blessedness, there is no ego or desire or attachment psychologically, and the Atman, that fragment or spark of God's Consciousness within, is free from any kind of non-Christlike, non-Krishna like, or non- Buddha like manifestation, for it is at one, in harmony of Soul of God, the Mind, Emotions, and Will of God. And if in thought, word, and deed we don't go against the truths of the Beatitudes, we remain constantly in that state of Blessedness.

This is the same state of being known in the religion of Hinduism as "the state of Yoga." It is a state where our Atman, our Christ within, is free to roam and influence metaphysically both the inner and outer circumstances of our existence, things of both mind and matter, as our personal supplier, provider, and protector, the one who meets all our needs.

And I say, all our "needs", because at times what we desire is not necessarily what we need for our wellbeing. For what the human flesh "thinks it desires" is not necessarily what the Atman within "knows we need". And as such, in this state, the state of Makarios or Blessedness, this state of Nirvana, the human being is "as a God."

We read in the New Testament's Book of John, Jesus in quoting Psalm 82 said to his disciples who followed his way and his will, "but ye are Gods." To be in that state is to be in a state of complete detachment from all egoic inclination. It is the state of being that the Buddha referred to as a state of non-attachment, a state of non-obsessing about our circumstances or our relationships; we are then able to "go with the flow", even when the storms of life assail us.

The Apostle Paul in speaking to the people of Philippi put it this way: "I have learned the secret of being content in any, and every situation, whether well fed or hungry, whether living in plenty or in want. I can do all this through him, who gives me strength."

Nirvana common, the state of existing or being to which all Buddhists aspire, is the cessation of desire, and hence the end of suffering, Nirvana in Sanskrit means the blowing out being understood as the extinguishment of the flame of personal desire, the quenching of the fire of earthly life. The Beatitudes in that sense could be likened to the kindling wood that reignites the previously quenched spark of Divine Consciousness within us, thus turning the deadened embers of the past through energetic transformation into a "full blown bushfire of blessedness" in the future. It is the death and resurrection principle at work."

Now regarding the fourth Beatitude, "Blessed, joyful, nourished by God's goodness, are those who hunger and thirst for righteousness, those who actively seek right standing with God, for they will be completely satisfied," it is helpful to understand the following.

For most people righteousness is a synonym for virtue. To most people it refers to being of moral character, having an inclination to act the right way in all situations, to do the right or righteous thing in every circumstance. We set aside our own egoic driven desires in favour of doing what is right.

But in the Israel of Jesus's time, righteousness was something much more dynamic than that. Metaphysically it could be likened as a force field: an energetic or vibrational state of being, charged with a Holy Presence. To be "in the righteousness of God" as the term is used in the Old Testament, means to be directly connected to this vibrational field, to be anchored within God's own aliveness. The Apostle Paul described this as "being made alive in Christ.

There is nothing subtle about the experience of being in a state of righteousness; it is as fierce and intransigent a bond as one would get in the picking up of a downed electrical wire after a storm.

To "hunger and thirst after righteousness", speaks to an intensity of connectedness. It is a deep yearning. Jesus promises that when the hunger arises within you to find your own deepest aliveness within, God's aliveness, it will be satisfied, in fact, the hunger itself is a sign that the bond is already taking place.

When we yearn, we come into sympathetic vibration with a deeper heart-knowing. I spoke in the previous chapter about how the heart is an organ of alignment; it connects us. Yearning is the vibration of that connectedness. In this beatitude Jesus is not talking about doing virtuous deeds so that you'll be rewarded later; he is talking about being in connection with your fundamental yearning, the yearning of our Soul to be in complete alignment or harmonisation with the Soul of God.

So in terms of our own spiritual growth, whilst it is good to have a historical understanding of the basis of the religion of Christianity, for example the birth, life, death, and resurrection story of Christ, if one lived solely the Beatitudes applying them to their daily life, it would be sufficient to speedily progress one in the evolution of their state of personal consciousness. And if one wants a greater understanding of the metaphysical nature of our existence then time spent in silent contemplation of these Beatitudes would be most helpful.

When we choose to consciously evolve our spiritual life, we will find ourselves becoming more intuitively wise in our thinking, which means our choices become more often than what was the previous case, the right choices. And we don't "shoot from the hip" in thought or deed as the saying goes, as we previously had done.

We find little things begin happening, blessed things, good things, that many in the early stages of their evolutionary journey through consciousness may dismiss as simple co-incidences, when in truth they are the hand of Infinite Intelligence coming into play.

We are being made "alive in Christ." Our old self, now fuelled by Infinite Intelligence, renewed daily, through a regular discipline of meditation in the Beatitudes, is transcending to a new self to a new state of being and with that a new state of living. These self-transcendent results that emerge from our growth in harmonisation with the Christ within are not co-incidences, but simply God's synchronistic Essence at work anonymously.

The literal meaning of psycho-spiritual self-transcendence is:

"A human being's act of overcoming the limits of the individual self and its ego driven self-interested desires, through spiritual contemplation and reflection and ongoing practical application".

Authentic spirituality is not about asking God to change you, it's about your choosing to change and using the tools that Infinite Intelligence has provided for that process. And all of that support can be found in the blessed outcomes that Jesus predicted as the result of our living the Sermon on The Mount, the Beatitudes.

One important aspect of the study of any ancient literature is the literary genre under which they fall. Genre is a key convention, guiding both the composition and the interpretation of writings. Whether or not the gospel author sets out to write a novel, a historical account, or a biography of Jesus, has a tremendous impact on how the author's writings ought to be interpreted. Some recent studies suggest that the genre of the Gospels, are to be situated within the realm of ancient biography.

And naturally the ancient writers were subject to the existing rules or laws of the day, the laws of the Roman government and of their own institutionalised religious brand if they had one. And as such those ancient writers were careful not to veer too far off the lawful path in terms of freedom of speech, so as not to be accused of seditious behaviour. Seditious conspiracy, conspiring against the authority or legitimacy of the state, is still a crime in various jurisdictions as it was in the days of Christ.

Now as I just touched on with regards to rules or laws, there are two possible ways to approach them. There is "the letter of the law" and there is "the spirit of the law." To obey the letter of the law is to follow the literal reading of the words of the law as did religious leaders in the Old Testament days and as do some still in this present day. The Roman government, through harsh punishment methods upheld the letter of the law.

After the coming of Christ this is where things got muddied. Some religious leaders, particularly those of Catholic and later Muslim origins, fearing not only governmental retribution but also loss of status with their followers, refused to allow the spirit of those laws, life principles that Jesus or Muhammad taught, those with a metaphysical influence as well as physical aspect to them such as the power and principle of love, of compassion, and of forgiveness, to be the final guiding principle in all decision making.

Certain religious leaders through fear of Government retribution refused to allow the "spirit of the law" to have preference over the "letter of the law". They continued to strictly advocate for the punishment principle to remain in force making no allowance for the forgiveness principle.

They refused to let go of their focus on the letter of the law. They focused totally on the letter of the law and turned the letter of the law into what is known as religious jurisprudence, and the church's own crime and punishment rulebook entered the picture, which usually landed in each case a sentence somewhere between the act of excommunication by a religious body or a public burning at the stake or a public crucifixion. depending on what was deemed the severity of the offence.

Understanding that this was the case in the day when the Gospels were written, and as such recognizing that the umbrella of hesitancy would have held sway over the authors as they set about writing the Gospels, I turned my attention later in life to other teachings of Jesus. Primarily to teachings that had been secreted away at the time because of the controversy and retribution to the author that would have occurred with their publication. In particular I commenced exploring the Gospel of Thomas.

THE GOSPEL OF THOMAS

The Gospel of Thomas of Christianity is an extra-canonical sayings gospel. A biblical canon is a chosen set of religious texts that form a particular book of scriptures. Different religious groups include different books in their scriptural canons. The Upanishads canon of Hinduism does not contain all the teachings of Krishna or of the Hindu sages of old. The Dhammapada of Buddhism canon does not include all the teachings of the Buddha. And the New Testament canon does not contain all the teachings of the Christ era.

What we now know as the Bible, contains a group of religious texts chosen by the early Catholic Church bishops with the exclusion of many other texts such as the Gospel of Thomas.

You see the Catholic Bishops of the day were the final arbiters in the construction of the Bible, the final decision makers as to what should be included and what was to be set aside, and texts such as the Gospel of Thomas were rejected because the hierarchy of the early Catholic Church felt its teachings did not align with the established Catholic dogma and doctrine. Christianity was not alone in this practice of isolating ancient scriptures that did not align with their institutionalised dogma and doctrines, and subsequent binary bias.

The Gospel of Thomas was discovered or dug up by a farmer in a field on a property near Nag Hammadi in Egypt in December 1945. It was among a group of books that were found and subsequently named the Nag Hammadi library. Scholars believe it was buried centuries ago in response to a directive from the Catholic Church that it was to be included as part of the Vatican's Index of Prohibited Books.

The Index of Prohibited Books, known as the Index Librorum Prohibitorum, established in 1557 by Pope Paul IV, was a list of books that Catholics were prohibited from reading on pain of excommunication. Certain books were prohibited because it was deemed they contained material considered dangerous and contrary to their faith, differing from established dogma and doctrine, and as such repugnant to the church authorities.

Victor Hugo's Les Miserables was one of the most recent books added. The 20th and final edition of the Index appeared in 1948 and due to ongoing intense public scrutiny any further changes were formally abolished on 14th June 1966 by Pope Paul VI.

Hitler also adopted this policy of book prohibition, as one of his tools for controlling the thinking of the people and following the practical example of the Catholic authorities, on May 10, 1933 with encouragement from his German Minister of Public Enlightenment and Propaganda Joseph Goebbels, the world witnessed university students in 34 university towns across Germany burn over 25, 000 individual titles.

The works of Jewish authors such as Albert Einstein and Sigmund Freud went up in flames, alongside other prohibited books from authors such as Ernest Hemingway and Helen Keller, whilst students gathered and gave the Nazi salute.

The burning of people and any literature they had written or were connected with, was a long standing policy of religious and political authorities for centuries in a vain attempt to not only obliterate the people, but to obliterate any thoughts they may have held and written down in the form of a book so as to prevent them from any further influence.

It was done purposefully to prevent further interference in the power and influence that the established religious institutions or government organizations wielded at the time. And as such the Gospel of Thomas was one that was buried, by monks it is believed, to hopefully preserve its message for future generations.

Unlike the canonical Gospels, the Gospel of Thomas is not a narrative account of the life of Jesus; instead it consists of over one hundred logia (sayings) attributed to Jesus, sometimes stand alone, and sometimes embedded in short dialogues or parables; thirteen of its sixteen parables are also found in the Synoptic Gospels, Matthew, Mark, and Luke.

When this Nag Hammadi discovery first came to light, the church hierarchy and some religious scholars of the day treated it with a little disdain, because it seemed so different in construction from the Gospels that the church had become accustomed to. They were used to orthodoxy, the generally accepted theory, doctrine, or practice, and these scriptures seemed so unorthodox.

The Catholic Church in the construction of the New Testament had staked its reputation on its choice of acceptable scripture for the masses to read, and in terms of the Gospels selected for the New Testament, that orthodoxy must not be disputed. As such for some of the church hierarchy the first inclination was to dismiss any newly discovered teachings as fake teachings, a tactic still used in this day by many politicians when adverse publicity about themselves or their party comes to light.

But researchers discovered that indeed some of the teachings that were found even enhanced some of the oldest teachings of Jesus. Some scholars believed that they might be even older than the teachings found in the Gospels.

Now the following is extremely important for us to understand. The primary difference between the Gospel of Thomas and the Gospels in the New Testament that we have become used to, is that the teachings in the Gospel of Thomas were of a *sophiological* nature, rather than a *soteriological* nature. I spoke of this in the previous section about the Christ, but it is really quite important for us to understand and bears repeating.

The Christianity of the West as witnessed in the traditional Gospel teaching, favoured the concept of *"soteriology"* which is a word derived from the Greek *soteria* meaning "salvation."

Soteriology is the branch of theology dealing with the study of salvation. The term is also related to the Greek *soter,* meaning Saviour. And as such the majority of westernised Christianity agree that salvation and with that the heaven hell eternal life principle, was and is made possible only through the crucifixion, death, and resurrection of Jesus the Christ.

But the original Christianity of the East, the birthplace of Christ, saw things radically different from the Christianity that evolved in the West. The West saw God as "a giver", but the East saw God as an "expressor." Whilst western society mainly saw Jesus as "the giver of God's eternal life," eastern society with their own established religious and cultural beliefs, saw Jesus as "the expression of Divine Energetic Life," and as such the Master of a Divinely Energetic lifestyle, or Master of Consciousness.

The Christianity that was birthed in the East, the birthplace of Christ, was not one of *soteriology,* but rather a religion of *sophiology.* The word *sophiology* having its root meaning in the word Wisdom, Sophia being the Greek word for Wisdom. You could say for the earliest Christians of Eastern religion, Jesus did not come as the Saviour, but as the energetic life giver and the dispenser of Divine Wisdom. In the original, Aramaic story of Jesus, his followers saw his life as a living expression of Divine Energy, similarly as did the followers of Krishna and the Buddha.

In the original Aramaic records of the story of Jesus and his followers, there was no use of the word salvation it was all about being "made alive in Christ." It was all about the Divine enabling of ourself to become expressions of God's Image through the indwelling Christ and thus expressors of Divine Wisdom.

In the East salvation was understood to be a bestowal of the Energetic Consciousness of Christ, and to be saved was to be made alive through him in the present moment, not to be saved from hell and gain entrance to heaven in some future moment after death.

Hence the Gospel of Thomas doesn't have a biographical slant to it as do the traditional Gospels. It is not a birth to death life story slant on Jesus. It is not the narrative that you find in the other gospels, and its slant is not toward the miracles and healings that he carried out in his life journey.

Rather it is simply a collection of Jesus's sayings that have a transformational and transcendent aspect to them. And as you sit quietly and contemplate these sayings, they reveal a greater understanding of the metaphysical nature of the Christ's existence. You begin to see that Jesus was not just the Master Messenger of Truth but that he was The Master of Consciousness Transformation.

The entire Gospel of Thomas consists of 114 short sayings including teachings from the orthodox canonical Gospels as well as a selection of the beatitudes and parables, that many Christians are aware of, but in addition we see many teachings that have not been included in the Gospels nor appeared anywhere else in ancient literature.

All together, they paint a picture of Jesus teaching continuously the theme of "singleness" or Advaita as it is known in Indian religious philosophy. Advaita is simply the "principle of non-duality." Advaita argues that there is no duality; that the mind, awake or dreaming, moves through maya, meaning illusion, and that non-duality or Advaita is the only final truth.

Thomas is remembered historically as the apostle who travelled east to Persia and India, and it is noticeable that the teachings in the Gospel of Thomas have a distinctly "eastern" fragrance to them as they focus on the unification of one's consciousness.

Unlike some of the Advaitic or non-dual teaching of the East, but still complimentary to them, they set forth a vision of wholeness in which this physical plane is neither a mirage nor a trap, but rather an integral part of Divine Reality with a unique and indispensable role to play. "Singleness" or "Non-Duality" is achieved by mastering that role.

The teaching here relies on the classic wisdom schematic of "the great chain of being and becoming." As we evolve or get psychologically and thus consciously closer to the Divine, we integrate and carry with us the consciousness gained at lower levels of being. Thus life, this animated living breathing life that we exist in whilst we are alive on earth becomes primarily in terms of importance, an evolutionary journey of our own personal consciousness.

It is all about displacement not destruction. We do not "destroy" or dissolve our lower nature, the activities of a lower level of consciousness, in that lifelong process, because energetic influence cannot be destroyed only transformed. Rather we absorb them into the mix, enhance their good elements, and suppress or veil their offensive elements.

It is not a question of complete removal, but rather of unification, with those elements of our higher nature that are expanding or evolving always having ascendancy in the unified relationship. Always having dominion in the workings of the Soul, our mind, emotions, and our will.

The Gospel of Mary, which is a part of the Nag Hammadi collection discovered alongside the Gospel of Thomas, is a non-canonical text (not included in the Canon of The New Testament) discovered in 1896, in a fifth century papyrus codex. Both the New Testament's Book of Ephesians and the Gospel of Mary use the term "and the two shall become one".

As usual the early church fathers in their interpretation of this teaching in Ephesians focused on the physical aspect of its meaning, teaching that it was all about leaving our parents and taking up a marriage partner. This was the intent of institutionalised teaching in the early church in an attempt to remove all aspects of the metaphysical from Christ's teaching to bring it all back to the fleshly aspect of human life.

Logion or verse 22 of the Gospel of Thomas also references the "two shall become one" principle. It tells a story of a time when Jesus saw some infants being nursed at the breast, and he said to his disciples: "These nursing infants, are like those who enter the Kingdom". The disciples asked him, "then shall we become as infants to enter into the Kingdom?" Jesus answered:

"When you make the two into one, when you make the inner like the outer, and the high like the low, then you will enter the Kingdom."

Non-dual Consciousness evolution is all about the making of the two to become one." It is about the harmonisation of our Soul with the Soul of God. The merging of our ego consciousness with Divine Consciousness, but not the complete dissolution of our ego consciousness, for how could we see all other human beings or life forms as being worthy if we had no sense of our own worthiness and at times unworthiness. But it is a sanctified or consecrated ego not a de-sanctified one.

In the early stages of this dissolution the ego will dance back and forth for a time, between "self-consciousness" and "Divine Consciousness", between Lower Self and Higher Self, and the unification will find a few cracks appearing, as the usurping attitude of the lower nature frantically tries to hold on to its place on the Throne of our Soul.

The Apostle James in the New Testament spoke of this as being "a state of double mindedness." And in the story of the temptation of Jesus in the wilderness in the Gospels this dancing scenario is described as "the devil departing until a more opportune time". Until a more opportune time in your physical and psychological journey through life.

To see the teachings of Jesus through the lens of the Gospel of Thomas, at first may be disconcerting particularly if our thought processes have been over climatised with the institutionalised church's interpretation about the life and teachings of this Divine Messenger the Christ, but that need not be so.

However I find nothing in the Gospel of Thomas that contradicts any of Jesus's teachings in the canonical gospels. Rather it rounds them out metaphysically and creates a newfound sense of awe as we see just how original and subtle his understanding of Divine things really was. He was the first truly integral teacher to appear on this planet. As we take a fresh look at these teachings at first perhaps unfamiliar and strange, we will eventually be catapulted forward again in our journey to Nirvana, along a path that rings with the power of Truth and Wisdom.

THE TEACHINGS OF THE BUDDHA
THE TRIPITAKA AND THE DHAMMAPADA

Buddhism has various sacred texts, the most important of which are the **Tripitaka** and the **Mahayana Sutras.** The Tripitaka is the primary holy text for Theravada Buddhists, while Mahayana Buddhists revere The Mahayana Sutras. The Tripitaka, or "Three Baskets," is a collection of three canons: the Vinaya Pitaka (monastic rules), the Sutta Pitaka (teachings and discourses), and the Abhidhamma Pitaka (philosophical and psychological analysis).

The Mahayana Sutras encompass a vast range of canonical texts, including the Prajnaparamita Sutras (Perfection of Wisdom), the Lotus Sutra, the Avatamsaka Sutra, the Pure Land Sutras, and the Vimalakirti Sutra, among others. There are also other texts in the Vajrayana tradition, such as the Tibetan Book of the Dead, which Vajrayana Buddhists revere.

A Canon is simply a collection or list of sacred books accepted as genuine. The Pali Canon is maintained by the Theravada tradition in South east Asia. The Chinese Buddhist Canon is maintained by the East Asian Buddhist tradition, and the Tibetan Buddhist Canon is maintained by the Tibetan Buddhist tradition. They are all some of the most important Tripitaka in the contemporary Buddhist world.

These sacred texts of Buddhism discuss a wide range of topics, including the teachings of the Buddha, ethical conduct, meditation, the nature of reality, the path to enlightenment, and the nature of suffering and its cessation. They also guide monastic life and the community of practitioners.

The texts' ages vary, but it is believed that scribes wrote down most of the Tripitaka between the 1st century BCE and the 1st century CE. However, the oral tradition potentially dates to the time of the historical Buddha in the 5th century BCE.

Likewise, the Mahayana Sutras were composed between the 1st century BCE and the 5th century CE. The original language of the Tripitaka is Pali, an ancient Indian language closely related to the Sanskrit of Hinduism. The Mahayana Sutras were written in various languages, including Sanskrit and Gandhari.

According to traditional history, the teachings in the Tripitaka were transmitted orally by the disciples of the Buddha and later written down by the monastic community. The authorship of the Mahayana Sutras is more complex, as some texts claim to be the direct teachings of the Buddha, whilst others are sayings of various Buddhist masters or celestial beings. Translations of Buddhist texts have indeed changed over time, as they have been translated into numerous languages and adapted for different cultures.

Major Buddhist sects, such as Theravada and Mahayana, generally respect and study each other's sacred texts to some extent, recognizing their shared roots and the value of diverse perspectives. However, they may prioritize their own core texts and interpret them differently according to their respective traditions and beliefs.

The Dhammapada, a collection of sayings of the Buddha in verse form and regarded as one of the most widely read of the Buddhist Scriptures, is the best known and most widely esteemed text in the Pali Tipitaka, the sacred scriptures of Theravada Buddhism.

The word Dhamma or Dhammapada is a Pali word, Pali being the language of the Buddhist scriptures of Ceylon, Burma, and Indochina, and corresponds with the word Dharma of the Sanskrit language, Sanskrit being the classical language of South Asia one of the oldest Indo European languages and the sacred language of the religion of Hinduism.

Substantial documentation exists for this language the earliest of which, known as the Vedic Sanskrit, dates back as early as 1700 BC (1700 years before Christ), when Sanskrit is believed to have been the general language of the greater Indian subcontinent in these times. The word Dharma of the Sanskrit language corresponds with the word Dhamma in the Pali language similarly you might say as the Italian language is connected to the Latin language, the language of the ancient Roman Empire.

Behind the word Dhamma there is a far deeper meaning that many in Buddhism and in Hinduism don't commonly realize. In its true meaning Dhamma or Dharma comes from its Sanskrit root DHR, which means "to support and to remain supportive". It is a moral law which never ceases, a spiritual law of righteousness. It corresponds with what Christianity would describe as "the all-inclusive will of God."

You could call the Dhammapada a collection of Divine Principles or Divine Laws of the Universe, Laws of Truth that support and remain supportive, that never cease to exist and function, laws of a reciprocal nature that support and sustain all the physical and psychological aspects of all existing life form; thus enabling each to function wholly and happily in a peace filled way, as each individual life form navigates the earthly aspect of its eternal pilgrimage of individual consciousness.

As such you could call the contents of the Dhammapada a definitive "Way of Life" for all spiritual pilgrims. If you wanted to relate this to Biblical language, you might say that the Dhammapada is "the Way and Truth of God," as expressed by Jesus when he said, "I am the Way, the Truth, and the Light."

In both the Pali and the Sanskrit language and in the words of Jesus it suggests footsteps to walk in, or a path or a way (of life) to walk on. Thus in Buddhism the collection of sayings known as the Dhammapada declare the "pathway of God", what you could call the "psychological and behavioural" pathway that one must walk in order for one to reach Nirvana.

It is a part of the greater Truth that the Apostle John was speaking of when he said, "you shall know the Truth, and that Truth will set you free." Free from what? Free from attachment to and reaction to circumstantial experience that creates fear and uncertainty, and thus free to enter a state of Nirvana, a state of Divine Bliss, a transcendent state in which there is neither suffering, desire, nor sense of self, and a person is released from the effects of karma and the cycle of death and rebirth.

It is recognised by most Buddhist scholars that each of the sayings that are recorded in this collection known as the Dhammapada were made on a number of different occasions as the Buddha was responding to a specific situation in his own life or in the lives of those in his community of followers.

The Buddha left his home, and set out on a great consciousness adventure, the same adventure that many spiritual people have set out on in their quest to get closer to the Infinite. You could say that in that journey, having put his hand to the plough, even though he had many setbacks, he never looked back. He never yearned for his previous life of wealth and prosperity and privilege.

Jesus we read in the New Testament's Book of Luke said: "No one who puts a hand to the plough and looks back is fit for the Kingdom of God." He was not speaking of being eternally unfit. He was referencing that we may at times stall in our pilgrimage of consciousness and for some come to a complete stop for a while, so that we are not in the moment progressing, but nevertheless the path to Nirvana, the peace supreme, always remains open to us.

When Jesus said, "not fit for the Kingdom of God," he was not talking about some sort of Divine decree that prohibits one from entering "heaven," he was speaking of the person's unfitness or ineligibility at that time of looking back to manifest Kingdom Principle in their daily lives because their focus is elsewhere.

The early church fathers of the Christian church wrongly and perhaps one could think deliberately to preserve their church influence, referenced those words of Jesus to the Old Testament teaching regarding Lot's wife, a Biblical character, a disobedient woman who was turned into a pillar of salt for looking back to see the destruction of Sodom and Gomorrah as she and her family were fleeing.

That teaching is of a parabolic nature, but the church has used her story over and over again in their exegesis of the scriptures, as an example of what happens to anyone who chooses a worldly life over salvation or backslides after a salvation experience. Which completely negates the Principle of Divine Forgiveness, for even if one looks back for a while, with a realignment and a re-prioritising of one's life, Nirvana can be reached in one's lifetime.

And even if at times there is a stalling or even a regression, the goal remains reachable. Even in the last hour of his life upon earth, man can reach the Nirvana of Brahman, man can have peace in the peace of God." And the Buddha did finally arrive, with tradition telling us that the Buddha's search became realised whilst sitting under the Bodhi tree. The Bodhi Tree is now a religious symbol in Buddhism due to its prominence in the story of the Buddha's enlightenment.

In that moment the Buddha understood the total peace and happiness found in Nirvana or the greater reality. He came to an understanding of the True Self within, the Kingdom of God within that waits silently to be recognized not only as our source of existence, but also the support for our ongoing existence in our earthly pilgrimage of consciousness back to our Source, Pure Consciousness.

Which then saw him pour out his joy of being liberated in the following two verses of the Dhammapada: "I have gone round in vain the cycles of many lives ever striving to find the builder of the house of life and death. How great is the sorrow of life that must die. But now I have seen thee housebuilder: never more shalt thou build this house. The rafters of sins are broken, the ridgepole of ignorance is destroyed. The fever of craving is past: for my mortal mind is gone to the joy of the immortal Nirvana."

The Buddha was speaking of the union of his Soul with the Soul of God. A complete harmonisation of the Mind of Man with the Mind of

God. A transcendence and with that a transformation in terms of peace and joy. The same transformation that the Apostle Paul is speaking of when he said to the people of Rome, "and be transformed by the renewing of your mind." And the Buddha was experiencing the same joy which caused the Apostle Paul to cry out as seen in the New Testament Book of Corinthians, "death where now is thy sting."

Both the scholars of the Buddha and the followers of the Buddha, accept that the spirit of the Dhammapada, is the spirit of the Buddha, and that same spirit wants us to stop doing what we're doing if it contradicts the will and way of Divinity; and the same Spirit wants us to step off the "wheel of becoming" so that we can "rest harmoniously in the centre of Being."

The message of the Buddha in the Dhammapada is a message of joy. The Buddha had after much searching finally found a treasure, and he wants us to follow the path that leads to the treasure he found. The Buddha tells us that we are in deep darkness, but he also tells us that there is a path that leads to light. He wants us to arise from a life of dreams into a higher life, where humanity loves, and does not hate, where humanity helps, and does not hinder or hurt.

The Buddha's appeal is universal, because he appeals to reason, and to the universal in us all: but as he says in the Dhammapada 20, verse 276:

"It is you, who must make the effort, for the great of the past can only show us the way. The one who achieves a supreme harmony of vision and wisdom, only does so by placing spiritual truth, on the crucial test of experience; and only experience can satisfy the mind of modern man."

The Buddha encourages us to watch and be awake, and he wants us to seek and find. In the Dhammapada we can hear the voice of the Buddha, encouraging us, inspiring us, and motivating us to press on to Nirvana, each verse in it being like a small star in the radiance of eternity.

The Upanishads of Hinduism are the Path of Light; the Bhagavad Gita of Hinduism is the Path of Love; the Dhammapada of Buddhism is the Path of Life, and the teachings of Jesus are a composite of all three. If the question were put to Jesus by a spiritual seeker desperately trying to discover the right path to follow, as to which way to follow, Jesus would not have pointed that individual to a specific religion, a specific place of worship, or a specific religious ritual.

Jesus might wisely and most probably would have simply answered that question with the following words as recorded in the Book of Matthew:

"Seek ye first the Kingdom of God that is within you, and his righteousness, and all these things shall be given and shown unto you."

"This is what you shall do; love the earth and the sun and the animals. Despise riches, give alms to everyone that asks, devote your income and labour to others; hate tyrants, argue not concerning God, and have patience and indulgence towards all people.

Re-examine all you have been told at school or in church or read in any book and dismiss whatever insults your own soul; and your very flesh shall be a great poem and have the richest fluency, not only in its words, but in the silent lines of its lips and face, and between the lashes of your eyes, and in every motion and joint of your body."

— WALT WHITMAN......POET, ESSAYIST, JOURNALIST.

Conclusion

〜🙢〜

What is needful?
Righteousness, and sacred learning and teaching.
Truth, and sacred learning and teaching.
Meditation, and sacred learning and teaching.
Self-control, and sacred learning and teaching.
Peace, and sacred learning and teaching.
Ritual, and sacred learning and teaching.
Humanity, and sacred learning and teaching.

— THE TAITTIRIYA UPANISHAD

Stoic philosophy was a School of Philosophy, founded in Athens in the early third century BC. It is a philosophy of personal virtue ethics, asserting that the practice of virtue is both necessary and sufficient, and is the only true way to achieve lasting happiness in preference to momentary pleasure. It emphasises that one flourishes by living a truly ethical life.

To live a virtuous life, one must conform to moral and ethical principles. One must be morally excellent or upright, or as ancient religious scriptures termed it "righteous." The Stoics are especially known for teaching that "virtue is the only good" for human beings, and that external things, such as health, wealth, and pleasure, are not good or bad in themselves, but only have value as material for virtue or virtuous behaviour to act upon.

So in simple terms that means, it isn't the attainment of money or personal wealth that is the problem, it isn't the attainment of some sort of political power or social influence that is the problem, the problem lies firstly in the ethical nature of how we attained that personal wealth or power, and secondly in the ethical attitude underpinning what we prioritise to do with that personal wealth or power.

Similarly with personal relationships. Whilst the incessant desire for a personal relationship can be a problem, whether or not virtuous behaviour underpins all our relating in the established relationship can in fact be a far greater problem. When virtue is absent on a continuing deliberate basis in the family dynamic, thus begins to rise the ugly head of the snake of domestic violence, which more often that not will eventually sadly, strike.

The ancient Psalm 55 of the Old Testament tells us that:

"Whoever walks in integrity, walks securely, but he who makes his ways crooked will be found out".

Jesus in his lifetime was the personification of kindness, a key virtue. Kindness is part of the Nature of God and as such a dynamic part of God's Natural order of things, being mentioned more than 80 times in the Book of Psalms, not just purely as an ethic or duty that must be grasped but more so as an expression of personal virtue that flows from and is rooted in love, which is at the heart of all virtue.

The Apostle Paul in the Christian New Testament gives six virtues that every human being regardless of race or gender should pursue: righteousness, godliness, faith, love, steadfastness, and gentleness. The imperative "pursue" is also a present tense command. Every day in every situation we must follow those virtues that are contained in the measure of God Consciousness that we have all been given.

The great virtues taught by the Buddha were: the act of sharing, ethical morality, patience, renunciation, wisdom, diligence, truthfulness, determination, loving-kindness, and equanimity, and he perfected these to the most difficult and advanced level.

And the Hindu Bhagavad Gita 16, Krishna speaking, lists twenty-six virtues of a saintly nature, that should be cultivated for elevating ourselves to the supreme goal: they are fearlessness, purity of mind, steadfastness in spiritual knowledge, charity, control of the senses, performance of sacrifice, study of the sacred books, austerity, straightforwardness, nonviolence, truthfulness, absence of anger, renunciation, peacefulness, restraint from fault finding, compassion toward all living beings, gentleness, modesty, lack of fickleness, vigour, forgiveness, absence of covetousness, fortitude, cleanliness, bearing enmity toward none, and absence of vanity.

"Virtue by simple definition, is the moral excellence of a person".

Virtue ethics, though it leaves a place for rules, laws, consequences, and outcomes, focuses mainly on the inner qualities of the individual, those things that lead to the behavioural manifestations of the individual. One of the most well-known proponents of virtue ethics in the history of the world was the famous Greek Philosopher Aristotle, teacher of Alexander the Great. Similarly we could say was Krishna, who we see in the Bhagavad Gita teaching Arjuna his moral responsibilities, as did Jesus teach his disciples their moral responsibilities and those around him who had ears to hear.

Morally excellent people have a character made up of virtues such as love, honesty, respect, courage, forgiveness, kindness, and compassion. In Christianity, in the teachings of Christ, we see that the love between man and God is the highest virtue, and loving our neighbour is its equivalent. The concept of Jesus, as a virtue ethicist is not a new one. Most philosophical thinkers in the ancient world were virtue theorists in one way or another. Even the Buddha and Confucius were not inconsistent with the belief that character was central to ethos.

The Stoics also held the belief that certain destructive emotions are birthed as the result of errors of judgement in financial matters or elsewhere such as in relationships, simply because those judgements are not underpinned by virtuous attitudes and behaviours. They believed people should aim to maintain a will, that is in accordance with nature, or the natural order of things, being the only way to avoid falling into unethical self-survivalist attitudes and behaviours.

Because of this, the Stoics emphasised that the best evidential indication of a virtue led successful life was not primarily witnessed in what a person achieved, in what a person said, or in what a person had, but rather in how a person behaved, and those behaviours had to be in accord with the natural order of things or what we call the laws of nature.

And since they believed that everything was rooted in nature or natural universal law, they stressed that to live a good life, one that leaves a lasting legacy, one needs to have an understanding of the natural order of things which then leads to a deep desire or yearning to lead a virtuous life.

Not just the physical natural order of things, but also the psychical/mental natural order of things; those things affecting or influencing the subconscious and the conscious awareness or perceptions of the human being, which of course eventually lead to specific physical or emotional behaviours.

So how do we set about changing our behaviours to align them with the principle of virtue ?

Firstly we must accept that the world has conceptualised God, mainly due to the activity of egoic energy forces that insist on keeping people unaware of the true nature of their existence, to prevent humanity from discovering its true reality. And if we appear to at any stage be getting closer to a revelation of this inner consciousness, our true reality, these egoic forces will divert our attention away from impending Krishna,

Christ, or Buddha Consciousness, to perhaps a religious experience, or some other kind of spiritual experience.

It too eventually being discarded as the egoic mind, having withdrawn temporarily to await until a more opportune time, begins once again its campaign of distraction and procrastination through desire and attachment to the world of form.

Since birth we have relied on engaging with new knowledge and new experiences to fulfil the yearning of the Voice of Consciousness within, to bring its creative healing nature to our conscious level of awareness. This manifests in a constant state of varying degrees of uneasiness you might call it.

This uneasiness is the yearning of God's Spirit within us, the Christ within saying, "I've had enough of these endless conceptual experiences; I want to return back to the beginning when all was well in the Garden (metaphorically speaking), to my original, at birth, psychological connection with God or Pure Consciousness."

But, since Consciousness is in the first instant compelled to think of itself and express itself through the person, which is the reason the person was given dominion over all things in the beginning, shortly after you wake up to the truth of who you really are, the true persona of your being, those personality patterns of your egoic mind will progressively be seen as less important and progressively more and more lessen their grip on your life; the grip that manifests as a continuous pulling force towards ephemeral things, visible things that you can attach yourself to either psychologically or physically to obtain a measure of pleasure from.

To try to help the people of his time Jesus taught the conflicted and confused crowds with words such as, "the Kingdom of God is within you," and "seek ye first the Kingdom of God," and the Apostle Paul seemingly with less patience than Jesus in trying to explain this to the citizens of Corinth, said in what appeared to be an underlying tone of frustration, "don't you understand that your body is a temple and that the Spirit of God dwells in you?"

Both Jesus and Paul were basically saying to the people, "look you are struggling to live a virtuous life, but I can show the way. Seek first to understand that all the qualities of a virtuous life are embedded in the Kingdom of God that is within you. Seek first to harmonise them with your inner and outer existence and all the virtues of that Kingdom will automatically manifest, they won't have to be strived for they will simply just be. That is the natural order of things. It's called Grace. We draw near to God, and thus God draws near to us. (James 4:8).

Yet many spiritually inclined people including Christians, Hindus, and Buddhists, in their search for spiritual truth fail to recognize the Cosmic or Universal Nature of life, merely settling for an intellectualised understanding of their chosen religion. What you could call settling for a literalised interpretation of the wonderful wisdom truths in their particular Holy Book, rather than a metaphysical interpretation of them. Which means then that the supposed virtuous life that is a part of living a truly spiritual life, is continually impacted on by non-virtuous behaviour of some kind.

Preferring what is called the milk of the word rather than the meat, the flesh of life rather than the Spirit. But the mysteries of the indwelling are found in the meat and not in the milk, in the Spirit and not the flesh, and that meat is embedded in us already.

Once we come to an understanding that our inner self, our innermost consciousness or breath is cosmically joined to our immortal nature, our higher self, Pure Consciousness, and come to accept that our lower nature and its identification, fascination, and co-operation with visible form and all the material aspects of our life is just a passing phase that can be transcended, then the captivity to a life of personhood with its accompanying stresses ceases. We may have through desire and attachment made some ill informed decisions in life that led to our current circumstances, but that can, through Grace, be turned around very quickly.

In the Book of Matthew in the Beatitudes that I spoke of in an earlier chapter, we see the words of Jesus, "blessed are the poor in spirit."

He used the word Blessed, what was he meaning? The meaning would more easily be understood if one reads it this way. "Blessed are those "who recognize that they are poor in spirit." He was talking about those who recognize that they have made either a wrong investment spiritually or perhaps made no investment at all spiritually.

Poverty of spirit is the result of someone having made an incorrect investment on behalf of his or her Soul. He was speaking of psychological poverty, poverty of the mind. If one is poor in terms of food sustenance there is a hunger for food. If one is poor in spirit there is a hunger for spiritual food, and if one shows a hunger for spiritual food God will bless them and give it to them. That is what Jesus meant when He said, "Blessed are the poor in spirit." The church can't satisfy this spiritual hunger, good works alone can't, and giving financially to the church can't.

The only thing that can satisfy spiritual hunger is a relationship or partnership that we are responsible to establish; a partnership or harmonisation between our Soul and the Soul of God. Between the attributes of our Soul, our mind, emotions, and will, and the attributes of the Soul of God, God's mind, emotions, and will, which brings about what is referred to in Eastern religion as a state of enlightened being or a state enlightenment.

"The process of the establishment of that harmonisation or partnership is "our personal pilgrimage of becoming," and the achieved partnership is "our enlightened or transcendent state of Being."

The central component of our "pilgrimage of becoming" is the process of mind renewal. If the mind has not been renewed or transformed to a new level of conscious awareness, no amount of religious ritual will enable us to complete our personal spiritual pilgrimage towards a more ethics based virtuous life. Their will always be obstacles threatening and stalling our progress.

Getting our thought life right, is the major component of the Atonement process in Christianity and the Enlightenment process in

Eastern religion, and all this is accomplished through a psycho-spiritual partnership: a deliberate partnership between our will and the willingness of the Spirit of God or Brahman within. It's as simple as that.

A psycho-spiritual partnership occurs when the psychological and spiritual qualities of being human are accompanied and reinforced by practices adopted to enhance the psychological and/or spiritual wellness of a person. The process of psycho-spiritual transformation is synonymous with spiritual emergence or spiritual awakening, and this journey is acknowledged by various spiritual traditions and beliefs systems around the world.

So, in the words of Jesus as written in the Gospel of Thomas of the Nag Hammadi texts:

"Become a disciple of your mind, which is of the Father. I am come to give sight to those who seek after right-mindedness. Understanding is hidden from the heart and only revealed to the mind".

And in the words of Krishna from the Bhagavad Gita:

"One must deliver himself with the help of his mind, and not degrade himself. The mind must be the friend of the conditioned soul (the renewed mind, emotions, and will), and not the friend of the unconditioned Soul (the unrenewed mind, emotions, and will)."

And the words of the Buddha from the Dhammapada:

"With our minds, we make the world. Speak or act with kindness, and happiness will follow you as surely as a shadow follows the person who casts it."

The essential way to successfully and virtuously navigate both this earthly kingdom without and the Heavenly Kingdom within, is through the harmonisation of our Soul, being our Mind, Emotions, and Will, with the Soul of God, God's Mind, Emotions, and Will. This is the Divine Blueprint for a virtuous, healthy, happy, peace filled pilgrimage. I use the term "peace filled" and not "peaceful", because true Divine Peace does not indicate the absence of trouble, rather it speaks of maintaining a supernatural rest in the midst of the antics of the enemy.

And to understand the practicality of that blueprint before we develop enough intuitively to automatically tap into it, we in the first instance simply have to spend time in re-educating the thoughts of our mind, so as to harmonise our everyday thoughts with the thoughts of God.

We were conceived in silence, born with silence, and as we grew up, we lost the silence and were filled with words and sounds. We for a short time as babies fresh from the womb, lived in our hearts, and as time passed, we moved into our heads. Now, the reverse of this journey is enlightenment. It is the journey from the head back to the heart, from words and sounds, back to silence; getting back to our innocence, in spite of our imagined intelligence, which for some is really ingrained ignorance.

To do this we re-educate, realign, transcend, and eventually completely transform the thoughts of our rational mind through an applied focus on the thoughts of chosen messengers of Divine Thought, who have in their respective lives most influenced the spiritual existence of the world since recorded time. And the more we psychologically ingest their teachings, the more they become the automatic response in our time of need.

How can this be achieved? It can be achieved through contemplative reflection in those Divine Messages revealed through those Divine Messengers of the Divine Mind, Krishna, Christ, and the Buddha. Messages, that not only correspond and reaffirm each other but all with an eternal purpose to realign the Mind of Humanity with the Divine Mind of Infinite Intelligence.

During my time on the road that I spoke of in the Preface and Introduction of this book, to deepen my understanding and subsequent experience with the metaphysical side of humanity's existence, midst the all-embracing early morning sunrises over the ocean, and early evening sunsets over the landscape I spent time, my personal sacred time, reading and in a contemplative way reflecting on these teachings of the masters. And during these times two interesting things began to happen which continue to this day.

At various times as I was reading and reflecting on teachings in a spiritual book, such as The Bhagavad Gita, The Dhammapada, the Upanishads, or the Quran, certain verses, paragraphs, or passages, or sometimes even just a few lines on a particular page, would jump out at me, gripping my attention. You could say that the seed kernel of Wisdom embedded in the outer chaff and debris of overall information in the passage had separated itself, and the true spiritual message was revealed.

What sort of outer chaff and debris? Historical chaff, mythological chaff, allegorical chaff, institutionalised chaff, doctrinal chaff, or even the writer's rational thought bubble chaff, perhaps flavoured with institutionalized bias. Outer chaff and debris which the egoic self sometimes uses to hide, smother, or veil the truth and intent of the small kernel of Wisdom embedded within the teachings.

But even more interesting, many times in that moment of realisation, my mind would immediately align that particular passage of words from the Bhagavad Gita or the Dhammapada or the Upanishads, or the Quran, with a verse or passage from the Bible, more particularly from the teachings of Jesus or the Apostle Paul of the New Testament, or from the Psalms or Proverbs of the Old Testament, all of which I had read and meditated on in the early morning hours many decades before as I set about getting to know the Wisdom teachings in the Bible.

It was as if the Spirit was, in desiring to demonstrate the truth of what I was contemplating, cross-referencing the passage I was reading with a passage from the scriptures of a different time and era spoken by a different spiritual master, to demonstrate to me the timelessness and ageless influence of that specific sliver of spiritual truth.

It may have been cross referencing my immediate meditation with something Jesus had taught, or some Wisdom from the Book of Psalms or Proverbs, or even something said by one of the Old Testament Hebrew Prophets such as Isaiah, but because I had not visited that passage in the Bible for a long time I had imagined I had forgotten it.

After initially being puzzled by this, I came to realise later that what was occurring was the realisation of one of the most important truths that Jesus had ever given to his disciples regarding their ongoing personal evolution of consciousness, since he would not be around in physical form to guide and instruct them.

Jesus on the eve of his crucifixion told his disciples that when he was gone he would send them the Holy Spirit, to be "in them and with them, who would teach them all things and bring all things back to their remembrance."

Bring what things back to their remembrance? Bring back the eternal Wisdom of the sages from past ages lying in stillness in that spark of Divine Consciousness within them. Why? To demonstrate the eternality of God's Wisdom, that no matter in what era it is birthed or through whom it is birthed, if it is True Divine Wisdom, it has the seed of eternality embedded in it.

The Old Testament Book of Provers says: "The beginning of Wisdom is simply this, get skilful and Godly Wisdom, this is pre-eminent." Then goes on to say, "however with all your acquiring of True Wisdom, get understanding, actively seek spiritual discernment, mature comprehension, and logical interpretation."

These incidences in my contemplative times indicated two things to me. Firstly they reaffirmed to me the eternal nature of God's truth, that no matter in what era, in which religious culture, or through what spiritual messenger it was originally birthed, Divine Truth is timeless and ageless. And secondly they reaffirmed to me that there is only one source of unwavering Truth and Wisdom, and that source is "the mouth of God," and not the mouth of man unless what that man or woman is saying aligns or agrees with God's original intentional message.

Sogyal Rinpoch the author of The Tibetan Book of Living and Dying best described this intuitive voice from within when he wrote: "Two people have been living in you all your life. There is the ego, which is garrulous, demanding, and calculating, and there is the hidden spiritual being, whose still voice of Wisdom you have only rarely heard or attended to."

The Kingdom of God within you is the storehouse of Divine Wisdom and Truth, in which pearls of wisdom lie waiting to emerge at the appropriate time, and they are intuitively given to you at the right time by the Holy Spirit or Shiva, the active agent and enforcer of the True Wisdom of God or Brahman.

What is the Holy Spirit or Shiva delivering? It is delivering to our conscious mind the Wisdom of the Krishna, Christ, or Buddha Mind, laws pertaining to virtuous ethical behaviour. And it can happen in simple moments of contemplative reading of the timeless teachings of Krishna, Christ, and the Buddha.

How do we know that they have the answers?

We know because "the Fullness of God dwelt in them bodily."

What are we doing through contemplation and reflection, through prayerful reading of the teachings of Krishna, Christ, and the Buddha?

We are imprinting them on our conscious awareness, veiling the old ego thoughts from appearing. We are progressively renewing our mind.

I have spoken on the process of contemplation and not meditation. It is important to understand that contemplation is not meditation. Meditation is a movement of thought, limited within a circle, but in contemplation, there is a silence of thought. Meditation is the mental activity of the thinker; contemplation is the silence of the poet.

Saint Teresa of Avila, 1515 to 1582, also known as Saint Teresa of Jesus, was a Carmelite nun and prominent Spanish mystic and religious reformer. In her own personal pilgrimage of consciousness, she discovered and taught four ways of prayer, which can be compared to what the Yoga Sutras tell us, or to the Buddhist way of meditation. The Yoga

Sutras are "threads of Wisdom" that weave the garment of a meaningful, purposeful, and ethical life.

She speaks of our making a garden, where we plant the seeds of our good works in life. That garden must be watered by the waters of love. Those waters of love can be drawn in either of four ways: one, out of a well with buckets, a laborious way; two, by using the wheel of a windlass, a machine for drawing water; three, by the waters of a stream; or four, by rain from heaven, the easiest way.

These four ways, correspond to recollection (the well), meditation (the windlass), contemplation (the stream), and union (rain). Recollection requires attention and concentration. In meditation, the mind thinks, but the thoughts are limited to a definite object. In the third stage, there is contemplation, a much higher stage. Saint Teresa called it, the Prayer of Quietness in the Silence of the Mind. In this state we are in the regions of poetry and art where there is greater joy and love; and this cannot be reached by thought. Thought is not true silence, because thought is sound in one's head.

Then finally there is the fourth stage, "the rain from heaven" stage. This stage goes beyond the stages of recollection, meditation and contemplation, and is the culmination of the highest state of consciousness that a human being can reach. It is a stage where our ego centric lifestyle of "becoming" has completely ceased, and a new phase of simply "being" has begun. This was the stage the poet William Wordsworth was at when he wrote the following words, in his work, Lines Composed Above Tintern Abbey:

That serene and blessed mood, in which the affections gently lead us on,
Until the breath of this corporal frame, and even the motion of our human blood,
Almost suspended, we are laid asleep, in a body, and become a living soul;

While with an eye made quiet by the power of harmony, and
the deep power of joy,
We see into the life of all things.

In this state of union, both the knower and the known are one, in complete harmony. Ego consciousness has disappeared, retreated into the shell of its own self-interested existence, for The Mind of Man is totally immersed in The Mind of God, and with that in a complete state of rest. Or as the Bhagavad Gita 6:19 says:

"Then his Soul is a lamp whose Light is steady, for it burns in a shelter where no winds come."

The Old Testament's ancient Psalmist described it this way:

"O God, you are my God, earnestly I seek you; my Soul thirsts for you, my body longs for you, in a dry and weary land where there is no water. I have seen you in the sanctuary and beheld your power and glory."

Choose to water the Garden of your own Soul in whatever way suits your current level of consciousness, and virtuous attitudes and behaviours will become the norm for you. Choose the well, the windlass, the stream, or the rain. But it is profitable to the Soul to choose at least one in the first instance with the eventual aim of being able to at chosen times voluntarily embrace the water of rain, a state of quiet reflection beyond contemplation. To ignore them all is to ignore the thirstiness of our Soul and continually leave it open to the divisive influence of the ego. Be blessed in your endeavours.

"Take time to reflect on your own place and part in the universal oneness that is all. That creative and supporting oneness from which we all arise and that same oneness to which all Souls having conquered death will return. The ultimate reality of who I am is not "what you see is what you get," it is simply "what you don't see, "I AM" and what you don't know "THOU ART."

Daily Spiritual Pointers and Practices

❦

"Step off the "wheel of becoming" so that you can
"rest harmoniously in the centre of Being."

❦

1. Regularly Feed your Soul with the Teachings of the Masters.
Choose the right version of the New Testament or the Gospel of Thomas
that you feel comfortable with. I find the Amplified Version of the New
Testament is the most comprehensive. And choose the right language
translation of the Bhagavad Gita or the Dhammapada that you can
relate to. And spend some time each week quietly contemplating these
teachings.

**2. Always greet the new day with gratitude, with some sort of gratitude
dialogue.**
The day should always be greeted with a "Good Morning God" attitude
and not with a "Good God it's morning" attitude. Starting off the day
with positive intent engages Divine Law and makes all our goals easier.
Our thought process has to be aligned with God's thought process from
the get-go, which is, "in everything give thanks for this is the will of
God concerning you." (1 Thessalonians 5:18 and Colossians 3:17.) I have
attached my personal morning prayer of Gratitude and Intent that takes
only 5 or 6 minutes to complete.

3. At every opportunity engage with the Holy Spirit, Shiva, talk to the Spirit in your mind.

Commit your day to the guiding Hand of the Spirit. Talk to the Spirit if you need to make an important decision. Seek guidance. If you practice it regularly enough it will eventually become an automatic response in any situation similar to a child who has an imaginary friend they continually converse with. It does not have to be some sort of disciplined prayer routine, just quiet, relaxed, silent or audible conversation. Cast your cares upon the Holy Spirit because She cares for you. That's why She is called the Comforter.

4. Live life deliberately focused on everything that comes into your life.

If you are talking to someone give him or her your full attention. If you are doing something give the task your full attention. Fully engage with everything that comes before you. This will minimise the opportunity for you to get lost in trivial and wasted thought. Give the present moment your full attention. Live life deliberately and not just accidentally as most people do.

5. Take some time, at least once a week, to get "lost in stillness."

What do I mean by that? Take time out from the inner and outer noise of the universe and spend time with the stillness of the universe. You may decide just sitting quietly breathing rhythmically or meditatively is what you need to do. Or take a walk at the beach and drink in the peace, or a walk in the park, or just a walk down the street, but not in this instance as a means of exercise, rather as a means of observing in a non-judgemental way the universe you live in, the goings on around you. Stop occasionally and sit on a park bench, and simply observe.

6. Take time occasionally to deliberately examine your thoughts, to observe your thoughts.

It does not have to be a regimented routine just do it when you think of it. You will be amazed at how many trivial and useless thoughts you entertain all the time. Just occasionally stop, step back and become 'the observer' of your current thought and it will surprise you how much you are living through your mind thinking about past events or future scenarios and expectations, usually with some regretful or anxious connotations.

Then immediately say to yourself or out loud if you can, "my mind holds only what I think with God, a child of God can suffer nothing, I am that child." Actions like this are all part of the renewing of the mind process, which is the key component of the Atonement process.

7. Take a moment every day to deliberately forgive someone.
During the day at any particular time you think of it take a moment to forgive deliberately and sincerely someone, anyone that comes to mind. At first you will find yourself choosing only those who you have minimum psychological discomfort with, then as you progress you may or should deliberately move on to the more difficult ones. It is a powerful spirituality influencer, an energetic force for not only your good but for the good of the beneficiary of your forgiveness. The measure that we are forgiven is always in accord with the measure of forgiveness we extend.

8. Go for a brisk walk and take some deep breaths as you do
Develop a habit of getting some sort of exercise daily. It has all kinds of health benefits mental and physical. Does not have to be strenuous. Does not have to be of the Arnold Schwarzenegger type. Just a brisk 30-minute walk will suffice. Remember life is all about finding harmony and balance in everything.

SOME SIMPLE TIPS TO HELP ONE RISE ABOVE EGO MIND IDENTIFICATION

1. PAY ATTENTION...Listen to the voice in your head continuously.
2. PAY ATTENTION...To repetitive thought patterns.
3. PAY ATTENTION...To your current emotional state, your feelings.

It will surprise you how many trivial, destructive or negative thoughts you filter through your mind impacting on your emotions.

AS YOU DO THIS

Recognize that there is a voice there and here I am listening to it or recognize that there is an emotion present and here I am feeling it. Don't try and fight it just observe it, like a teacher in a classroom who gives an occasional glance in the direction of a misbehaving child whilst saying nothing.

1. DON'T dwell on the thought or feeling.
2. DON'T analyse the thought or feeling to see where it's coming from.
3. DON'T judge the thought or feeling.

JUST OBSERVE IT

1. Watch the thought almost in a way letting it know you are watching it but not embracing it.
2. Observe and feel the emotional energy it produces inside of you. Identification with the mind gives it energy; observation of the mind withdraws energy.
3. Try to avoid conversations with others that push for an opinion on or a judgement against some particular situation or person. These things are all manifestations of the ego mind.

"Remember thoughts and emotions feed each other. If we habitually entertain a particular thought we give it energy, spiritual energy, power to create after its own kind. We turn what should be just a passing potential energetic influence into a present moment impactful kinetic influence".

If we reject that thought with words or thoughts like "my mind holds only what I think we God," or "I am as God created me, the son (or daughter) can suffer nothing, I am that son," (or daughter), or "I have been given the Mind of Christ," then we will de-energise, deflate and destroy the potential kinetic energetic influence of that thought, and it will eventually disappear totally."

When the thought is gone the emotion goes with it, and the energy that is withdrawn from your mind will turn into peace filled presence. Life will physically and emotionally feel a whole lot easier to navigate.

The Morning I AM Prayer

A PRAYER OF GRATITUDE AND INTENT

The following is my early morning wake up discipline that I have been carrying out every day without exception for years now, to the point where I know it off by heart. It is a combined **"affirmation of gratitude and prayer of intent"**. Gratitude and Intent are both powerful energy forces that operate according to Divine Law and over time can have a huge impact on your life.

Gratitude, the word itself, comes from the Latin root *gratus*, and *gratus* is also the root of related terms such as Makarios or "Grace," the subject matter in Chapter 10 . It's Proto-Indo-European root *gwere* means "to praise, to celebrate, to be in contact with the Divine."

In the renowned neuroscientist, author and spiritual teacher Deepak Chopra's article titled "Sowing Seeds of Gratitude to Cultivate Wellbeing," the co-authors reference clinical studies that prove the positive effects of gratitude on the recovery of patients with symptomatic heart failure.

Science had been providing for many years now clinical proof supporting what many religions and spiritual traditions have been predicating for eons, that gratitude does you good. In his article Deepak also draws a powerful association between the physical and mental wellbeing that comes from an ongoing attitude of gratitude and the subsequent development of a higher level of consciousness.

Intention is the starting point of all our dreams and is an energetic force within itself that fulfils our needs.

"Intention is the present birthplace of future behaviour."

Everything that happens in life begins with an intention thought. The sages of India observed thousands of years ago that our life is shaped and impacted on by our desires which intention comes forth from.

Intention in Sanskrit the ancient language of India is called Samkalpa; literally meaning "what you create in your mind with will, desire, or imagination".

"Intention is more than a mere thought. It is an energetic influence caused by desire, and then moved by the will in the direction of a specific purpose or goal."

The classic Vedic text known as the Upanishads declares:

"You are what your deepest desire is. As your desire is, so is your intention. As your intention is so is your will. As your will is so is your deed. As your deed is so is your destiny."

Jesus said:

"Seek (desire) first the Kingdom of God, and all the things you need shall be added to your life."

The Buddha taught that "right intentions" are threefold: intentions of renunciation; intentions of goodwill; and intentions of harmlessness. These three intentions are the opposite of the wrong intentions of desire, ill-will, and harmfulness. Wise intention is one of the steps of the Buddha's eightfold path, and it might be the most important one. Wise intention is what keeps our lives heading in the right direction.

Buddhism affirms the overarching importance of good intentions. Synonymous, with good karma, positive intentions have the power to lead to better future circumstances and the possibility of liberation.

"An intention is a directed impulse of consciousness that contains the seed form of that which you aim to create."

Like real seeds, intentions can't grow if you hold on to them. Only when you release your intentions and plant them into the fertile depths of your consciousness, can they grow and flourish.

The morning prayer should be recited out loud or read slowly and silently to oneself. It takes less that 5 minutes each morning, but you will find over time it will be the most valuable 5 minutes of your day that you will ever spend. Try to keep focused on each part of the prayer as the morning mind does have a tendency to drift out of immediate focus into thoughts about the day ahead.

The prayer covers many areas that we have discussed in this book including Holy Spirit or Shiva engagement, our thought processes, the Mind of Christ or Krishna, the intuitive mind and the rational mind, creativeness, forgetting the past, forgiveness, achieving balance and harmony, embracing stillness and having respect for our body, our personal instinctively operating earthly vehicle for the manifestation of God's creative pleasure.

I follow this with what I term my Prayer for Virtuous Behaviour, which is basically the Prayer of Saint. Francis of Assisi slightly adjusted. Saint Francis of Assisi, born in Italy in 1182, was a Catholic friar who gave up a life of wealth to live in poverty. He established the Franciscan Order of friars, and the women's Order of The Poor Ladies.

Not only did he care for the poor and sick, but he preached multiple sermons on animals, and wanted all creatures on earth, including humans to be treated as equals under God. His work was hard, menial, low-paid work, yet he never passed a collection plate when he preached, nor asked the public for money. His life and message was uncompromising and simple: greed causes suffering for both victims and the perpetrators.

⁂

THE MORNING PRAYER OF GRATITUDE

I am grateful Lord of the universe for today. I am grateful today for who I am, I am grateful today for where I am, I am grateful today for everything I have, and I am grateful today for what I am doing right now. I am grateful for the Holy Spirit who you sent. Holy Spirit I align my will with your will for my life and ask that you would today guide my thoughts, guide my will, guide my reason, guide my intent and guide my actions and behaviours that they be in accord with God's will.

I am grateful Lord of All to open my eyes today, I am grateful for another day to live my life, for a new start. I am grateful to feel the breath in my lungs and the beating in my heart. I am grateful Holy Spirit for today, for the opportunities in the next twenty-four hours; I welcome the chance to do something amazing and creative with the day today.

I choose to make the most of today, I energise my thoughts, I focus my intention, I remind myself of how far I've come and believe that I will go the distance today to whatever goal or vision I have in mind. I remind myself of achievements accomplished successfully and channel my focus to today only and the present moment only that I might make the most of the next twenty-four hours and not be bothered as to what comes after this.

I am grateful Lord of All for this body and vow to treat it well today. To eat well, to nourish it well, hydrate it, exercise it, stretch it, move it and relax it. I am grateful for the Mind of Christ within me, for my intuitive mind and my rational mind and vow to use them both well and harmoniously, to focus on learning, to applying knowledge gained, to reflect, and to hold myself accountable.

I place my rational mind in subservience to my Christ Mind. I commit to staying humble, I agree to talk and think well of others and myself and to channel my focus in conversation only to the positive. I commit to let go of wasteful thinking, to let go of dwelling on the past where there are no more lessons to be learned, to let go of fear and anxiety of the future and instead focus on what I can control, my own attitudes and my own thoughts, my own intentions and behaviours.

THE PRAYER OF SAINT FRANCIS
(with last two line additions by author)

"Lord, make me an instrument of your peace.
Where there is hatred, let me sow love; where there is injury, pardon;
Where there is doubt, faith; where there is despair, hope;
Where there is darkness, light; and where there is sadness, joy.
O Divine Master, grant that I may not so much seek to be consoled,
as to console; to be understood as to understand; to be loved as to love.
For it is in giving that we receive; It is in pardoning that we are pardoned;
And it is in "dying to our false self", our sense of mortality, that we fully realise our true self," and embrace our sense of immortality."

www.ingramcontent.com/pod-product-compliance
Lightning Source LLC
Chambersburg PA
CBHW051713020426
42333CB00014B/971